EMPOWERED
with MARY

EMPOWERED
with MARY

Affirming Full Personhood in the New Millennium

By Barbara Horton Jones

PELICAN PUBLISHING COMPANY
Gretna 2000

*The word "Pelican" and the depiction of a pelican are trademarks
of Pelican Publishing Company, Inc., and are registered
in the U.S. Patent and Trademark Office.*

Library of Congress Cataloging-in-Publication Data

Jones, Barbara Horton.
    Empowered with Mary : affirming full personhood in the new
millennium / Barbara Horton Jones.
      p. cm.
    Includes bibliographical references and index.
    ISBN 1-56554-496-X (alk. paper)
    1. Mary, Blessed Virgin, Saint. 2. Christian life. I. Title
BT602.J66 2000
232.91—dc21   98-55536
                                                             CIP

Manufactured in the United States of America
Published by Pelican Publishing Company, Inc.
1000 Burmaster Street, Gretna, LA 70053

To my family,
especially Bill, Patrick and Barbara, and Stephen

Contents

Acknowledgments 9
Introduction 13

1 Mary—An Archetype for Full Personhood 15

Part One: Mary as an Individual

2 Inner-Directed Mary 37

3 Creative, Artistic Mary 57

4 Thinking Mary 77

5 Faithful Mary 105

6 Individuated Mary—Being Close and Separate 131

Part Two: Mary in Relationship

7 Words to Say It—An Assertive Mary 151

8 Mary and Joseph in Relationship 171

9 Maternal Mary 191

10 The Power and Virtue of Sexual Mary 213

11 The Power of Loving Presence in the Midst of Suffering 233

12 A Balanced Mary—Wholeness and Power 255

Notes 277

Bibliography 283

Index 285

Acknowledgments

*T*HOUGH THIS HAS BEEN in some ways a very solitary journey, there are many whose support has been deeply appreciated along the way. First, my husband, Bill, who has enthusiastically supported not only this book, but also the various steps that, unbeknownst to us, were necessary foundations to its writing. These steps included my embarking on a new career some years ago by entering graduate school in psychology. Then, when I woke up one fine day with a dissertation idea that was likely to be more time-consuming than the original plan, he did not hesitate to encourage me to proceed. I would not have tackled the longer dissertation without his and our children's support. Finally, Bill has offered steadfast encouragement, contributed to my thinking process in the areas concerning Joseph and Mary's relationship, and read the manuscript as it developed, making helpful suggestions. His joy in the work as it developed has been especially touching to me. Thank you, Bill.

Patrick contributed in a most basic way by marrying Barbara Ann, whose questions first stirred my interest in this topic. He and Barbara also read and discussed with me the earliest versions of the ideas, and the book proposal itself, giving me helpful feedback. They have both provided helpful insights concerning Catholic perspectives. Stephen, either off on his own adventures or engrossed in the very different world of aerospace engineering studies, has nonetheless consistently offered words of encouragement and support, as well as the supportive prayers of a young man whose priority is to serve God.

My sister Beth DeVan and her husband Ben have been

supportive sounding boards and consultants at various points along the way, especially regarding certain theological matters. My mother's love of ideas as they related to the crucial matters of how we find meaning in life has contributed to my own interests, as has my father's clarity of thought and love of knowledge. Thank you, Janet and David Horton.

A number of friends and colleagues have provided stimulation, useful critique of ideas, and support. They have given me comments from numerous faith perspectives, including Jewish, Catholic, Protestant, and Episcopalian. Their backgrounds encompassed evangelical, charismatic, liberal, and conservative views. They have provided distinctly feminist and non-feminist comments. My thanks and appreciation to all of you. You enrich my life, and I am grateful.

Special thanks to Margaret Solomon, a wise woman and dear friend whom God uses in many ways. Dr. Wayne Viney, scholar and psychologist, provided helpful comments and critique on the manuscript. In addition, his expert mentoring of me in the method of examining the Biblical record from a psychological perspective was an indispensable foundation to this work. Others in the psychology department at Colorado State University who were supportive of this type of scholarship and/or who created the kind of atmosphere where intellectual freedom was supported are thanked and commended.

My agent, David Spilver, provided encouragement to proceed with these ideas. He was a sounding board, and often gave wise counsel to a first-time author. Dr. Milburn Calhoun, publisher and president of Pelican Publishing Company, expressed enthusiasm for the manuscript and has taken a special interest in shepherding the book through the publishing process. Jim Dunn, my editor, has provided sensitive, intelligent, and timely editing. My appreciation and thanks to these key persons.

In therapy, my approach has been to be a participant-observer, as I learned in my training. This means I am actively present, person-to-person, in the therapy process, and I am at the same time observing that process. The observation allows me to make comments and interventions based on my training and expertise as a psychologist, hopefully in a fairly objective way. The participation allows for the person-to-person interaction and caring that is so essential to the healing and growth process. In writing about Mary, I have strived for a similar blend of participant-observer. I am an active participant in the Christian faith, and at the same time I am examining (the observation part of the process) the scriptural record from a psychological perspective. Just as in therapy, such an approach has its advantages and its risks. The challenge is to not let the participant portion wipe out the more objective part of the process, but to keep the two in balance. As a participant in the faith, I acknowledge and thank God for any and all parts of this book that speak in truth. As a participant-observer, I take full responsibility for the content.

Any examples given based on clinical cases have been written to protect confidentiality, and thus identifying details may have been changed. This is also true regarding other examples.

In discussing God, I have typically used the masculine pronoun or the name Father if a pronoun or parental title was given, because that is how the Biblical translations typically handle this matter, and because Jesus used the term "Father" to address God. As discussed in the book, this does not mean that there are not important, scripturally based aspects to the God of Abraham and Sarah, of Jesus and Mary, that are today regarded as feminine.

Introduction

*A*S A THERAPIST, I am sensitized to the fact that the very words that bring healing to one person can bring confusion or hurt to another. The challenge and the luxury when working with an individual is to speak in a way that respects who that unique person is and how best to communicate in a way that can be heard, received, and used at a particular point in that person's journey. As a writer, the desire to connect individually with readers remains deeply embedded in my heart, yet the luxury of choosing ways of expression geared to fit a particular individual or even a particular group does not exist, except at the risk of making the message less accessible to another individual or group. Paul wrote to various groups, sometimes expressing the same truths in different ways, according to what he knew of the needs, personalities, and cultures of the churches he addressed. When the Romans received a message from Paul, it was written in a style they could easily understand. When Paul addressed the Greeks in the Athens marketplace, he spoke in a way that communicated within their world-view. This is an issue of particular importance in writing about Mary, the mother of Jesus, because individuals and groups have distinctive ways in which they have come to approach both the scriptural record and Mary herself.

Indeed, within my own family there is a diversity of reactions to what I have to say. My hope is that those parts that are helpful and illuminating to you will be taken in and used, and those parts that are not will be put aside. As a friend of mine likes to say when we have led groups together, "Approach this like eating fish—eat the meat and leave the bones." May the meat nourish and none of the bones stick in your craw!

Chapter One

Mary—An Archetype for Full Personhood

*L*IKE A TROUBADOUR, the heart sings out upon recognition of an archetype worthy of the soul. Human beings yearn for an archetype that calls us into balance, that meets us where we are and yet can take us where God calls us to be. Such an archetype must be plain enough to be recognizable by our simple hearts, and yet rich, mysterious, and wild enough that its essence defies capture, much less taming.

For contemporary women and men, the archetype must also be capable of embracing the complexity of modern human relationships rather than stereotyping the sexes into roles that stifle completeness. It must be an archetype for a lifetime, taking us from the ideals of youth to the seasoned wisdom of our final years.

Mary is the archetype of the one who says *Yes* to God—who assents to having God dwell within her. Thus, in Christendom, each of us is to be in some sense like Mary—we too are to have Christ within us.

Yet who is the woman on the donkey? And what does she have to say to us as women and men poised at the precipice of the twenty-first century? Can the Mary of old, the pregnant maiden on the beast of burden, shine a light that illumines the way for a postmodern people seeking to be whole persons in right relationship to God? Is the scriptural Mary up to such a task?

AN UNEXPECTED QUEST

These questions were brought to my consciousness several years ago during a conversation with a loved one. When I picked up the phone that day, with signs of early spring sending dappled light through the window, little did I realize that a new quest was about to unfold in my life, one that would directly affect the spring break I had been eagerly anticipating. My vibrant, endearing daughter-in-law was finishing her degree in psychology and women's studies. Raised in a loving, protective family, she was in a phase of exploring many issues and asking thought-provoking questions about her spiritual life and its place in her life as a woman. One question was about Mary, the mother of Jesus.

"What do Mary and her life have to say to women today?" was the essence of her question. We had both been brought up within the Christian faith, she from a Catholic background and I from a Protestant one, and each of us took our faith seriously. Yet, as we talked, it was apparent that neither of us had a very full picture of anything the scriptural Mary had to say to us today. Several important things stood out about Mary, of course. One was her faithfulness and willingness to bear the Christ-child. We both associated Mary with purity, but were unclear as to what relevance that had to our twentieth-century lives. Certainly we desired purity, but did Mary's life as recorded in Scripture have much that could help us in our struggles? And what was purity, anyway, when it came down to the nuts and bolts of it?

I had strong associations of Mary, pregnant and weary, on the back of a donkey. I also pictured her trusting Joseph to find a place where she might rest and give birth, as well as of her gazing in love and adoration at her firstborn son. My daughter-in-law had strong associations of the young virgin being visited by the angel. Now she had come across a book that asserted that the birth of Jesus was probably not a virgin birth, and that much of the story surrounding Mary and the early years of Jesus was myth, not to be taken as literal truth. Furthermore, not taking the story as literal truth was much friendlier and more liberating to women, the book seemed to say.

My curiosity and interest were rising. Spring break, a week I often took off from my private practice as a psychologist in this university town, had been set aside for writing. Instead of the project that was slated for work, I found myself, as I offered the week up to God, reading the Scriptures that referred to Mary. Using my training as a psychologist, and taking the Scriptures as they are recorded, I looked for fresh understanding for myself, and my daughter-in-law. The method of using the Scriptures as data and examining them from a psychological perspective was one I had been well mentored in while doing my dissertation on the topic of "Anger: Psychological and Biblical Perspectives," at Colorado State University. It felt good to be applying this method once more, this time poring over the Scriptures regarding Mary. I was enthused and invigorated by the discoveries I was making.

A richer, stronger, more creative Mary emerged as my unexamined stereotypes were washed away by the refreshing waters of new insights. J. B. Phillips, theologian and writer, challenged his generation when he declared, "Your God is too small." In the same way, my Mary had been too small.

Similarly, there is the story of a young man who refused to believe in God. He was sharing these views with Dr. Harry Emerson Fosdick, the noted pastor of Riverside Church in New York, some years ago. Finally, Dr. Fosdick asked him to describe this God in which he could not believe. Upon hearing the description, the minister exclaimed, "I don't believe in your God, either." Likewise, my stereotypes of Mary may not have related as much as I thought to the Mary that God chose. In short, I was being shown just what a remarkable woman God had chosen to bear the Christ-child.

Significantly, discarding Scripture or twisting it was not at all necessary to find a complex Mary who was able to challenge and encourage us by being a much fuller model for women and men than I had previously imagined. This seemed all the more remarkable to me, because I was not a stranger to these Scriptures, having read them many times. It was just that I had never had the eyes to see these things in quite this way before. Perhaps I hadn't been looking.

Illusions Unveiled

Erich Fromm, the social critic, philosopher, and psychoanalyst, whose interest in the meaning of life melds religion, philosophy, and psychology, may have an interesting perspective on why others and I had not seen these aspects of Mary before. He points out that every new system of thought is necessarily erroneous. The creative thought is a critical thought because it does away with an illusion and gets closer to reality. Yet the new thought must be expressed within the thought categories of the time . . . otherwise it cannot filter through and is "unthinkable."

Even our logic and reasoning powers are culture-bound. An example of this is that the word "atheism" did not even exist in tenth-century Europe, where the idea of a world without God was alien to thought. Interestingly, Fromm believes that societies depend on certain irrational assumptions in order to justify exploitation, and therefore each society depends on a distorted view of reality to some degree. Only in a Messianic society would these irrational assumptions not be necessary and rational thought be unhampered, Fromm asserts.

Following this line of thought, are there truths embedded in Scripture all along that have been unthinkable or unseeable to me and to many others? Has our culture and thought now developed to the point that we have eyes to see Mary and other Biblical women in a new light? A light that offers a fuller, more complete picture, both Biblically based and psychologically sound, which reveals more fully the real Mary that God chose and honored?

The principle of progressive revelation as we are ready for it is supported by the comments of noted Bible teacher and writer Dr. Everett L. Fullam. In discussing the words of Jesus in Scripture, he states, "Each sentence was jammed with truth that often would not be fully grasped for years, even centuries."[1]

Such a perspective also fits with what we know about developmental psychology. In our individual development, there is the awareness of new knowledge as our minds can comprehend it. Trying to teach a child skills before she is developmentally ready is a thankless task, frustrating for both the child and the teacher. This is why most people do not try to teach infants to read or to tie their shoes, for example. Once a child has moved on to a new developmental stage, however, trying to deprive him of the new skills that are natural to that stage is equally fruitless. Think of the difference, for example, of the eight-year-old boy who "hates" girls, and the eighteen-year-old young man who can think of hardly anything else.

I believe that there can be general parallels to this in cultural developmental stages, though these may not be nearly as well understood. At this stage in our development, the world culture is yearning for relevant feminine archetypes. The huge outpouring of sentiment and grief that overcame the globe upon the death of Princess Diana, followed by the massive swell of loving tributes to a departed Mother Teresa within the same week, are but two examples that attest to this.

Are there reasons for this response, beyond the obvious ones of a glamorous princess and a selfless nun? Both of these remarkable women, although very different in age and station, captured the hearts and yearnings of the world, in part because each sought to find and express the fullness of her life purpose in a way that both fulfilled her and benefited the world. In Mother Teresa's case, the emphasis was on the paradox of self-fulfillment by dedicating her life totally to God. In Princess Diana's situation, the paradox and the fascination concerned a woman who was graced with so much and loved by so many but who could not win the heart and fidelity of the prince she loved. It concerned her facing the powerlessness of that reality and learning to claim the power of her own person, her many vulnerabilities notwithstanding.

In some ways, too, Diana represented the women of this century coming of age. Much has been written about her insistence on finding ways to be herself rather than be stifled by outmoded forms. Both Mother Teresa and Princess Diana acted upon the world as women rather than simply riding the tides of traditional roles and expectations. Although their contributions (and interestingly, even their titles of "Mother" and "Princess"), were uniquely feminine, they transcended gender typecasting. Both summoned up strengths from within to do their work, and in so doing beckoned and called forth something from deep within others to do the same. Although in different ways and different degrees, they each expressed something of the discovery and claiming of empowerment.

Developmentally, the world, including Christendom, has largely seemed neither eager nor even capable of embracing the concept of empowerment for most women and some men in the last several thousand years. A change in consciousness, embryonic though it yet may be, appears to be occurring as we make the transition into the next millennium.

Paul says, "When I was a child . . . I reasoned like a child. When I became a man, I put childish ways behind me."[2] This appears to be true both for us as individuals, and for whole cultural groups. Studies of tribes and other groups suggest that whole cultures reach new developmental stages where fresh ideas and insights can be taken in, comprehended, and then used in ways that are beneficial to the people. With the advent of modern communication, it seems that such a shift may occur on a world scale, as we set aside old ways of thinking and embrace new ones about women and men.

DISCERNING NEW WINESKINS

Unfortunately, new ideas and thoughts are not always beneficial. So, how do we sort out the good from the bad? How do Christians, for example, discern when new thought corrodes the foundational base of their faith, and should therefore be exposed as faulty rather than being embraced, and when it is something God is calling us toward, asking us to "expand the borders of our tent" on the solid grounding of truth? When are new ideas calling us more fully into the kingdom of God and the abundant life Christ promised, and when are they seducing us away from that foundation?

As I have thought about these issues in the several years since writing the original thoughts about Mary, it has seemed to me that those who hold to scriptural truth must be willing to see it in the truest light possible for our time. If we do not have the courage and faith to do this with God's help, we lose valuable territory for God. Others embrace the new insights and take the lead, separate from the framework of Christianity. Those searching for guiding lights for their lives are confused when they see the church clinging to outmoded ideas that no longer shed the best contemporary light on Scripture.

Another consequence of lacking a willingness to see scriptural truth in the truest light possible is that extremes tend to spring up when something important is not examined this way. On the one hand are those who minimize and ignore Mary, while on the other hand are those who may exaggerate and distort her importance beyond what God intended. For example, some are now lamenting that so-called "channelers" report Mary is speaking volumes to them. *Newsweek* has alluded to the difficulty even those who are part of the Catholic Marian movement experience in trying to sort out what is real and what is extreme.[3]

Jesus spoke of needing new wineskins for new wine. Peter needed to lead the way for the Jewish believers in Jesus to accept the Gentiles into the faith, including the radically different practices of no longer mandating circumcision or requiring traditional dietary guidelines. In order to do this, first he had to be convinced by God of the rightness of these great changes. Peter needed both great discernment and spiritual openness to have eyes to see this new paradigm that God was initiating. God wanted Peter to be a state-of-the-art follower, and Peter was determined to follow God, in spite of centuries of a different and hallowed tradition that God himself had initiated. Peter's willingness to change in this way, and to strongly lead others to do the same, did cause controversy, but was necessary in order for him to both continue to follow God's best and to bring the good news to others.

At the time of Jesus introducing the new covenant as the fulfillment of the old, it also took great discernment to see where

God was leading. Again, when Peter accepted Paul's insight not to require circumcision, and received the vision that eating unclean food was now not only permissible but required in order to further the work of the kingdom, great discernment was needed. Believers needed to understand that God was indeed calling them to follow in this path. Those who did not were no longer able to serve God as effectively. Today, believers face many paradigm shifts. Some are seductive and ultimately destructive of the faith. Others are God leading us to new areas that can further the kingdom. The spirit blows where it will. Are we willing to follow?

It seems to me that as our society grapples with far-reaching issues, including family values and changes in women's and men's roles, the church must discern where the winds of the spirit are blowing. To the extent that we "blow it" rather than allowing ourselves to follow where the spirit blows, we find ourselves increasingly weakened and irrelevant, while not quite knowing why. More traditional churches find themselves frustrated, fearful, and angry that so many are finding frameworks for growth outside the Biblical framework, where they seem to thrive, if only for a season.

The exciting news about these issues is that God is ready with answers based on Scripture. Our Lord desires to go before us and show us the way. He wants to keep us state-of-the-art, walking in faith. We will make mistakes as we seek to follow, just as the early disciples did. He will be there to help us when we stumble or deviate from the path, just as he has always been, when we seek to follow him.

HAVING EYES TO SEE MARY

Having said these things, let us return to the issue of seeing Mary with fresh eyes. A compelling need exists to fully see the Mary revealed in Scripture. Otherwise, we cannot address the previously mentioned questions adequately, and we risk ignoring treasures that can provide the means of sustenance along our collective path into this new century.

I am reminded of Dorothy in *The Wizard of Oz*. She found herself whirled into strange places by frightening winds of change. In her heartfelt desire to return home, she searched the strange land in which she found herself for the return ticket to Kansas. Finally, her eyes are opened. The very shoes she wore as she searched tirelessly for the ticket are themselves that ticket home!

Like Dorothy's mysterious, powerful shoes, the archetype for which our hearts yearn may be right under our noses. We take her out at Christmas time, set her under the tree by the manger, and bask in the luster of the Christmas miracle. As the new year begins, we get back to the business of resolutions and goals while we tuck Mary away in the tissue paper, storing her away for another year. We read about her in Scripture, yet part of the scriptural Mary has remained in the shadows, noticed but not recognized by the heart's eyes as the archetype for which we long. As we begin to take another look at this woman on the donkey, we find power, inspiration, and mystery enough to engage us for a lifetime of growth.

Her life offers guidelines for women and men on living an empowered life in right relationship to God. Some characteristics of Mary have served as guideposts throughout the centuries since her life. Such traits as her faith, obedience, humility, and purity have been extolled and emulated by Christians. However, a key principle of health is balance. If certain traits, though wonderful and valid, are emphasized while others go unnoticed or even shunned, balance is lost and empowerment is not possible.

It is precisely this loss of balance that has happened with our views of Mary. Some traits that are evident in the scriptural account have remained in the shadows, so that we have not seen the full truth about the woman on the donkey.

Condemned to Perpetual Inferiority or Freed for Empowerment?

" . . . for all their beauty and power (and indeed because of them), the legends of Virgin Mary have condemned real women to perpetual inferiority." So goes the assertion on the back cover of *Alone of All Her Sex: The Myth and Cult of the Virgin Mary*. To the extent that this is true, it is because we have relegated part of Mary to the shadows. Yet, it is time to ask if this is what God intended, or does a careful examination of the Biblical record support a different view?

These are vital questions for contemporary women and men. Christianity has been a dominant spiritual and cultural influence in America and many other parts of the world. *Empowered with Mary* will not deny that *legends* of Mary may have condemned real women to perpetual inferiority. Rather, this work returns to the Biblical record, and finds strong evidence that, legends aside, Mary offers a compelling model and archetype of an empowered woman.

Approaching the Biblical account from a psychological perspective, we see that Mary serves as a strong, psychologically healthy role model for contemporary women. Her relationship with Joseph also yields a model of how men and women can relate in ways that honor themselves, God, and the couple relationship. Mary's *Yes* to God is an archetype for men and women desiring God to dwell within.

In this light, a portrait of Mary emerges that stands the test of time. She can speak to us in our dilemmas as we approach the complexities of life in this pivotal millennial time. Let us now explore the concept of archetype as it is used in this work.

ARCHETYPE, OH ARCHETYPE

An archetype, the dictionary tells us, is an original model or type after which similar things are patterned. It is a prototype, and one definition of prototype is an early and typical example. This term has been used in psychology to refer to profoundly deep as well as overarching models after which individuals pattern themselves. Jung refers to the importance of archetypes in the lives of both individuals and their cultures. He believed that archetypes are deeply embedded in our consciousness, and can hold powerful sway over our unconscious lives. This can be all the more reason for consciously examining an archetype. Part of the task of adulthood is reexamining old messages in the light of present adult knowledge, keeping what is good and true, discarding what is distorted, and completing that which is incomplete.

Archetypes can give us a blueprint for meaning in our lives. In order to relate to the truth of God's word presented in the Gospel, for example, we need models that can speak to our souls. That is one reason that the stories of the Bible characters have been preserved in Scripture. These stories not only reveal truths about God, but also provide models for helping us know how to relate to God, and what steps can help us in growing as persons in relationship to God. They put meat on the living bones of God's truth. It is not that we cannot relate to a loving God without them; it is that they can make it easier to know how to do this. They are another means that a loving God provides for us. Jung suggests that one reason for rootlessness in a society is a lack of being able to relate to the stories (myths) and archetypes of the past. These stories and archetypes must relate to where we are today. Otherwise they become either invisible to us or, even worse, irrelevant.

Archetypes can give us powerful permissions as well as potent prohibitions. Their power means that if we misunderstand the archetype, we can be shaped in ways other than the best God desires for us. As we have just begun to discuss, within recent years voices have arisen challenging the benefit of the traditional Mary archetype, particularly to women. The archetype is said to have been shaped by patriarchal voices that have used images of Mary to keep women in a position of inferiority. Bishop Spong, for example, asserts that any literalism must be swept away from the "nativity story" before there is any hope of the message being more positive toward women.[4]

This book takes a different position. As a psychologist examining the scriptural record, I believe that there are very positive and powerful messages embedded in that record that we have simply not seen and taught[5]. There are no doubt several reasons for this, and exploring them could in itself be the topic of a book. One of those reasons concerns the interactive nature of an archetype and the culture. In our own time, we are witnessing such a process in the life and death of Diana, Princess of Wales. Who she really was, with all her vulnerabilities and complexities, is shaping aspects of our culture, as both sexes have responded to her widely shared talents and dilemmas. Yet the media and our desires have also shaped our view of her, as she becomes bigger than life.

Thus, over time, archetypes not only shape us, but we as part of the culture shape them. This has led to criticism of the images of Mary by several who have made profound explorations concerning how those images have affected women through the ages. Let us briefly examine further the assertions made by two of these thinkers.

In *Alone of All Her Sex: The Myth and Cult of the Virgin Mary,* Marina Warner contends persuasively that Mary "represents a central theme in the history of western attitudes towards women."[6] It is perhaps because Mary became the "ideal of the feminine personified"[7] to the Western world that traits of hers that failed to fit into this ideal went unnoticed and that therefore women were deprived of a more balanced portrait of Mary. Psychology recognizes that both so-called feminine and masculine traits are present in varying degrees in each of us, providing a healthy balance. To extract all feminine traits from a man and hold up what remains as ideal or to extract all masculine traits from a woman and hold up what remains as ideal is to set ourselves up for unrealistic expectations and a hollow caricature of what God intends. It is this unrealistic idealization of traits that sets women up for any perpetual inferiority, not the reality of Mary herself as revealed in Scripture. Any message of inferiority is the result of the culture acting upon the archetype, not the archetype acting upon the culture.

It is also important to briefly consider further what Spong has to say in this regard, even for those who may vehemently disagree with his theology. In a stance similar to Warner's, he contends that the Christian church has been involved in the participation and support of women's oppression. "This oppression has been both overt and covert, conscious and unconscious. It has come primarily through the church's ability in the name of God to define a woman and to make that definition stick."[8] He then links this oppression to the illusions he says spring from the birth narratives in the Gospels, especially the account of the virgin birth. Thus both Warner and Spong see such views of females as a cultural and ecclesiastical sickness that weakens and hobbles women. Others, myself included, concur that a malady exists, but depart from the diagnosis and treatment prescribed by Spong. In considering these issues further, let us now turn to the concept of empowerment.

EMPOWERMENT

When I looked up the term "empowerment," the dictionary definition surprised me. The meaning given is "to invest with legal power, to authorize."[9] Empowerment thus means that someone has legal power, is authorized to do or be something. Our president, for example, is empowered to act because we have elected him or her to do certain things. When former president Nixon resigned from office, he immediately lost his authorization to act as head of state and became an ordinary citizen, with none of the power or authority to act as president from that moment forth.

Genesis 1:28 indicates that we humans are to have dominion over the earth. We have been empowered to have a certain role, over the animals and over the land and its resources. God has also empowered us as created creatures to have free will and to make choices. With empowerment comes the need for good stewardship. We are held responsible for the choices we make and for the use of our talents. In Deuteronomy, for example, God lays out key choices the people must make and the consequences of each. God urges us to choose life.

Some Boundaries Concerning Empowerment

In the book *Boundaries*,[10] Drs. Cloud and Townsend note that God has given each person authority over her own life, and that we are to use that authority responsibly. Thus to be empowered is in part to be responsible for our own lives. A metaphor they use has proved very helpful with both my clients and seminar participants in understanding aspects of empowerment: A person is like the owner of a house who is responsible for his or her own yard, but not for the yards of the neighbors next door.

For example, most of us don't get up on a Saturday morning, stretching, yawning, and looking out the window at the yard across the street, only to exclaim, "Darn it, old Wheeser has let his grass grow long again. I've got to cancel my plans for the game and mow his lawn. I bet he won't even notice I've done it, either." On the other hand, we know that it *is* up to us to care for our own lawn, whether we do it ourselves, or pay someone to do it for us. It is up to us to see that the garbage is removed, the flowerbeds planted, and the garden mulched. Furthermore, if someone should steal the barbecue from our yard, violating its boundaries, it is up to us to call the police. There are also times when we offer to help out with a neighbor's yard, knowing they have a new baby, or are away. In some emergency circumstances, what would be normally be intrusive becomes the necessary, loving thing to do.

Now transpose this picture to our psychological yards, with our feelings, thoughts, talents, and actions within our own boundaries. Likewise, the feelings, thoughts, talents, and actions of others are within *their* yards, not ours. While most of us have learned the rules for handling our green and grassy yards, we are often less clear about the boundaries and guidelines concerning our psychological yards. How many of us dissipate our time and energy attempting to manage other people's yards, while our own yards go unattended because we don't have time and energy to see to them?

Thus we are empowered to take care of our own "yards." We are not empowered to go into other people's yards inappropriately, trying to take care of their feelings, thoughts, and behaviors. To attempt this leads to exhaustion and lack of power. As we give up trying to control others and take responsibility for our own lives, our power increases.[11] Mary can be seen as a woman who paid attention to her own yard, rather than what others thought she should be doing with that yard. Likewise, by focusing on her life purpose rather than on what others should be doing in their yards, she was empowered. We will explore ways she accomplished this in the following chapters.

Another limit to empowerment as described by the Bible is that we are created beings who remain under God's sovereignty. It is when we accept the limits of our power and then work fully within those limits that we accomplish most fulfillment. The problem has been that we are sometimes not aware of our God-given empowerment over our own lives. Women in particular have traditionally not been brought up to recognize and exert that authority.

Several more examples can help us further absorb a common understanding of empowerment. Picture an individual with the talents to be president and to exercise the requirements of that office well. Without the empowerment of office, that person will not be in a position to use those talents.

Next, picture a person who is a queen, but has been raised to believe she is a peasant. She has been taught the virtues of being a good peasant, but had no preparation for how to be a ruler and exercise power of state. Although a queen by virtue of having legal authorization, until she gets the message that she is indeed royalty, and begins to move into that role, she will not fulfill her proper destiny. In order to make use of her empowerment for the good of her country and for her own good, she must: 1. Know about and accept her role; 2. Learn how to exercise her role wisely. To the extent that women have not realized their God-given authority over their own lives, and have followed models that were also portrayed to them as virtuous for not having such authority, they are in the position of the queen who believes she is a peasant.

Someone once observed that it is no accident that so many of the stories passed along the generations in hopes of transmitting wisdom to our children are about a young prince who sets off to seek his fortune. After encountering many trials and passing many daunting tests, the prince returns to claim the kingdom and the princess.

Such tales can be seen as models for gathering the skills and talents needed to take care of one's own kingdom or yard, as in our previous metaphor. Interestingly, the princess can represent either a literal life companion, or the integrating of a balanced set of masculine and feminine traits into the person. Having completed this set of developmental tasks, the prince is now empowered and can have dominion over his own kingdom. Thus, these stories deal with a second aspect of empowerment, the developmental skills needed to exercise authority, even over one's own life. An infant or young child is not terribly empowered, for example, even if she is the princess! Such a royal child must grow into the power of her rightful role.

Because Mary has been seen as a model for women throughout Christendom, it is vital to see that she is empowered by God in certain ways that have gone largely unnoticed throughout the centuries, and that she, even in the midst of a patriarchal culture that limited roles for women, claimed and exercised her empowerment. Women (and men) have often found themselves not utilizing their full empowerment, either because they, like the queen above, did not know their true state, did not accept their true state once it was known, or were unequipped to use it wisely.

As we see ways in which God empowered Mary and in which she exercised that authority in her life, we can begin to see anew the ways in which God has empowered us. Mary becomes a model who helps us develop as the full persons we were uniquely meant to be, not a model who invites us to become stereotypes of her. She helps us recognize the authority we have been given, models developmental skills and their use, which allows her to use that authority wisely, and shows us how these skills are put to use over a lifetime of consistent choice. As we identify with this Mary we become empowered alongside or with her. Let us now turn to a brief overview of the remainder of the book.

A Glance Forward

The scriptural record affirms a psychologically whole Mary who stands as an effective, powerful archetype of full personhood, capable of guiding and inspiring contemporary individuals. Succeeding chapters each focus on a particular aspect of Mary that contributes to this psychological whole. The Biblical account is explored with regard to each area, integrating psychological perspectives to help us further understand its significance to our lives. I have chosen to focus on those traits that are grounded in the scriptural record as they became apparent to me. The list of traits does not claim to be exhaustive. Some of the traits covered are widely associated with Mary already, and some have received far less attention. Many are cast in a somewhat different light by the perspective taken. It is this casting that illuminated Mary in a more relevant light for me.

With Mary, as with each of us, the individual self develops over time, and it is this self that can then form strong adult roles and relationships. With this developmental sequence in mind, the chapters are divided into two portions. Part One deals with Mary as an Individual, and Part Two deals with Mary in Relationship.

Part One identifies and explores those traits that make up Mary as an individual, forming the foundation of her personality. This section describes a strong, inner-directed woman who is therefore able to say a healthy *yes* to God. The paradox of a healthy inner-directed person being more fully capable of submission to God is explored. Mary is also a gifted woman who gives us a glimpse of her creative, artistic side. In addition, she possesses an intellectual side that is able to think in clear, complex ways. This part of Mary has often gone particularly unnoticed, and can thus be especially affirming to those thirsty for affirmation of this facet of their being.

The nature of Mary's faith, and the key role it played in her life purpose and in binding the other aspects of her personhood together, is also explored in this section. Mary as an individuated person, one with her own identity, is next described. How Jesus himself affirmed this trait in her and, by extension, in us, is discussed. How does the Christian concept of dying to self relate to the psychological concept of developing the true self? This sometimes puzzling paradox, with its important ramifications to our self-esteem, is also explored.

Having examined these traits found in the scriptural record, we then move on to Part Two of the book, which focuses on Mary in relationship with others. Mary's assertiveness and the wise ways she implemented this skill are explored. The topic of Mary and Joseph in their couple relationship then draws us into the question of how the newly emerging traits we are discovering fit into a marriage that honors God and each member of the couple. If a woman is inner-directed, intelligent, and assertive, how does this affect her relationship with her mate? What are the traits that God chose for Mary's spouse, and how did the two of them forge a common life purpose?

The all-important role of parenting by Mary and Joseph is then explored, with an emphasis on parenting principles that we can also implement as modern parents. The issues surrounding Mary as a fully sexual woman are explored, with questions addressed about how this affects attitudes towards our own sexuality. Lastly, the power of Mary's loving presence in the midst of suffering helps us learn about the simple power of being fully present ourselves when a loved one suffers.

Having sought to separate and bring forth from the shadows traits of Mary's that have seldom been noticed, as well as to further explore traits that we have long associated with Mary, the last chapter weaves the various strands back together in the whole person, allowing us to see the importance of balance.

My work and my joy have been to study and to apply my own professional and personal perspective to Mary's Biblical story. You too are invited to actively engage yourself in her story and these perspectives. As you do so, not only insights about Mary, but about yourself and your relationships can take seed, or burst forth in full flower, as the case may be. Is there a hidden part of yourself that has been seeking the safety of the shadows but is ready to emerge as you find affirmation for it? Or is there perhaps a wild part that can seek more form and discipline at this stage of your life? It is in this interactive work with powerful stories that fruits are realized in our own lives.

Enough of previews! Activating our wits, opening our hearts, and girding up our souls, we are ready to explore further these ancient Scriptures jammed with truth about Mary and, by the mysterious power of those timeless words, ourselves.

Part One

Mary as an Individual

Chapter Two

Inner-Directed Mary

In the sixth month, God sent the angel Gabriel to Nazareth, a town in Galilee, to a virgin pledged to be married to a man named Joseph, a descendant of David. The virgin's name was Mary. The angel went to her and said, "Greetings, you who are highly favored! The Lord is with you."

Mary was greatly troubled by his words and wondered what kind of greeting this might be. But the angel said to her, "Do not be afraid, Mary, you have found favor with God. You will be with child and give birth to a son, and you are to give him the name Jesus. He will be great and will be called the Son of the Most High. The Lord God will give him the throne of his father David, and he will reign over the house of Jacob forever; his kingdom will never end."

"How will this be," Mary asked the angel, "since I am a virgin?"

The angel answered, "The Holy Spirit will come upon you, and the power of the Most High will overshadow you. So the holy one to be born will be called the Son of God. Even Elizabeth your relative is going to have a child in her old age, and she who was said to be barren is in her sixth month. For nothing is impossible with God."

"I am the Lord's servant," Mary answered. "May it be to me as you have said." Then the angel left her.   Luke 1: 26-38 (NIV)

*S*O BEGINS AND ENDS the fullest gospel account of this momentous and remarkable event, which we call the annunciation.[1] Our purpose in looking at this extraordinary encounter between a young woman and an angelic messenger of God is to discern what Scripture reveals about the nature of this young woman chosen by God to bear the Christ-child. We also want to discover any message this passage contains concerning the relationships between Mary and herself, between Mary and God, and between Mary and others. Such discoveries can inspire and empower us, serving as guideposts as we relate to ourselves, to God, and to others.

With this perspective in mind, what do we notice? For one thing, God chose a woman who is able to be present physically, spiritually, emotionally, and intellectually at this encounter with God, to be the mother of the Messiah. This full presence enables her to say a meaningful *Yes* to her Lord. In addition, Mary possessed the confidence and strong sense of self to agree to this radical plan directly, without consulting even her betrothed, who would certainly be greatly affected by such a decision.

This suggests a young woman with a strong sense of inner direction. Mary provides an example of this trait for all individuals, especially women who have hungered for Biblical models that can speak to the many facets of their contemporary lives. God and Mary, through Luke's gospel account, send the message that God is pleased with strong, confident, inner-directed women who choose out of that individuality and strength to follow their Lord.

In this chapter we will examine more closely how the annunciation passage and other passages on Mary support these findings. Answers to the following four questions are explored: What does it mean to be inner-directed rather than outer-directed? What does it mean to be fully present physically, spiritually, emotionally, and intellectually? What are the implications for us that Mary agreed directly to this plan without consulting others? What are the implications of the fact that God dealt directly with Mary in a culture where men were typically the decision-makers?

INNER-DIRECTION VERSUS OUTER-DIRECTION, IN MARY'S LIFE AND OURS

As an inner-directed person, Mary is able to listen to her own inner conscience and sense of who she truly is in making life choices. She does not need to be dependent on human approval and guidance in order to make this crucial personal decision. This does not mean that others are not important to her, or that she may not at times seek out the support and advice or help of others. It does mean that she has trust in her own abilities to make decisions that are in accord with her own life values and life purposes. She has a sense of self that allows her at times to not go with the crowd, the general trends, or even the cultural expectations.

The description of Mary in the above paragraph also describes what it is to be inner-directed. What are some ways that Luke's account reveals this quality in Mary? When Gabriel visits Mary, she listens, discusses the practical question of her virginity with the angel, and then not only accepts God's plan with the words, "I am the Lord's servant," but also actively joins in the plan by saying, "May it be to me as you have said." We are told that all of this takes place in one episode. Mary does not ask for time to "get back with you on this" so that she can further mull the matter over, or discuss it with Joseph or other trusted loved ones. Trusting her own perceptions, she does not question the veracity of the angel's message or whether this visitation could really have happened. She trusts both God and herself.

In contrast, an outer-directed person will base her decisions on what people or forces outside of herself direct her to do. She is not likely to look within herself and seek, with God's help, the choice that is right for her. The wisdom of her choice therefore depends on whom, or what group, she is choosing to follow. Her allegiance may switch, depending on the mood of the dominant person or group.

An outer-directed young woman in Mary's position might have a very difficult time believing that the visitation of the angel Gabriel even took place, since no one else witnessed it, and it certainly did not conform to usual experience. Perhaps it wasn't real. How likely would such a woman have been to agree to bearing the Christ-child when it would obviously be difficult to explain to all around her—the people she loved and counted on, the gossips in the village, the acquaintances who

had expectations of her? What would the elders in the synagogue say? She might even be stoned for this development!

Mary's ability to be inner-directed is particularly striking
because it is quite likely that she was still in her teens, the time
in our lives when we have a natural tendency to be outer-
directed. Young people often go through a time when doing
what their friends are doing seems to be of crucial importance.
In addition, her culture was one with relatively more emphasis
on family and community and less emphasis on rugged indi-
vidualism than American culture.

Some Contemporary Examples

Nan did not particularly have any desire to smoke marijuana
or drink alcohol during her high-school years. She preferred
eating popcorn and sipping soft drinks with her friends. When
she finally found herself hanging out with friends who represented the "with-it" attitude she admired, she was surprised to
learn alcohol and/or marijuana were a part of the weekend
scene. Although uneasy, she put aside her own preferences and
values because it seemed obvious to her that declining to
partake would set her apart from her newfound friends.

Lou, on the other hand, was also pleased when she began to
be included by the same group. She, too was uneasy when it
became apparent that drugs and alcohol were an assumed part
of most parties with her new friends. She tried participating
without partaking of these substances. The teasing about this
was fairly casual, and Lou could withstand it, but soon found
that she was bored and restless being the only one who wasn't
high. Before too long she found other outlets that were more
comfortable. Initially, Lou felt sad about this, but soon found
other friends with more compatible tastes for fun. Although
there was a cost, Lou possessed the strength to live with an
inner-directed choice.

Other situations can be more subtle. For example, in one
church, there was a women's sewing group that made blankets
and other items to send to missions. Jennifer loved to sew and

greatly enjoyed the time conversing and sharing with the other women while making a worthwhile mission contribution. Marcy did not really like sewing, but felt after prayerful consideration that this was a good place for her to get to know some of the other women in her church, and chose to go for this reason.

Nancy found herself attending the sewing group after being invited by several friends. The event bored her, and she had a vague feeling that this was not the best use of her time and talents, but she did not want to let her friends down. Also, she could not think of a good excuse not to go. Nancy's decision was outer-directed rather than inner-directed. Though Jennifer and Marcy had different reasons for participating, both had made inner-directed decisions.

People can also choose to be "Christians" for inner-directed reasons or for outer-directed reasons. Some choose because they grew up with that expectation and found it comfortable. It is a rather easy, automatic choice for them, rather than a radical commitment to the risen Lord. For some it may help business and social life and be a way of educating their children within the traditional faith. They give lip service and are even sincere within a very limited framework.

Others have grappled in one way or another with the assertions of Christ and had a personal encounter where they made a conscious and life-directing decision, whether this happened in small increments or in the context of a specific, memorable choice.

Melanie was in college and fell in love with a young pharmacy student. During their courtship, Phil went to a Christian retreat more by happenstance than conscious choice. To his surprise, he had a radical life-changing experience and returned to Melanie an enthusiastic new Christian. Melanie had grown up a part of the church, but was doing some searching and exploration on her own at that time. She began feeling pressure from Phil to accept Christ in the same way he had, and to declare her faith in the same way, especially as they began to seriously consider marriage. To further complicate matters, Phil's new mentors told him that he must marry a Christian wife (and defined this in a very specific way) so he would not be unequally yoked, and he was anxious to fulfill what God wanted him to do in this instance. He was also strongly desirous of marrying Melanie.

Finally Melanie felt forced to tell Phil that while she loved him and wanted to marry him, any decisions she made about God must be because of her love for God, not because of her love for Phil. Otherwise, she would not really be putting God first, but her love of Phil first. That was the wrong order, she felt. Melanie needed space to grapple with her own spiritual issues and make her recommitment in a way that was right between her and God. If Phil could not give her that space, she felt that she needed to end the relationship, at least until she had resolved the matter with her own integrity.

Phil was driven to take this matter before the Lord in a different kind of way. Eventually, he prayerfully decided that he respected Melanie's need to make her own faith decision in her own way, and could highly respect her integrity to not be pushed into a decision prematurely out of her desire to not lose him and their love together. When Melanie did come more fully into her own faith, it was a strong, inner-directed decision that has stood the tests of time. Phil, too, had moved from an outer-directed decision encouraged by his friends to an inner-directed decision where he did not abandon the serious considerations his friends brought up, but searched prayerfully for what was right for both himself and Melanie within the context of those Biblical principles.

In this case, God gave Phil a peace about continuing the relationship with Melanie, even though she was at that time unable to articulate her faith in the way that he, Phil, would like. Melanie resisted making an outer-directed decision about her faith in order to please Phil. Phil moved toward an inner-directed decision regarding his marriage choice, one in which prayer and self-examination were important components.

These examples may help illustrate that Christians can make the same decision for either outer-directed or inner-directed reasons. Seeking to follow God's will is an important added dimension for Christians. When someone dialogues with God about God's will, and makes a free choice about it, based not only on whom God is, but also on whom he or she truly is, that person is making an inner-directed choice. Mary gives us a model for this kind of choice-making.

Many psychologists agree that obedience or submission has most significance when it is the act of a strong, free individual, empowered with true choice. We will see even more evidence that Mary fits this model. First, however, let's look at another powerful illustration of the significance of a strong, free individual choosing freely to submit to God.

The Example of Jesus

The choice of Jesus to die on the cross was such a significant, powerful gift. He could have said no. Instead, after a tormented night at Gethsemane spent dealing with this free choice, he accepted God's will. Jesus allowed himself to be captured, tried, and crucified.

At many points, he could have found freedom. For example, had he chosen to defend himself at the trial, he possessed the verbal skills and powerful logic to win an acquittal. Both his brilliant answers to other questions and his ability to evade capture in previous situations illustrate this.

The Paradox of Choice and Obedience

Had Jesus been trapped without a choice into a painful, unfair death, his dying would have been more akin to the tragic deaths of so many in our violent world today who are victims without a choice in the matter. His sacrificial act is partly so awe-inspiring because he freely chose to die, knowing the outcome would bring salvation to those he loved. Mary's act of obedience also has this noble ring of free choice. As we can see from the examples of both Mary at the annunciation and Jesus at Gethsemane, neither Mary nor Jesus made blind, mindless choices to do God's bidding. They freely chose God's plan in the context of being fully who they were and dialoging with God in ways that honored God and themselves. Their choices were ultimately both inner-directed and in submission to God's will. This was probably one reason they so pleased God.

Thus, for believers, there is a paradox involved in being inner-directed. We are committed to obeying God, and yet we choose out of our own freedom and inner-directedness. In obeying God, we honor and become more fully our true selves.

Of Costs and Benefits

To further illuminate the shades of Mary's inner-directedness, we turn now to another Scripture. Luke's account of the annunciation is immediately followed by the account of Mary visiting her cousin Elizabeth. Recall that the angel Gabriel has told Mary of Elizabeth's pregnancy. This visit, too, appears to be an inner-directed decision to seek out someone who will understand and support her during this perplexing, although wonderful, time when her pregnancy is a fact and when Joseph is still likely having a very difficult time dealing with it.

Joseph apparently believes Mary has been unfaithful to him and resolves to quietly divorce her rather than cause her public shame. We are not told whether Mary explained the angel's visit and the circumstances of her pregnancy to Joseph. We are only told that he became aware of her pregnancy and for a time did not understand.

Thus the person to whom she was betrothed and from whom she would most likely have sought support and love was not available to her at this crucial time. Being inner-directed and obedient to God is not without its costs. The strain of this situation might well have been too much for a more outer-directed young woman. Here Mary had to trust the reality of what she had seen and experienced with the angel and the Holy Spirit without validation from the man she would marry.

Although inner-directed, Mary still had need of key individuals to understand and support her. Being inner-directed is not the same as being a loner, although there are times when it seems that may be a consequence of being true to ourselves and to God! Mary was part of a culture where individuals were deeply embedded in community life. Mary had the wisdom to seek out Elizabeth, probably one of the few kindred spirits who could understand something of her experience and be supportive. How gracious of God to provide this older woman who could emotionally support the younger Mary and be a mentor to her. How gracious of God to provide a kindred spirit with whom Elizabeth could share her own pregnancy during the time that Zechariah was unable to speak due to his questioning of the angel's announcement of Elizabeth's pregnancy.[2]

Mary, Elizabeth, and the silenced Zechariah likely had much fellowship and spiritual growth as they praised God and wondered at what awesome and mysterious things God was doing in their lives. In addition, it is possible that Elizabeth was an influential older woman in Mary's family, one who could help pave the way for Mary's acceptance in the family.

There may be times in our lives when our motives and our behaviors are misunderstood by the very ones we love, in a similar way to Mary being misunderstood by Joseph. If we have made an inner-directed choice seeking to obey God, we still yearn to be accepted and understood by those around us. Yet we may find ourselves needing to do what Mary did—accept God's plan, regardless of the possible consequences. She could not control Joseph's reaction or force him to change his mind, yet she still followed God's plan for her life.

What she could do was give Joseph space, release him to God, and not rely on her betrothed for support during this period. However, she did not languish during this time, but sought out, with God's help, circumstances and people with whom she would be able to flourish in spite of the situation with Joseph. Later, when Joseph had a change of heart due to God's message in a dream,[3] Mary was able to reestablish the close relationship with Joseph. She was able to be close to Joseph without giving up her true self.

Contemporary Examples

Working this process out in our own lives is always unique to our particular situation. Pam faced a dilemma when she broke up with the man her parents and friends had assumed she would marry. Her parents were shocked, and not so secretly feared that Pam had missed her best chance for happiness and security. After all, Pam was twenty-eight, and not getting any younger! Then, when Pam decided to study art through a master's program that included time in Italy, her parents disapproved, for reasons Pam could not fully comprehend. Sad that her parents seemed resentful and angry about her choices, Pam nevertheless went ahead with her plans. She would have greatly valued their love and support expressed to her at this time, but they were unable to express these qualities in the midst of their distress. Somehow, Pam realized on a deep level that she needed to make these choices for herself. She also felt at peace about her decisions spiritually. Reluctantly, she realized she could not change her parent's reactions. Nevertheless, it was lonely boarding the ship to Italy without either a special man or her parents to wish her bon voyage.

For the first several days on the ship, Pam felt withdrawn and sad. She even felt torn by the uncertainty facing her. What if her parents were right? Perhaps her dreams were grandiose. As the voyage progressed, Pam began to strike up conversations with other passengers. One of these encounters blossomed into friendship with a female writer who resided in the same city where Pam would be studying. The two continued their friendship upon reaching their destination, and the slightly older, more established woman became a mentor to Pam, introducing her to a variety of interesting artists and writers.

When Pam returned to the United States, her parents' attitude had mellowed, and they were actually showing some pride in their daughter's art. The three of them were able to relate warmly, with more acceptance on the parents' side that Pam would continue seeking God's will for the unique expression of her life. Pam, for her part, had been willing to give her parents the freedom to disagree, and even withhold expressions of love. Releasing them to God, she had gone her own way, seeking other support. That act of releasing helped her be open to reestablishing a close relationship when they were ready.

Sometimes, of course, we may do our part, and yet our Joseph or our parents may not have a change of heart. We may have to accept that in a world of free choice and woundedness, others may not change. In such instances, it can help to realize that Jesus himself had to face such circumstances when so many were affronted by his choices. Mary made her choice without knowing what the full outcome would be. Let us now examine how her ability to be aware in this situation helped her with her choice.

BEING FULLY PRESENT

A major factor in Mary's ability to make the free, inner-directed choice to bear the Christ-child was her ability to be fully present spiritually, emotionally, intellectually, and physically.

Our ability to be fully present in a situation is one important measure of psychological health. Luke's account tells us that Mary "was greatly troubled at his [the angel's] words and wondered what kind of greeting this might be."[4] This distress and bewilderment indicates that her concerned reaction was to the content of his greeting, rather than the potentially upsetting effect of a visitation by an angel. Apparently, even in the face of such an awesome and overwhelming experience, she kept her head about her and was able both to think, and to let herself react emotionally to the content of the message.

For Mary, both head and heart were present at this event. Her initial emotional reaction was to be troubled. Intertwined with her emotional response was the intellectual response of wondering. This response by Mary was perceived by the angel, who then was able to both reassure her and give her further information. Gabriel reassures Mary with the words, "Do not be afraid." He then goes on to tell her about the reason for his visit. Her presence in both emotional and intellectual ways allowed the angel to reveal more and for her to take in this information and reassurance. By being in touch with her own processes, she could allow God to minister to her and was able to benefit from that ministry.

Mary's next response is also an aware, thinking one. "How will this be," she inquires, "since I am a virgin?" She desires to talk with God about this situation before agreeing. She does not beat around the bush, either, but asks the practical question of how she can bear a child since she has not experienced sexual intercourse. This indicates Mary was able to be direct in her approach, participating in understanding the situation rather than following from a naive, child-like position. God chose a woman who could speak up in thoughtful, forthright and healthy ways.

Notice the balance here. Mary voices her ideas without claiming them as definitive. She is dialoging with God, rather than either doubting or refusing him. Some have found themselves questioning God in a way that drew consequences, apparently because they were asking out of doubt.

For example, as we have seen, Luke 1:18-25 records how Zechariah asked a very similar question when told by the angel Gabriel that he and his wife Elizabeth would have a son. Zechariah inquires, "How can I be sure of this? I am an old man and my wife is well along in years." In this instance Gabriel gave a very different reply. "I am Gabriel. I stand in the presence of God, and I have been sent to speak to you and to tell you this good news. And now you will be silent and not able to speak until the day this happens, because you did not believe my words, which will come true at their proper time." Of course, one difference in Zechariah's situation is that he was already married and had been praying for a child, so there was not a need for him to consent to the birth.

In contrast, Mary's question seems to have been accepted not as springing from a doubtful heart, but from a genuine need to understand and be a part of the decision-making process. Apparently, Gabriel was able to see a crucial difference in the motives of Zechariah, even though both asked very similar

aring God, and the ability to be attuned so that we can hear
It is possible to have one ability without the other.

rst, Mary was able to be open to hearing a message from
clearly. The Bible often speaks of the importance of
ing eyes to see and ears to hear. It speaks of how God has
rned to speak to God's children, but they either refused or
re unable to listen. We also see how during the exodus from
gypt the Israelites begged Moses to be the intermediary for
hem and God—the presence of God was too overwhelming
nd frightening for them to be able to handle it. They were
unable to be open to hearing from God directly.

Another facet of being spiritually present is not only to be
open to hearing from God, but the ability and stance of being
attuned spiritually. To be in the presence of God often took
much purification, and a walk with God over time that built up
one's ability to handle closer contact and survive the experience. It seems, for example, that the years Moses spent living
quietly with the priest Jethro and his family in the desert herd-
ing sheep were a time of preparation not only for the work God
called him to do, but also for developing the ability to be
present and hear God's voice in the burning bush.[5] His faith
and ability to be attuned to God were further built up as he
followed God's instructions in leading the slaves from Egypt,
until he was able to spend long periods of time with God on
God's holy mountain.

Yet God also spoke to children such as little Samuel,[6] dedi-
cated to the temple at an early age by devout parents and under
the tutelage of a priest. This child was also able to discern and
be present with God, though he was at first unsure of the source
of the voice, thinking the priest was calling him. Somehow, in
his trust and innocence, the young Samuel was also attuned to
the voice of God and open to hearing that voice clearly.

Dante, in "Paradiso" 13, gives a wonderful metaphor for the
readiness that can enable us to be prepared to hear God. In his
day, a signet ring was impressed upon warm wax to put the seal
of the sender on a letter. No matter how beautiful and well-
made the signet sign was, if the wax was of poor quality or the

questions. This desire and willingness to di[...]
God's messenger) is another sign of psycholo[...]
itual health. Mary was not only thrilled to be [...]
she was now able to own her part in the dec[...]
Christ-child. She was acting in adult mode.

Now let us consider Mary's ability to be presen[...]
we do so, it becomes more obvious how all the[...]
intertwined. Being present physically was necessar[...]
be present in the other ways. What do we mean by be[...]
physically? Some Biblical figures report fainting wh[...]
encing an extraordinary spiritual event, such as a vis[...]
an angel. There is no indication that Mary reacted in [...]
She was able to be present physically in this most basic [...]

Most of us have ways of zoning out, checking out, bein[...]
to lunch," etc. Sometimes we may experience this in our b[...]
in terms of getting suddenly sleepy, of getting fain[...]
nauseous, or becoming too fidgety to remain in a situati[...]
Sometimes we block or short-circuit the uncomfortable sens[...]
tions by using such things as alcohol, drugs, food, or coffee.

For example, one of the things I often do when I sit down at
the computer to write is get up very shortly thereafter and fix
myself a cup of tea. This probably serves several functions. It
allows me to direct my fidgeting energy into a physical activity—fixing the tea. Tea has a comfort factor for me as well, and
it involves imbibing something. All of these factors probably
help divert and channel my anxiety about actually sitting down
to write, something that I love but that can also invoke feelings
of anxiety.

Even this relatively safe activity brings up feelings that can
divert me from being fully present. I manage these feelings
with fairly harmless techniques. In more nerve-wracking situations, however, I might find myself getting faint or dizzy
because it is too overwhelming for me to be present bodily in
that situation. Mary was able to be present and to be aware of
feeling troubled without her body being overwhelmed.

What does it mean to say that Mary was able to be spiritually
present? We will explore two facets of this: the ability to be open

temperature was not right, the image of the ring would not come out clearly on the wax. In order to hear God clearly, we usually need to be prepared and have the ability, by God's grace, to be receptive to his message. Otherwise, we are like the wax that cannot receive a clear image of the signet ring, no matter how desirous the sender is of making a clear imprint.

By having the necessary qualities, again because of God's grace, Mary was able to receive a clear message from the sender. We are not told if this was because she regularly studied Scripture, devoutly prayed, and lived according to God's precepts, but these are all likely.

An example that suggests further differences in being attuned to God's messages to us involves Christ's appearing to Saul on the road to Damascus.[7] Here, Christ came to Saul in such a powerful and direct way that he was blinded. In Mary's case, we are told of no adverse effects. It is likely that at least in part she was able to see and hear this appearance of the angel with no ill effects, because she was spiritually attuned already, used to being open to the presence of God, and seeking God's will for her life.

Thus we see a strongly inner-directed Mary, able to be present physically, spiritually, emotionally, and intellectually at this encounter with God, and to say a meaningful yes to God because of this. Mary and her archetype provide a beacon for all individuals, but especially to women who have hungered for such a model. This event vibrates with the clear message that God is pleased with strong, individuated, inner-directed women who choose out of that individuality and strength to follow him. Let us focus now on one example of God's validation and respect for Mary's inner-directedness.

GOD AND MARY—A DIRECT LINE

To appreciate the impact of the example that follows, we need to see it in the context of contemporary scriptural interpretations and related practices. Several years ago, I was involved with a small group of colleagues who were integrating

Christianity with therapy. We would gather every few weeks for a time of both personal sharing and lively discussions about a wide range of subjects related to our professional interests. From time to time we had ardent discussions about the role of women in the church and within marriage. One person in particular had been influenced by what I'll call the "chain of authority" concept, which has long been a teaching within some Christian groups.

According to this concept, God speaks to us humans in an ordered, "chain of authority" way, a way that is part of his design. The chain goes from God to the man, as head of the household, then proceeds from the man to the wife. The chain could then go from the man directly to the children or from the man to the woman as wife and then from her to the children. The Scripture traditionally cited to support this idea is I Corinthians 11:3, where Paul states "Now I want you to realize that the head of every man is Christ, and the head of the woman is man, and the head of Christ is God."

What Paul says here must be interpreted in terms of the whole of the New Testament. By way of contrast, there is also a tradition of strong arguments by believers that Paul's overarching message is **mutual** submission and equality of men and women under God. This tradition cites such Scriptures as I Peter 2:9 regarding the royal priesthood of all believers, Ephesians 5:21 regarding mutual submission, and Galatians 3:28 regarding equality of both male and female in Christ. Our present focus is not to thoroughly discuss this important issue.

I believe, however, that the annunciation passage adds an intriguing perspective that must be taken into account as we seek to understand what Paul acknowledges is the mystery of the marriage relationship and how it reflects our relationship with Christ. Let us examine Luke's account, searching for insights in this area.

One of the first things noticed is that God spoke to Mary directly, through the angel Gabriel. God did not speak to either of the men in her life, her father or her betrothed, to get consent for Mary to bear the Christ-child. God did not even say, "Now that you have agreed, let me inform Joseph or your father before we proceed further." Mary also answers God directly, without saying, "I am willing Lord, but let me get Joseph's blessing or permission." Neither does she say, "I am willing Lord, but let me get my father's blessing or permission."

It is interesting that Mary, highly favored by God, did not feel the necessity to follow the normal "chain of authority" concept. In her culture, Mary would have been under the head of either her father or of Joseph her betrothed, or of the nearest male relative. Yet in this very important instance, where God is choosing Mary to be the mother of Jesus, neither God nor Mary uses this chain of authority model.

What can this mean? God seems to act with great care to fulfill law or custom where he considers it important. For example, Jesus insists that John baptize him, even though it is not necessary in the usual sense, since Jesus did not need to repent of any sin.[8] Jesus wants to fulfill the usual requirements as a model. Since Jesus states that he does only what the Father directs, we can assume it was also God's intention that he fulfill this requirement.

However, in the annunciation God does not act through the chain of authority, nor does Mary, even though they could have done so to model or follow tradition. Mary hears God's call directly, and makes her decision on her own, without consulting others. This is especially remarkable since saying *Yes* would directly affect her relationship with Joseph in major ways! As we grapple with godly roles of men and women within marriage, within families, and within the church, the truth of this example must be taken into account as part of the gospel record, and as having bearing on this matter.

Is it possible that we need more respect and awe for the mystery that exists between the polarities of various positions on this aspect of marriage and women's roles? Much of what Jesus taught us was in the form of parables and through the use of paradox. Both of these teaching methods make themselves open to various levels of understanding. They also can perplex and puzzle us. Even the twelve disciples were sometimes perplexed and didn't "get" the essential kernel of what Jesus was communicating to them.

Whatever Paul's various statements about marriage and about women mean, they surely also involve the concept of paradox. Just as Jesus made such an apparently contradictory statement as, "So the last will be first, and the first will be last,"[8] so some of Paul's statements appear to be contradictory. When this occurs, do we sometimes desire clarity over truth and choose only one side of the paradox as our position? Is it possible that we must somehow take into account both sides of the apparent contradiction or polarity in order to live out the balance and mystery of God's truth?

How often do we try to extract a different kind of truth from statements that may involve paradox, and then make it dogma for everyone? While Biblical truth certainly has boundaries, how often have we "pulled in the borders of the tent" God has given us, robbing ourselves and others of the needed spaciousness provided by God to live within the mystery of God's truth, between the creative tensions of the paradoxical polarities? On the other hand, have not some stretched the borders of the tent until the fabric has strained and perhaps ripped? How do we find the balance?

As we shall see later in the book, Mary seemed to be comfortable living in the spaciousness of the tent provided by God, without stretching it beyond the capacity God intended. Her inner-directedness, emphasized in this chapter, does not exclude other rich facets in her relationship with Joseph.

When we look further at relational Mary, we will explore how she was able to act independently yet also be part of a couple. I believe she provides guidance and modeling that suggest ways we can better understand the blessing of living in God's kingdom on Earth within the mystery of the paradox of inner-directedness and submission. The example we have just explored is one that should neither be omitted from our awareness nor overemphasized as Mary's only mode of relating. Rather, it is an important lesson that can add to our understanding of a rich and complex woman.

SUMMING UP

The annunciation story reveals some very important facets of Mary's character, facets that begin to fill out the portrait of a woman with whom modern women can relate in ways we may not have previously understood. Not only is Mary a shining example of virtuous traits that have been traditionally extolled in women, but she is also an example of some positive non-traditional traits about which we as a culture still feel ambivalent when it comes to the female sex.

It can be very affirming for women desiring to be both fully themselves and fully God's to realize that God highly values inner-directedness, and that Mary not only affirms this, but can serve as a model who lives this trait out in a way that honors God and her true self. Indeed, Mary's inner-directedness is a foundational part of herself that sets the stage for her to exercise other gifts and to possess the strengths and traits necessary in raising the Messiah. Likewise for us, inner-directedness may be a foundational part of ourselves that helps us become the true self God intended, and that helps us bring forth Christ into the world.

Chapter Three

Creative, Artistic Mary

SEVERAL YEARS AGO, I began to study the person and work of a profoundly creative woman. I discovered, rather to my amazement, that this female author produced what I believe to be the most widely published poem by a woman of all time. Although she was young and often thought to be uneducated, her work contained remarkably complex thinking. Her awareness of some of the paradoxes in life indicated a depth that many much older never attain. The poem indicates she pondered theological and psychological matters with both spiritual and social awareness. This seemed no small order for one poem, created by a young woman while pregnant with her first child. Yet, although I had been aware of the woman and her work for most of my life, I had never thought of her in this context—the context of a profoundly creative artist.

If only I had realized the significance of this woman's work earlier, what an encouragement that might have been for me. As I began to ask others who were familiar with her, I found that they, too, were surprised at this discovery. They had never thought of it or her in that way, nor had such an idea been presented to them before, although they too had often been taught something about her life.

Who is this enigmatic, creative author? Mary the mother of Jesus! Her *Magnificat*, also known as Mary's Song, reveals a beautiful example of her creative side, and her ability to let that creativity flow forth, sharing it with others.

Consider these facts: the Bible is the best-selling book of all time; the New Testament has a huge market of its own; and Mary's Song is sometimes published apart from the totality of Scripture. Therefore, I submit that this is the most-published poem by any female author.

In the Scriptures, we get only a relatively small glimpse of Mary. Verses including her are often read during Advent, when the focus is largely on Jesus and his birth. Until launching into a focused study on Mary herself, I had seen these Scriptures primarily as arrows pointing to the arrival of our Savior.

It is almost as if someone in a beautiful, sumptuous banquet hall had much with which to be delighted. There was a large keyhole in a door in the room, which was noticed as part of the totality of the room, but never received much direct attention. Then, one day, the person needs something more, and as she begins to search around the room for it, she notices the keyhole. Curious, she bends down and puts her eye close to the beautiful brass opening. To her fascination, as she presses close and peeps through, she is able to see treasures in another room, and the "something more" she needs is provided.

Mary's Song is like that keyhole. Her song is there as part of what is offered in the sumptuous banquet hall of Scripture. Like the keyhole, when her song is focused on, more can be seen than at first meets the eye, and we begin to get a wider glimpse of who Mary is than we would if we did not take the time to examine the poem closely, as a tiny window into the creative soul of Mary.

THROUGH THE KEYHOLE

Let us bend now, and begin to look through the keyhole. As we scan the new room, we will first examine the context of Mary's Song. We will look at issues regarding the originality and inspiration of the poem. What it means to us that Mary displays this type of creativity is explored. We will then consider the nature of creativity as it relates to Mary's poem and to us. In addition, ingredients that encourage the creative process will be

explored. From this glimpse through the keyhole we will begin
to see how all these factors flow into guideposts for us today.

Context of Mary's Song

Peering through the keyhole, one of the first things noticed
is the context of Mary's Song. Luke relates that after Mary is
visited by the angel of the Lord and consents to bear the
Messiah conceived by the Holy Spirit, she hurries to the town
in the hill country of Judah, where her older relative Elizabeth
resides. Entering the home of Zechariah and Elizabeth, Mary
greets the older woman. Upon her greeting, Luke records that
two things happen: the baby in Elizabeth's womb leaps, and
Elizabeth is filled with the Holy Spirit.

This leads Elizabeth to exclaim: "Blessed are you among
women, and blessed is the child you will bear! But why am I so
favored, that the mother of my Lord should come to me? As
soon as the sound of your greeting reached my ears, the baby
in my womb leaped for joy. Blessed is she who has believed that
what the Lord has said to her will be accomplished!"[1]

And Mary Said—Ownership

The account next records the simple words "And Mary said
. . .,"[2] which graciously give her credit for these words in the
song. In this book, I am using the Biblical account as data to
examine from a psychological perspective, rather than engaging in various theological debates about the accuracy of the
Biblical record.[3] Within this framework of the Biblical data,
some questions have been raised about Mary's Song. One question concerns the originality. Is Mary simply quoting other
Scripture, and does this invalidate the song as an original work?
Another question concerns authorship. Wasn't the song
inspired by the Holy Spirit and therefore not really Mary's in
the sense of an original work? Did she not merely utter the
words as the instrument of the Holy Spirit?

These questions are worth considering. In her song, Mary

began by quoting Hannah's song at the birth of Samuel, in 1 Sam. 2:1-10, as well as integrating some other Scriptures from the Old Testament. This indicates her knowledge of Scripture and her ability to creatively assemble and weave passages into her own creation. It is symbolic of the fact that all of us "stand on the shoulders of others who have gone before us," and it is the particular way we assemble the pieces from our unique perspective on top of those shoulders that is our creative contribution, with perhaps some new pieces woven in.

On the other hand, while acknowledging whatever roots from the past are in the poem, we need to avoid the conclusion that this was not an original poem. The poem stands on its own, expressing a fullness of meaning that applies to the present situation Mary is in, and its significance for her and the world.

Turning now to the second question, that of authorship, we can also acknowledge that inspiration was a factor in this song. Yet it is interesting that with Zechariah's Song, which follows shortly after Mary's in Luke, it is specified that Zechariah was filled with the Holy Spirit and prophesied. Likewise, when Elizabeth responds to Mary's greeting, Luke states specifically that she was filled with the Holy Spirit. Yet Mary's Song simply says "And Mary said." I wonder if this is at least in part because God honors Mary's autonomy and creativity. In wooing Mary, God does not want words solely put into her heart and soul by God, but by her own creative process responding to God's love and call.

I believe we can see this song as a valid creation from a young woman who was responding from the depths of her own heart and soul to the wonder of God's mighty act in her life, in the life of the Jewish people, and indeed in the world. Just as training and discipline in any artistic endeavor show themselves in the work, any training and discipline she possessed regarding knowledge of the history of her people and theological understandings she had of the plan of God manifested themselves as part of her creativity.

We can give Mary full credit for the artistic, creative aspects of this poem, just as we can give other poets and writers credit for their work, even when it is no doubt inspired. Many artists will give credit to a source of inspiration for their work, and yet rightfully own the work. It is the paradox of humbly acknowledging the source of inspiration and yet also acknowledging the role of artist. I stress this because Mary's Song may not have received notice as a creative work because of the historical cultural tendency to not notice fully creative, artistic aspects of women's work. Perhaps because our age is now able to more fully celebrate these gifts in women, we can begin to more completely appreciate and celebrate this creative, artistic side of Mary.

Significance of Mary's Creativity for Us

Seeing Mary in this light provides a different perspective of her as a person. In addition to her very important and creative work as the mother of Jesus, she had an additional creative side—her own expressive work apart from that of growing and parenting her child. It suggests she cultivated her creativity and artistic talents in their own right. Mary as the chosen bride of God sends a powerful affirmation to all concerning the validity and value of these traits in women.

In any culture, the wife or bride of a popular, beloved figure often sets a trend that other women strive to follow. Recent examples in American culture come from the impact of Jacqueline Kennedy as the first lady on American fashion and sensibility. Now, a generation later, we are still seeing her impact, as well as the influence on fashion and style when her son, John F. Kennedy Jr., chose a bride. *Newsweek* devoted a cover and major article to his new wife, suggesting that she was an icon mainly because she had been chosen by him. The magazine then noted in detail items about her hair color and cut, her fashion sense, and the "rules" she had used in courtship. Had she telephoned him frequently or played hard to get? The implication was that her behavior could serve as a model to other young women.

How much more is Mary a model and influence for us to follow. How much greater her impact; sometimes subtle, sometimes more visible. As we have seen earlier, Marina Warner and others speak to the power of ideas about Mary to have profound impact on the lives of women, sometimes in ways not helpful to women. Such observations about how Mary has been seen culturally highlight the compelling need to fully see the Mary of Scripture. Her artistic, creative side is a vital part of that picture. Let us now examine why affirming this part of Mary and of women is of such crucial importance. To do this we need to examine the nature of creativity, its role in our lives, and the benefits of helping it to flourish versus stifling it.

THE NATURE OF CREATIVITY

An essential part of God's nature is that of Creator. Indeed, it is one of the basic ways of describing and addressing God. Creator God, and God, Creator of the universe, are primary ways of honoring the nature of God in our prayers and worship. It is because of this part of God's nature that the world we live in and our very selves exist. The created world, including ourselves, is seen as the outflowing of a loving, creative nature. God created it, and saw that it was good. This suggests satisfaction in not only the finished product but in the process of creating itself.

One dictionary[4] defines creativity as the act or process of bringing something into being; of producing through artistic or imaginative effort. Creativity is characterized by originality and expressiveness; it is imaginative.

Scripture tells us that we are made in God's image, and it seems one key characteristic of that image is the ability and desire to create.[5] Thus, from a scriptural point of view, the creative part of us is a core part, and we honor God when we express that part within the bounds God designed.

Jesus states that he glorified God by doing the work that God had given him to do. God gives us work in accordance with our gifts, including our particular creative gifts. We not only glorify God when we develop and express these gifts, we express a core part of who we were meant to be. This can be a most satisfying and personally unifying experience. It promotes our growth, happiness, and development.

In discussing creativity, the noted Gestalt therapists Erving and Miriam Polster state, "At times of union between awareness and expression, profound feelings of presence and wholeness of personality, clarity of perception and vibrancy of inner experience are common."[6] For them, the union of awareness and expression are essential components of creativity, and when they come together, the effect can be almost magical. Returning to Mary's Song, she was aware of her feelings—that her spirit rejoiced in God. Her awareness of her feelings of joy and thankfulness to God was a key component of the creation of this song. It led to a desire to express this awareness. Her feelings desired to flow over into an expressive, creative act.

A key part of the creative process, then, is the ability to be aware—not only of the world around us, but of our response to that world within ourselves. Psychology teaches that if we repress our feelings or awareness in some areas of our life, it affects our ability to be aware of other feelings and our awareness of life in general. Thus those who do not allow themselves to feel sadness or anger also tamp down their ability to feel peace and joy.

Luke's account indicates that Mary allowed herself to be in touch with a range of feelings and awareness. For example, she was aware of being greatly troubled initially when the angel addressed her, and she gave herself permission to ask a relevant question about the situation. She asked how the angel's announcement could be, since she was a virgin. She also seems to have been profoundly in touch with her joy and praise to God as she receives Elizabeth's greeting and affirmation of her pregnancy. It is probably no accident that allowing herself to be aware of troubled thoughts and emotions and to express them appropriately also allowed her to be profoundly aware of her feelings of joy and to find a beautiful means of expressing these feelings.

Mary's Song indicates that she had an awareness of the history and theology of her people. This suggests training and discipline in the study of Scripture and the historical, theological richness it conveyed. Herein lies another component of creativity. In most areas, the quality of the creative product is related to training and discipline. This often requires time and effort devoted to learning, study, and practice. Thus the raw creative talent and urge is shaped into something that can eventually give more satisfaction to both the creator and the recipient of the creative expression. Mary's Song radiates in part because of her knowledge of Scripture, her awareness of her people's history, the prophecies concerning the Messiah, and her study of the nature of God. All of this knowledge and understanding came to play as her creative expression poured forth.

All of this implies that Mary and/or her parents had made a priority of devoting a significant time to foundational learning and skills that could then flow forth in quality work. It affirms the importance of this basic choice for education and training in women in order to develop their creative talents. Since most scholars agree Mary was a teenager at this time, it affirms the role of parents in supporting the training of their children, girls and boys alike, in areas of talent. Fortunately, our society has made great strides in affirming the importance of this for both boys and girls. Mary's artistic ability affirms the need to continue vigorously in this direction. There have been long periods of history where women have not been seen as worthy of this type of training and have not been encouraged to develop foundational skills for creative expression in this way. The degree and quality of training Mary received may well have been the exception rather than the norm for the young women of her day.

We have been looking at two components of creative, artistic works—awareness and training. As the Polsters note, the creative person is not seeking to simply reproduce what is seen in the world: "He combines the reality 'out there' with his inner experience and the synthesis is a discovery, even for himself."[7] In looking at Mary's Song, we can see this process at work. She combines the reality of scriptural knowledge, insights into God's plan, understanding of people and how they work, and of the unique experience she has just lived through with her own inner experience, and synthesizes all these parts into a creative expression and discovery, if you will.

This song is more than the sum of its parts. Together, it forms a creative whole that expresses something both prophetic and original about her understanding of God's act in gracing her with the conception of Jesus. It is a beautiful love poem to her beloved God, celebrating this unique act and the many ramifications it has for herself, her people, and the world. It celebrates as well the wonder of God's notice of her and love of her.

Often artists do not fully know what they are about to create. They discover the artistic piece in the process of creating, as they use their awareness and training. The sculptor Rodin spoke of liberating the sculpture from the stone, a process of discovery as he engaged in working with the marble. Likewise, Mary probably did not fully know what she was about to create, but discovered the poem within her depths in the act of creating it. Thus the creative whole has an integrity and artistic unity that is more than a mere compilation of various parts. It combines intellectual activity and keen insight with artistic expression and creative understanding. Mary's Song stands on its own, unique in history, as the creative utterance of the one woman who was a fulcrum point in the greatest act of God touching humanity.

Because Scripture gives ownership of this song to Mary in some way different than when words are uttered by someone primarily as a vehicle for the Holy Spirit, it validates that this was a real and vastly respectful dialogue between the maiden and the Lord who loved and respected her. This Lord did not deign to put words in her mouth, but accepted and celebrated her original, creative praise and love as expressed in her love song. All of us know what a joy it is to receive expressions of love that come from the hearts of those that are dear to us. It means more to us by far than if we had penned the words for them and they had signed them, however truly they might agree with the words. In this same way, this poem was Mary's gift to God, and God cherished it as something authored by her rather than something supplied to her.

This wonderful gift of the capacity for original expression that God has given us was used by Mary to honor God in a special way that signing off on God's words could not. For me to imagine God's thrill in receiving this gift is also to begin to get a sense of his thrill in my humble creative expressions that are offered to him, inspired by him, and yet my own, offered to him. It is a stunning affirmation of the joy that each of us can give God when we lovingly offer up our creative gifts to him.

Ingredients Fostering Creative Talent

Two ingredients encourage awareness, and therefore the creative process. These ingredients are a safe place and an affirming place. Awareness of our feelings, sensations, and thoughts can be blocked and stymied if we experience it as unsafe to be aware of them. As young people, we often tend to shut down our feelings, sensations, and thoughts if we experience disapproval of them in our home and other caretaking environments. We mightily want to please our caregivers. In some cases, little ones fear anger and abandonment if their feelings, sensations, and thoughts are expressed.

On some level young children realize that they literally cannot survive unless their parents provide them with care and the necessities of life. Ironically, it is often the most sensitive, creative children who may be especially aware of subtle messages that parents disapprove of their creative efforts or interests. Such children may voluntarily give up parts of themselves, believing (accurately or not!) that this will please their parents. These parts may then be pushed from children's awareness and become part of what some psychologists call "the lost self."

As adults, we have the grown-up task of reexamining such early decisions and reclaiming lost talents and portions of ourselves that may be important, authentic parts of whom God created us to be. This can be one of the most exciting aspects of therapy for many individuals. I remember a charming gentleman, a successful manager and engineer, who began to discover sensitive, feeling parts of himself that he had not paid attention to for a long time. One day as he sat across from me in the therapy office, his eyes glowed warmly and he said with enthusiasm and wonder, "I'm trembling when I come here because it's so exciting to make these discoveries." He was now at a place where he could joyously welcome home some lost parts of himself. It was finally safe to do so.

It appears that the young Mary had a safe place where she could accept her own feelings, thoughts, and sensations, and learn how to express them in appropriate ways. This basic requirement is a great boon to the creative process. In addition, there appears to have been a safe place to focus on the foundational skills she needed to support her creativity.

The second ingredient mentioned was affirmation. Those who affirm and respect our essential creativity and talent can be key supporters of our creative process. Those who are able to do this without unduly shaping or controlling our creative expression give us a gift indeed. Most of us, children and adults, bask in the glow of simply having those parts of ourselves noticed. Thus the parent who puts the childish drawing on the refrigerator, or delightedly reads aloud the simple poem their child has written, affirms the creative expression of the child.

GUIDEPOSTS FOR OUR CREATIVE SOULS

What, then, are the guideposts for the creative and artistic parts of our souls and spirits that we glean from our study of Mary?

Making the Choice to Honor the Creative in Ourselves

The past is done, and the future not yet to be. What we have is the present and hope for the future. In the present, whatever the past, we can make the conscious choice to honor the creative part within ourselves and to find ways to nurture this part. For some, this begins with a commitment to find and reclaim lost parts of the creative self. This part must first be uncovered and identified. We may need to give ourselves permission to be aware of leanings or yearnings we have not trusted, much less listened to for some time. For some, it involves discovering new, emerging parts of ourselves that may not have so much been lost, but that at this stage of our lives can be developed if we will welcome them and give them a place in our lives. Sometimes this can mean a shift in the emphasis of what is creatively expressed in us.

Maggie expressed her creativity at one stage of her life by sewing clothes for herself and her children, with even an occasional shirt for her husband, as well as decorating the home and cooking creative meals that included originally designed cakes. These were only some of the ways that she expressed herself in caring for her family. At a certain stage in her life, a deep need for a different kind of creative expression began to tug at her awareness. She experimented by taking art classes of various sorts, and eventually discovered that working with stained glass was extremely satisfying for her. She continued to develop her skills in this area. As the children began leaving home, she found that she was directing more and more of her creative energy to working with the stained glass, an activity that was developing into a business where she created commissioned works for selected individuals and businesses. Her natural interests in other areas of creative expression began to take a backseat to her avid interest in this new area.

Glenn was a successful car salesman who had poured his energies into both creative ways of selling cars and into work in his shop during the first twenty years of his adult life. He was beginning to sense less avid interest in these areas when he was laid up after a skiing accident. With a leg in traction for weeks, someone gave him a set of watercolors and he began to "fiddle" with them, out of boredom as much as anything else. To his amazement, "fiddling" with watercolors began to light up his life, and eventually led to a full-time career as a watercolor artist.

Both Maggie and Glenn discovered new interests at a certain time in their lives. Neither feels their present career was necessarily the one they should have been doing earlier, but are quite comfortable that it's the one for them now. Zena, on the other hand, had a talent for inventiveness with gadgets from the time she was a young child. She was always assembling or disassembling something in the family home. As she became a young woman, this trait was strongly discouraged in her family as not a fit thing for a young lady, and Zena, interested in boys and being attractive to them, complied. Later, she found herself depressed as a young wife and mother, working in a job she didn't care for. During her therapy for depression, she began to realize that neglecting this key part of herself was contributing to her depression. As she welcomed back this part of herself and eventually got training in engineering, her depression diminished. Here is an example of someone who was not encouraged in a key part of herself and who needed to reclaim that part and to honor it.

Find or Take Time For the Creative Part

Make a commitment to give some portion of time to this important part of you. It may involve a portion of time each day or each week that you work into the present fabric of your life. Caroline devotes an hour four times a week to her creative writing. On those mornings she rises an hour earlier to do so. Max devotes several weekends a month to his writing, as larger spaces of time work better for him. Jim and Regina both enroll for classes periodically in their areas of creativity. Nan is exploring different avenues of creativity, and each week sets aside time in her daily planner to pursue this work.

Seek Out a Safe and Affirming Environment

Seek out an environment where you can expose this part of yourself safely. Some of this may involve making your inner environment safe, and not putting yourself down for your interest and your lack of instant expertise! If you can silence the inner critic, half the battle may be won. Your talent does not have to be earth-shattering to deserve this safe place to grow and flourish. I think of creative expression in several different categories. One is the level of creativity where the individual (or group of individuals) breaks new ground that benefits society. This level of creativity includes major new theories, new schools of painting, or major new inventions, such as the airplane was at the turn of the nineteenth century. Another level of creativity is that which develops new varieties within some category. For example, some create new types of aircraft, using the general model of a groundbreaking prototype.

Yet a third level of creativity is that which most of us are able to do. It involves unique, creative expressions of ourselves in some area that can be satisfying to ourselves and others, but that does not necessarily break new ground. I remember a Spiderman cake I made for one of our boy's birthdays, with a freelance version of the superhero. It was a huge hit with the young partygoers, who collectively decided that they all had to have a part of the cake that had Spiderman himself on it. Thus, it took some creative cake cutting as well! This cake was fun and gratifying for me to create and was a genuine gift of love to my son, but it did not break new ground of any sort. Nonetheless, it was a valid creative act.

A dear friend of mine recently sent some postcards of some new creative work she is doing, juxtaposing parts of one photograph onto another to create new scenes. As she described this work to me, she shared how deeply satisfying it was to her. She stated that it did not matter what anyone else thought of this art form in order for it to have meaning and importance to her. Something about this particular way of expressing herself was very important to her at this time in her life, and she was honoring that. She was creating a personal, safe environment for her to do her work, and was sharing it with those who were likely to affirm her in her creative process.

Another friend was working within a group setting of friends and acquaintances. The group got together for each member to work on her own scrapbook commemorating a major journey the group had shared together. My friend became immersed in the creative possibilities of the task, and began to produce beautiful, artistic renditions of the shared journey on her pages. To her consternation, this evoked negativity, almost scorn, from other members of the group. Perhaps her level of creativity threatened them. Whatever the reason, the group did not encourage her creative expression in this area, and it was not a safe, affirming environment in which to flourish.

A woman I once worked with experienced anguish as she began to realize how a barren, repudiating early childhood environment had squelched her artistic enthusiasm. Now a mature woman, she began to see that this was a lost part of herself that was sadly not nourished or welcomed by her husband either. She was beginning to glimpse how important this part of her was to creating a whole sense of herself, and the imperative for finding some safe environment for expressing a piece of it. She needed to give herself strong permission to seek out a safe environment where she could do her art, as well as some supportive friends who could encourage her.

Persist and Be Patient

This can be a hard one for me personally. I want instant success! Likely the foundation for Mary's Song involved persistence with regard to the years of learning that helped shape her mind, making it a ready instrument to produce this work. Likely there were times when she needed to be patient that her work and training, whatever form it took, would produce something of value. Could she have had any idea as she patiently studied, for example, that her persistence and patience at this task would lead to a song that would have a major impact over the centuries? Yet there is worth in persistently learning the fundamentals and patiently developing our talent. While our efforts may not have impact over the centuries in the same way that Mary's Song does, there is value in honoring the creative side of ourselves by developing it.

Take the Freedom To Express Creativity

No one said to Mary, "Won't you please compose a poem to commemorate this event?" She took the freedom to share this gift to her God and to her relative. She had the confidence to joyously share this gift. We need to find ways to do the same with our gifts. As we begin to validate and honor our own creative gifts, whatever they may be, and free ourselves from critical inner voices, we can begin to explore this wonderful, core part of ourselves.

CELEBRATING A NEW BALANCE

The traits that I had been taught about Mary included her faithfulness, her purity, her obedience, and her maternal nature. These traits were what the church and the culture valued in women and therefore wished to transmit, through the example of Mary, to the young women of my generation, as well of those in other generations.

My particular coming of age took place in the sixties. Some in my generation heeded the message, and sought to fulfill the traditional roles this Mary—the faithful, pure, obedient, and maternal one—exemplified. For some in that group, this appears to have been satisfying and fulfilling. Their gifts and natural disposition fit comfortably within these parameters. For others in this category, disillusionment and dissatisfaction set in. It may have been vague or unspoken, leading in some cases to mild but unrecognized depression. It may have taken a more virulent form, leading to upheaval, and in some cases shattered lives and families.

Some in my generation chucked that and most other "chuckable" values they could get their hands on, seeking a more liberated life, free from what they saw as the stifling shackles of such a limited model, served up, they felt, by the hierarchical, patriarchal white males. This could lead to discarding the church and its teachings altogether, along with value in time-honored institutions like marriage and the traditional family unit.

Some of us, uneasy with either of these responses, trudged our way somewhere in-between, yearning in perhaps rudimentary ways for guideposts that would enable us to be both faithful and free, both pure (whatever that meant in our age!) and creative, both obedient to the call of God and to the call within to be true to ourselves. We yearned to have creative, unique parts of ourselves validated and celebrated, or at the very least heard. Not seeing many of these sought-after guideposts, we forged our own ways, in various fashions, with varying degrees of satisfaction.

For the Mary I now see, I thank God. What taste God has in women after all! I can dare to be a little spunkier because I see some of that in Mary. I can be validated in my creative writing efforts when I see how God celebrated Mary's creativity. After all, he was no doubt her agent, I fancy. Without his spiritual nudge, how likely is it that the men of that age would have thought to include Mary's Song? Hooray for Luke, who was sensitive to that urge!

There is theological precedent and spaciousness for women to express a fuller range of talents and creativity to be expressed with this Mary as our model. As we can develop eyes to see this Mary and hearts to embrace a more full picture of her, the way is paved for the children of God to see more diversity of talents, needs, and yearnings in Mary's sisters, and to celebrate that. All of this is solidly grounded in Scripture and in the life of a woman beloved and chosen by God. It is not that many parts of the church have not been moving in this direction. Rather, it is that having God and Mary point the way surely doesn't hurt.

In a wildly popular book, Clarissa Pinkola Estes, therapist, writer, and storyteller, urges women to "Insist on a balance between pedestrian responsibility and personal rapture. Protect the soul. Insist on a quality creative life."[8] Her book has been criticized by some because her spiritual grounding does not appear to be in the Scriptures. Yet why are women flocking to this and other creative works that affirm the importance and even necessity for the soul of insisting on a quality creative life? I believe it is in part because women are starving for this important and crucial validation. Too many have not found such validation and encouragement within the church, within the culture, or within their families. They have not been helped to see the value God placed on creativity within Mary and her exercise of this gift from him. The evidence suggests that both God the Father and Jesus the Christ affirmed and valued her for this.

Balance is crucial. It is not that our former picture of Mary was wrong; it is that it was incomplete. Seeing her creative side in a fuller way adds a piece to the reality of Mary as a complete and balanced person. We desire to be complete. That is how God created us—with a desire to move toward completion and to be all he created us to be. A more complete picture of Mary encourages and informs our own development toward this completeness and growth. Created in God's image, we have a thirst to fan the God-given spark of creativity within us. Freud's infamous question "What do women want?" and his wise understanding that men need love and work come together for us here, even though the connection apparently eluded Freud. Women also were created to desire love and work. An important and valid part of work for many women is the profoundly creative work of bearing, birthing, and raising children. Hopefully, the fathers and many others contribute to parts of this important work. The quality of the creativity becomes woven into the character and being of the child. Like any creative work, the sensitivity as to when our part of the work is done is also crucial.

Depending on the woman and the situation, this may be the main focus for a period of time, or it may be the dominant theme in a complex musical piece in which other parts add richness and variety, each to the other. Recently, in a discussion touching on these topics, a friend commented, "I still believe that women were created to marry and have babies." At least one other friend murmured assent.

I deeply believe that is one of the rich and wonderful purposes for which many women were created. It is equally true that one of the life purposes for many men is to marry and father babies. However, just as we learned in the Westminster Catechism, the chief end of man (as in humanity) is to glorify God and enjoy him forever. An important way we glorify God is to be all he created us to be, whatever our gender. This includes our creativity, as well as many other facets of our personality. Mary exemplifies that we as women can be creative in more than one way. We can be creative calling forth the depth of our intellect. We can be creative in exploring questions full of mystery and paradox. When we do so as his children, God delights in this.

Remember *Yentl*, the film starring Barbra Streisand, where she, as a young Jewish woman desiring to study, felt compelled to disguise herself as a young man? It was only in so doing that she could pursue deeper theological and philosophical knowledge. She had to choose between her femininity and her love of creative learning due to the strictures of her culture. Mary was not forced into such a contorted choice. She was able to be intellectual and creative while expressing femininity in its fullest form. The implications of the phrase "barefoot and pregnant" are thereby changed forever.

We can progress towards becoming all we were created to be in more than one way, within the traditional role of pregnancy and motherhood or outside of these roles. This does not have to be an either/or choice. The church can see, hear, and help women have creative "both/and" options, rather than limiting "either/or" choices. As the church grows in this dimension, it helps women honor God and ourselves, in the best sense of the word "honor." The Biblical celebration of the whole woman, rightly seen, helps give women a solid scriptural foundation for exploring and exercising our creative selves. Let us find ways to broaden and deepen this celebration.

Chapter Four

Thinking Mary

And Mary said:
>"My soul glorifies the Lord
>   and my spirit rejoices in God my Savior,
>for he has been mindful
>   of the humble state of his servant.
>From now on all generations will call me blessed,
>   for the Mighty One has done great things for me—
>   holy is his name.
>His mercy extends to those who fear him,
>   from generation to generation.
>He has performed mighty deeds with his arm;
>   he has scattered those who are proud in their inmost
>   thoughts.
>He has brought down rulers from their thrones
>   but has lifted up the humble.
>He has filled the hungry with good things
>   but has sent the rich away empty.
>He has helped his servant Israel,
>   remembering to be merciful
>to Abraham and his descendants forever,
>   even as he said to our fathers."   Luke 1: 46-55

MARY'S SONG, as we have seen, gives us a glimpse into the creative, poetic side of this remarkable young woman whom God chose to be the mother of Jesus. This poem, brief glimpse though it is, also reveals some other striking things about Mary that have often been overlooked—her abilities as a complex thinker and her intellectual giftedness.

Before going further, let's take a look at why this is an especially important facet of the full Mary archetype. I can't help but think of the old saying, "If God had meant for us to fly, he would have given us wings!" In our historical background, there were many good Christian folk who believed that women were intellectually inferior to men. This idea was widely embedded in much of the Mediterranean culture of the time. For example, Jewish religious writings often saw women as the cause of sin and death entering the world because of Eve, and wrote such things as "one should not trust a woman's virtue or intelligence, since sin came about through her."[1] The ancient Greek view of the intellectual inferiority of women also greatly influenced Christians around the time of Augustine in the fifth century. Thus, while the teachings and actions of Jesus modeled treating women with respect, including respecting their intellect, early Christianity soon largely abandoned that perspective.

These ideas of female intellectual inferiority were widely influential for centuries. Some of the sayings that derived from this influence included "A woman is to a man as a chicken is to a bird." An old European folk saying went: "A woman, a dog, and a walnut tree—the more they are beaten, the better they be." A bishop preaching a sermon before Queen Elizabeth I stated that many women were foolish, feeble, careless, witless, and, "in every way doltified with the dregs of the devil's dung hill."[2] As we can imagine, attitudes such as these would not be conducive to the flourishing of women's intellectual gifts! There were many who would have said, "If God had meant for woman to think, he would have given her brains!"

There were no doubt exceptions through the centuries where both some men and women held to different beliefs and acted upon them, valuing the intellectual contributions that women made. Furthermore, much progress has been made in recent times. Even so, work remains to be done. Many of us, both women and men, carry some remnant within us of this limiting view of women, and our culture as a whole is still influenced by traces of these ideas. Because these views in earlier times were often dispersed through church leaders, parts of the church have been slow to discard them in a conscious way. Even when these views are no longer actually held, if the intellectual side of women is less validated by society and by the church than the intellectual side of men, this important part of who God created us to be can dwindle from lack of affirmation and resources.

These are some of the reasons that women within the Christian tradition especially need Biblically grounded models of those who celebrate their intellectual giftedness in ways that honor God. Women have too often felt that society was telling them that showing their intelligence would somehow be threatening rather than welcomed. Mary can be an important guidepost linking God's affirmation of her giftedness to God's similar affirmation of women's intellectual gifts. We can all benefit by seeing that God did mean for women to think, and that by choosing an intellectually gifted woman to bear the Christ-child, God affirms the value of this characteristic in women.

In this chapter, we will first take an overview of Mary's song to see what it indicates about her thinking abilities. Then we will consider the quality of humility, mentioned in her song, and how that quality expressed in Mary likely provided a crucial balance for her intellectual giftedness. We will look at the implications of this balance for our lives. Next, we will explore several cultural influences that affect women's expression of their intellect. We will also examine some cognitive[3] developmental stages, to learn what these indicate about Mary's thinking abilities, and how these stages can serve as a guide for us. Finally, we will begin to look at the implications of this for women and the body of Christ as a whole.

OVERVIEW OF MARY'S SONG

What do we learn about Mary's thinking abilities from an overview of her song? We see that Mary is able to ponder theological and psychological questions. She has an intellectual grasp of Old Testament Scripture, and the history of her people, as well as a spiritual and social awareness. Her thinking process reflects what we know today about cognitive development, and indicates that she was a gifted young woman who evidenced mature thinking processes that many people do not achieve at any age.

Thus, Mary's thinking ability as displayed in her song is an important guidepost for women. It affirms that God values the intellectual abilities of women and that women can use these gifts, just as any other, in the service and praise of their Lord. I believe Mary's gifts in this area made an important contribution in at least three ways. First, she used them to glorify God, as in her song of praise. Second, her intellectual gifts were of crucial value to her family, and particularly in her role as the mother of Jesus. Third, this gift has blessed the whole body of Christ both in the benefit to us of her recorded song, and in the benefits we have all received from Jesus, who had the benefit of exposure to her intelligence and early tutelage.

Because we have so often been focused on characteristics such as her purity, faith, and obedience when we look at Mary, we may never have reflected on the intellectual giftedness revealed by her song. After all, the most wonderful thing about this poem is the glory Mary gives to God, and the awe she expresses that God has blessed her, his humble servant. Let us now look at this concept of humility.

MARY—BOTH HUMBLE AND GIFTED

What does it mean to be a humble servant of God? Mary's humility has been much extolled. It was likely an important balance to her giftedness as well as to the honor of the work God chose her to do—raising the Messiah of the universe. Let us explore the meaning of this term. The American Heritage Dictionary defines humility as "marked by meekness or modesty in behavior, attitude, or spirit; showing deferential or submissive respect; of low rank or station; unpretentious." These characteristics seem congruent with Mary's attitude and behavior toward God.

Webster's Dictionary includes "not assertive" and lists the first synonym as "insignificant." These characteristics do not seem so congruent with Mary. Historically, some believers have defined and valued humility as thinking poorly of ourselves. The prayer "May I know Thee, O Lord, that I may love Thee: May I know myself that I may despise myself," illustrates this attitude.[4] This is not the type of humility that Mary seems to have practiced—she is able to celebrate who she is and the wonderful favor God has shown her.

Theological scholar Michael Fox takes a different view of what the appropriate understanding of Biblical humility is. The word humility comes from the Latin root *humus,* which means ground, or earth. Humus, of course, is the dark, rich soil that can produce much growth. Fox suggests that, "humble means to be in touch with the earth, in touch with one's own earthiness, and to celebrate the blessing that our earthiness, our sensuality, and our passions are."[5]

This definition suggests an acknowledgment of our true place in God's creation, accompanied by a joyous celebration of that place in creation. It suggests acceptance and celebration that we are noticed, named, and loved by God in the midst of that very earthy, or grounded, place. It seems congruent with Mary's statement, "My soul glorifies the Lord and my spirit rejoices in God my Savior, for he has been mindful of the humble state of his servant. From now on all generations will call me blessed, for the Mighty One has done great things for me—holy is his name." Mary juxtaposes her humble state with the fact that God has been mindful of her, blessed her, and done great things for her. She is both humble and exuberant.

She is able to celebrate fully because of her sober knowledge of herself, neither elevating herself more than she is, nor despising who she is. Her connectedness to her earthiness and her awareness of her true place before God allow her to be awed by what God does for her and for us. It is this type of humility that helps ground giftedness, and yet allows it to flourish without the thistles of arrogance stunting its beauty.

CULTURAL INFLUENCES AFFECTING
GIFTED WOMEN

Women today particularly need models of those who celebrate their intellectual giftedness while remaining humble,
grounded, connected to the earth. Women have often felt that
society was telling them that showing their intellectual gifts
would be arrogant and "uppity," rather than humble and
responsible. It can seem to a woman that being humble and
responsible is one choice and that using their intellectual gifts
is another, and quite incompatible, choice.

Colette Dowling wrote about this issue in *The Cinderella
Complex,* a runaway bestseller published in 1981. In it she docu-
ments and discusses that many women feel that independent
behavior is not feminine. One of her conclusions was that
women must recognize the degree that fear plays in their lives.
Dowling believed that this fear has been built up due to many
years of social conditioning, and is so much a part of women's
psyches that we don't usually even recognize its presence. It is
so familiar, in other words, that like the proverbial water that
the fish would not think to describe, women would not think to
describe this part of their inner world.

Some talented young women are encouraged by loving
fathers to develop their talents until they reach adolescence.
Then they find themselves abruptly without the support they
have come to trust from this beloved parent. In fact, as Simone
de Beauvoir wrote about her own relationship with her father
when she reached adolescence, the very intellectual things the
father once encouraged may now seem to anger him. This can
be a jolting shock to the young woman, and undermine her self-
confidence. De Beauvoir writes, "I kept wondering what I had
done wrong. I felt unhappy and ill at ease, and nursed resentment in my heart."[6] This phenomenon of encouraging a young
girl's gifts and then abruptly switching to discouraging her has
been called the betrayal of the father by Dowling and others.

In addition, gifted young women often find themselves not
encouraged by their mothers, who may have had no encouragement for such things themselves. In some cases, the mother

may feel threatened and jealous at the possibility of the daughter developing gifts and independence the mother may never have had the opportunity to develop in her own life. In other cases, the mother may know all too well the price a young woman may pay if she develops her gifts, and fear that the daughter's choice will hurt her chances to have a happy married life and a family.

Women have feared that openly sharing their intellectual gifts and becoming successful in this realm would threaten others and put the woman at risk for being abandoned. The deep fear that a woman must choose between developing and celebrating her gifts on the one hand, and being beloved by a man on the other, has hindered many a woman in using her God-given gifts. An important study regarding this was conducted by a psychologist named Matina Horner in the late sixties. Having noted her own fear of success as she pursued her doctoral degree, Horner began to suspect that getting exceptionally good at something was somehow frightening to women. She was the first to name this phenomenon "fear of success." She realized that women can become so fearful at the prospect of success that the will to succeed shuts down. In fact, she found that the very women who have a high drive for success and are most capable of achieving are the individuals who develop the greatest fear of success. The results of her study indicated that women feared that doing well professionally would endanger their love relationships with men.

The bind that talented women and young women can feel over this dilemma may mean that they set aside their talents, letting them lie dormant rather than take the painful risk of not being successful in the area of love relationships. Thus, while using his gifts and talents is seen in our culture as enhancing a man's desirability by eligible women, it has often been seen as detracting from a woman's desirability.

Since some of these studies and theories are dated, are young women today faring better in this area? There is alarming evidence that, to the contrary, they may be faring even worse. According to psychologist and author Mary Pipher,[7] girls today face the same crisis of feeling the need to give up themselves, including their intellectual gifts, in order to fit in with their peer group, and in order to be seen as desirable by young men.

Also, a recent study commissioned by the American Association for University Women[8] found a precipitous drop in the self-esteem of young women in the adolescent age range. Both boys and girls have drops in self-esteem during the adolescent years, but only 29 percent of high school girls in the study reported being happy with themselves, while 46 percent of boys maintain high self-esteem. Several revealing differences between girls and boys in the study are that boys were twice as likely as girls to name a talent as something they liked best about themselves, while girls were twice as likely as boys to name a physical characteristic. Also, the biggest difference between the sexes in the study was that more boys than girls felt they were pretty good at doing a lot of things. The report notes that "Girls, aged eight and nine, are confident, assertive, and feel authoritative about themselves. They emerge from adolescence with a poor self-image, constrained views of their future and their place in society, and much less confidence about themselves and their abilities." Thus, girls seemed to switch to more emphasis on their physical characteristics and to place less value on other characteristics relative to this, including their intellectual gifts.

The Christian church has at times seemed to reinforce aspects of different or more restricted roles for women. For example, I remember reading as a young adult a Christian book where a respected male writer commented that it might be acceptable for a woman to work outside the home. However, this is only the case if all of her homemaking tasks are completed and in good order before she does so. Since the proverbial women's work is never done, this appears to be a stifling stricture to a woman exercising God-given talents that may be different from those expressed solely in the home. Such lack of encouragement for intellectual flourishing has not helped the body of Christ.

There is another factor that may inhibit women from fully exercising their intellectual talents. Both women and men have seen the model of using giftedness in ways that become overly controlling and rigid. Such characteristics have traditionally been seen as positive in men—"He's the take-charge type"—and negative in women. It has not necessarily been seen that it is possible to be a powerful woman without being a controlling woman.

Even with this background, we now live in a time when more and more women are celebrating and educating their intellectual gifts. For the Christian woman it is comforting and affirming that Mary has been there as a model all along, although we may not have been aware of this. As our awareness grows, let's begin celebrating the support and encouragement this can be to women who seek to develop their gifts.

COGNITIVE DEVELOPMENTAL STAGES

As we noted earlier, Mary in her Song gives evidence of thinking on a complex level. In order to understand this more completely, we need to know something about levels of complexity in thinking, also called levels of cognitive development. The idea of adults developing throughout their lives is a relatively new concept, historically.

For centuries it was assumed that once we became adults we had arrived at the final stage of growth, and would remain generally the same except for the aging process, which was a decline rather than growth. There was some recognition that we can grow wiser from having accumulated more experience, but it did not go much further than that. It was also often assumed that all adults were pretty much alike in their development and thinking, assuming they were at least of average intelligence. Now we realize that there are many differences in the complexity of how we think. Some very interesting work has been done on cognitive developmental stages by Jane Loevinger and her colleagues[9], looking at how our thinking can develop and mature in stages.

In order to better understand the significance of Mary's cognitive development as illustrated in her song, let us now look at these developmental stages theorized and researched by Loevinger. These stages also can serve as useful guideposts for us.

Since we are dealing here with normal adult development, we will focus only on Levels 3 through 6 of these stages, giving a brief summary of each.

Level 3—Conformist

At this baseline level we are completely normal. Level 3 thinking involves conformity to external rules. We do what is right because someone tells us to, and we look to others to make sure we're doing all right. We tend to be concerned about being nice or good, looking pretty, wearing the clothes that are in fashion for our group. Life can be pretty clear-cut at this level. We tend to see things in terms of black and white rather than shades of gray.

This level of thinking allows us to adjust to many situations and to be quite happy in most of them. We are not aware of many shades of feelings, and we do not explore the feeling part of ourselves much. We may be aware we are sad, happy, or mad, but we don't think about whether we are frustrated, angry, or anxious—we don't get into those finer gradations of feelings. Introspection is not something we do. If we break a rule, we feel bad because we broke the rule, rather than because we may have hurt someone. At this level we want advice from counseling, not help in finding our own answers. We want to be told what to do. We want stability rather than change.

Level 3-4—Conscientious-Conformist

As we begin to move into further development, we add other characteristics rather than leave the old stage behind. Thus we continue to function at Level 3, but build more ways of thinking on top of that. There is a big gap between Level 3 and Level 4, so a Level 3-4 has also been described. At Level 3-4, wanting to help others becomes part of our motivation, rather than only being motivated by wanting to conform.

We begin to think in terms of multiple possibilities. At Level 3 we might say, "When I visit my mother I feel happy." At Level 3-4 we might say, "When I visit my mother I feel happy sometimes."

Or we might say, "When I go out with my boyfriend I look good and I have a great time."

We think in terms of belonging at this level. We value understanding, but we don't get the details. There begins to be a sense of awareness of a need for solutions to some things. This tends to be vague rather than specific.

Level 4—Conscientious

At this level the conscience and self-evaluation emerges. We move from conformity with external rules to having our own standards for self-evaluation, and we have guilt for the consequences of our actions, rather than guilt because we broke the rule per se. We become aware that we are unique persons. Before this stage feelings and behaviors can be easily confused, but now we are aware of motives for behavior, and can see how feelings may underlie behavior.

A sense of responsibility emerges at this level. Also there is more complexity. "I am not very strong but I feel good about myself." Awareness of change, and of development and growth, occurs at this stage. We begin to have long-term goals and ideals at this stage, and there is concern for communication.

Level 4-5—Individualistic

Beginning with this level, the previous description of Level 4 still applies, but other characteristics of thinking are added. At this level, we gain respect for individuality and often begin to view dependence as an emotional problem. We become interested in social problems, and we are aware of differences between our inner life and our outer life. We are also able to make distinctions between process and outcome.

Level 5—Autonomous

Level 5 is involved with self-realization, and this is reflected in searching for goals and purpose in life. There is the need for autonomy. With this comes greater respect for others and a realization that each person needs to find his own way and be able to learn from his own mistakes. Thus tolerance emerges as a characteristic. We are aware of and develop coping skills in dealing with our conflicting inner needs. Our thinking shows increased complexity, a tolerance for ambiguity, the ability to think in broad scopes, and to be objective.

Level 6—Integrated

Level 6 adds the characteristic of transcending conflict and reconciling the polarities within ourselves, others, and the world. This involves integration and giving up the unattainable. It involves paradox, and living within the tension of the two sides of the paradox.

Now that we have a brief synopsis of these thinking levels, we can begin to see some of the impact of the ability to think in complex ways. As we move to higher levels of thinking, we begin to link emotions and intellect in decision-making. Thinking becomes both/and rather than either/or. We may see multiple possibilities and the pros and cons of each. We are aware of and can deal with ambiguity. "On the one hand I'd like to go to the mountains for vacation because of the sense of adventure, but on the other hand I'd like the beach for vacation because it can be so relaxing."

It is interesting to note that typically we find most intriguing and exciting the stage that is just beyond the one in which we are comfortable. Levels much beyond that are probably too difficult for us to understand or be interested in. Also, while we can understand levels below ours, and of course continue to operate in them some of the time, they are not likely to be as interesting to us on a consistent basis. The big exception to the last statement is when our children or grandchildren are operating at lower levels—of course we find that fascinating!

In our examination of the stages, we noted that paradox appears at Level 6, the highest stage. Let us now examine the concept of paradox further, because it has great relevance to Biblical truth, as expressed by both Mary and Jesus. The term "paradox" is defined as something that is beyond thinking or conflicting with expectations. A paradox often involves something that seems contradictory yet contains truth.

This is fascinating because Jesus himself was someone who conflicted with expectation and was beyond our thinking capacity to figure out. Certainly he conflicted with the expectation of the best scholars of the day, who had most deeply studied how the Messiah would manifest. In fact, it sometimes seems Jesus is Lord of the Paradox.

Many of Jesus's sayings involve paradox. "If anyone wants to be first, he must be the very last, and the servant of all."[10] "Blessed are the meek, for they shall inherit the earth."[11] Likewise, many of his stories involve paradox. At first these teachings don't make sense to us. They seem to be in contradiction and therefore impossible or not true. "How can someone be first and last?" we ask, scratching our heads and wrinkling our brow. This defies our categories! The meaning of these statements or teachings is a mystery to us.

There are some things in the stories and teachings that even those who are at the most basic level of thinking can be touched by, and learn from. Yet at the same time the wisest person can ponder the meaning of these rich teachings and still not fully plumb their depths. It is evident that Jesus was a master at all the levels of complexity of thought. Further, he knew the secret of teaching in ways that were profound, yet also able to benefit the person who was simple, but earnestly seeking the truth.

Now let us return to Mary and her Song. In this song, she links the present event to both the past and the future, indicating a prophetic sense about the impact of this pregnancy. She notes that from now on all generations will call her blessed because of what God has done for her—awareness of the future. She sees the significance of the pregnancy to the promises God made to Abraham and the other patriarchs ("our fathers")—awareness of the past. Thus she links both the past and the future to the present event of her pregnancy and God's gift to her and to all. She also links the particular—God's great act with her now—to the universal—God's mercy that extends to those who fear him in any generation. She seems to be involved here in reflecting on the meaning of life not only to herself, but also how her personal meaning fits in with the larger historical picture and with the larger purposes of God. This illustrates thinking at least at Level 5, where we begin to deal with self-realization and the purpose of life.

Mary is also dealing with several paradoxes in her song. She notes that God "has brought down rulers from their thrones but has lifted up the humble," dealing with the paradox of the mighty going down while the lowly go up. She also speaks about God filling "the hungry with good things" but sending the "rich away empty." Level 6 thinking involves both paradox and reconciling the polarities within ourselves, others, and the world. Here Mary is dealing with some of the mysteries of God that do not make obvious sense to us. Why would the rich go away poor and the poor go away rich? In the midst of her great joy and awe at being chosen, she acknowledges and celebrates the impact this has for her, and her focus then extends to the implications for all. Her ability to conceptualize while still being in the present moment is exquisite.

Many have speculated that Mary may have been as young as thirteen when Jesus was conceived. Certainly all agree that she was a young woman, and that the typical age of betrothal and marriage in her day was in the teen years. Since complex thinking often develops later in one's life, if at all, this makes her poem all the more remarkable.

There is some tradition that Mary was educated, knowing the Scriptures. The poem certainly evidences some knowledge of history, theology, and Scripture. Mary's possible young age makes the extent of her complexity of thought even more amazing. Truly this was a sensitive, gifted individual. When she pondered the things of God, it was on a deep level.

It can be expected that since she was capable of this level of thinking, her interactions with the growing Jesus helped shape the thinking capabilities of his young mind. God wisely chose a woman who had the ability to stimulate the brain of the developing child. We know now that such stimulation is an important ingredient for young minds to develop to their full extent.

IMPLICATIONS FOR WOMEN AND THE BODY OF CHRIST

We now come full circle in this chapter, returning to further exploration of how Mary's thinking abilities can be a guidepost for us today. What are the implications of this for women, and for the body of Christ as a whole? There seem to be implications in four areas. First, God affirms and celebrates the intellectual gifts of a woman, and wants us to develop this part of ourselves, just as the Lord delights in this part of men. Second, developed minds can better take in the fullness and mystery of God's truth. Third, as the body of Christ embraces these truths and learns to better affirm girls and women because of this, the church has a powerful evangelism tool for both women and men who find this important. Fourth, both the body of Christ and the world at large will benefit as women are encouraged to use this area of their gifts. Let us look at these areas in more detail.

The first implication—that God delights and affirms a woman's intellect and its development—has been interwoven throughout much of this chapter. God's desire for balanced wholeness is reflected in Luke 2:40, where the young Jesus is described as growing in wisdom, in stature, and in favor with both God and fellow humans. Thus his growth included the mind, the body, the spiritual, and the social.

The Hebrew world-view did not separate out parts of the person to the extent that we now do. They were probably the original mind/body advocates, understanding that each affects the other. A person's development of her mind is thus interwoven with her development as a whole person, affecting her emotions, her actions, and her faith. Further, we have seen that we can develop this part of ourselves and still remain grounded and humble, in the sense of being connected to the earth. Both Mary and Jesus accomplished this balance of being intellectually gifted and yet humble.

Yet, as we noted earlier in this chapter, many parts of the organized church and the body of Christ have not generally focused on Mary's strengths in this area, and have often not emphasized these gifts in women. Why has so much of this seemingly been lost? At this point, it is helpful to look in more depth at this important question, and historical background can add to our insight.

Historically, there has been an unfortunate tradition within the church to ignore or actively deny the intellectual gifts of women. By the time of Augustine in the fifth century, Christendom had incorporated much of the Greek idea that women were intellectually inferior and were incapable of discussing intellectual matters.

This has been given as one reason that homosexuality became so popular in Greece. Another male was more capable of carrying on a love relationship because women were so mentally inferior, it was thought. Women were necessary to give birth to babies, and care for them, but could not provide other ingredients of a full love relationship, the Greeks asserted. Of course, since most women were therefore deprived of education and intellectual stimulation, and treated as if they were intellectually inferior, this erroneous belief tended to perpetuate itself.

Because Hellenistic[12] thought was adopted by many of the early church fathers, they applied it as a lens through which they saw the world, including Scripture. Thus, any Scriptures that indicated the submission and quietness of a woman were emphasized, and those that did not fit their picture of women were barely noticed. Though much has changed since that time, these beliefs held sway strongly for centuries. They leave traces in the culture that may be hard to identify but that nevertheless influence us. This makes them all the harder to be dealt with in open ways.

Some churches have actively been working to remedy this. Other church groups still have a strikingly limited view of women and their gifts, which they may hold to as part of their interpretation of the Biblical view of women. But what about the churches that are more open and claim that they have changed?

What about the women in these churches who are assured that all is well and they are appreciated but who sense some nameless net entrapping the fullness of who they are even yet?

"Wait," some may say. "Are there such women? If so, why don't they simply find a church that does support the fullness of their gifts?" Addressing these questions is a complex issue. One possible reason for a woman not changing churches is that she may find she has opportunities for growth until she reaches a certain stage in her life and development. The church may have been largely supportive of her growth until that time. This would be similar to what has been called the glass ceiling phenomenon in corporate America. A woman seems to be progressing well, being accepted and promoted until she reaches a certain level—the invisible glass ceiling. When this point is reached, a woman who has previously maintained she has not experienced discrimination finds herself stalled. Men with her qualifications or less are progressing from this point onward, but she is not.

When a similar situation exists within the church, it can take time for the woman to recognize it. It may not occur until she and her family are interwoven into the life of that church community. Also, it can be very painful to choose to see this truth for a woman, because to recognize it and speak of it further separates her from the very body she desires to relate to in mutually supportive ways.

As all good teachers know, what we pay attention to we encourage to flourish. The long tradition of defining women in terms of more traditional values that have been praised as aligned with God's purposes and desires for women, at the expense of not encouraging women to risk developing intellectually, has no doubt influenced many a woman to bury her talent, at great cost to herself, her community, and the world. The church and the culture have all too often reinforced each other in these tendencies.

A church often may not know how to encourage this part of women, even if it claims to desire to do so. Just as there have been few models for women to develop in this way, there are even fewer accessible models for the church to follow in encouraging women. Yet part of this is that the very models that are available to us, such as Mary, have been only partially seen, when it comes to these traits. If we can begin to fully recognize and celebrate the strength of Mary intellectually, we have a powerful encouragement in our attempts to change this tragic pattern.

What about the second area of implications—that developed minds can better take in the fullness and mystery of God's truth? The New Testament instructs followers to put on the mind of Christ. While this instruction to all God's children has many facets, our particular focus will be that of thinking complexity. Having seen that Jesus functioned at the highest level of thinking complexity, part of putting on the mind of Christ would seem to be seeking growth in thinking complexity for ourselves, and encouraging this in our children and others we influence.

Thus the Bible seems to not only be affirming of women expressing their intellectual gifts, but actually commanding all of us, men and women alike, to develop our capacity to think at the highest level of which we are capable. Thinking and faith are not incompatible—we are to develop our capacities for both to the fullest, with God's help and transforming power. Biblical statements that the wisdom of humans is folly to the Lord need to be seen as saying that knowledge apart from belief in God and God's teaching can lead us astray and become folly. These statements should not be taken as devaluing the worth of a finely developed mind committed to God and transformed by God.

As our minds become developed and finely tuned in their skills, God can use them for increasing good when we are in submission to our Lord. The following story may illustrate this.

THE MAESTRO AND THE PEASANT WOMAN

Once upon a time, during the Middle Ages, there lived a maestro who was capable of playing beautiful music on a variety of stringed instruments. He delighted whomever he played for, and had played for queens, kings, and bishops, and well as at the castles of various lords and ladies.

While traveling, he found himself caught in a sudden and dreadful storm, which he and his servant barely escaped by leaving their traveling bags and running for their lives. As they continued down the road, wet and bedraggled, but thankful to be of one limb, a peasant woman saw them from her cottage near the road, and invited them in. She warmed them, gave them something to wear while their own clothes dried by her crackling fire, and fed them some of the simple but nourishing stew she kept warm by the flames.

The maestro, deeply touched and grateful for her spontaneous and unpretentious hospitality, spied a small stringed instrument hanging on the wall. He asked if he might see it, and the woman gladly handed it to him. He saw that it had been lovingly and carefully made, and that the strings were in good order. His knowledgeable eye saw that, simple though the instrument was, it had the capacity to play fine music when touched by one who knew how to bring out its best. Having ascertained this, he asked if the woman would care to hear some music. Delighted, she said yes. Sweet and melodious music enchanted her for over an hour, as her guest poured his talent into the simple instrument.

Because her little musical instrument was well taken care of and finely tuned, the woman was treated to some beautiful music by her accomplished visitor. In her simple cottage, she was treated to a personal concert such as many a king had never heard. The maestro, talented though he was, would likely not have attempted to play the instrument if it were not in the fine state of readiness that he found it. The music produced by a poorly strung and tuned instrument would not have delighted anyone.

I believe that our minds are similar to the stringed instrument. As they are developed and tuned to capacity, our Lord can best use them. If we are like an instrument that has not been kept in the best playing order, we may have some strings in disrepair, and God will be limited in the range and quality of music he can play compared to what he could do if the same instrument were fit and ready.

What of God's truth am I not getting because of mental blocks or because my mind has not been developed to its capacity in a certain area? This question is both chilling and hopeful to me. While I am hopeful of grasping the things of God, I am chilled by the question of how much of God's glory and love I and others miss because we do not have eyes to see the full picture—eyes receptive because of faith and finely trained or developed because of full intellectual development. The type of full intellectual development I refer to is very close to the concept of wisdom. Biblical wisdom appears to be a marriage of faith in God, honing of the intellect paired with study of Scripture, and life experience.

Yet while God desires growth in this way, he mercifully accepts where we are, and moves us forward as we allow it. As a teacher, I know that I will lose members of my audience if I try to teach things they are not yet ready to hear. While a graduate student some years back, I also had the exciting but sometimes frustrating challenge of teaching a large undergraduate psychology class at a state university. Some of the approximately two hundred students were bright and highly motivated to learn. They sat at the front, had read the assignments and been thinking about the concepts before class, because the topic fascinated them.

When I taught to their level, a portion of the class became restless and lost. Some did not have either the interest or the knowledge base to keep up. In addition, some had not developed the intellectual complexity to understand the concepts at that level. I had to back up, slow down, and simplify in order to reach more of the class. This could be disappointing to the students who had loved the intellectual stimulation of being taught at their level.

My respect for the master teachers who were able to keep all levels of their class intrigued and interested greatly increased with that experience! Jesus, of course, was one of those master teachers. Even so, at times he experienced sadness and frustration that so many did not understand what he was saying. Of course this is a matter of the heart as well as the head—some hearts were not open to his teaching, even if their minds were capable of understanding. Yet, how much would God share with us if our hearts were open and our minds were able to handle the complexity and richness of truth the Lord has for us? The Lord wants all of us—our hearts, minds, and souls.

What can we do to encourage our growth and development in our capacity to think complexly—to increase our capacity to take on the mind of Christ in this way? Mary's Song suggests that she had an awareness of her people's heritage and of Scripture. It suggests that she had a good vocabulary. Please note that thinking complexity is not about the amount of information we have stuffed into our heads, however. It is not necessarily about how much Scripture one has memorized or how much knowledge to which one has been exposed. Rather, it has more to do with how we use the knowledge we have. Are we able to integrate knowledge in helpful ways? Thinking complexity has something to do with how we take the knowledge we have about a variety of areas and organize it, perhaps even building on it and making our own contribution.

Interestingly, the study of Scripture is an excellent way to develop this capacity in ourselves, precisely because it contains so many levels of complexity. We are exposed to some ideas and truths we can absorb at our present level and to some, perhaps within the same story, that invite us into further growth. Using an example from the Old Testament, let's look at the story of David and Goliath. Very young children love such stories and listen attentively when told the basic story at their level. A child, being little, thrills to the story of how David, the youngest and smallest in his family, was chosen by God to fight the big mean giant, Goliath. Just as satisfying, David kills the terrible giant with only a simple rock and slingshot, because God is with David.

The young child can be expected to relate to the story at the Conventional level. David is good and the giant is bad. David trusts and loves God, which is the good thing to do, and God is with David to kill the bad giant. Everything is pretty black and white and uncomplicated, but thrilling and faith-building to the child. We can also see that the child's interpretation is true at that level of understanding.

A child, youth, or adult at the Conscientious level of cognitive development who reads the story will begin to see that David was a unique individual who had his own internal conscience, one that influenced him to take on this task to defend his God and his country. David knew he was not very strong, but he also knew that he was clever and that God was with him. Thus the story has somewhat more complexity.

At the Autonomous stage, the individual studying this story might be struck, in addition to the other aspects of the story, by how autonomous David was in making his decision and pursuing his task. No one else suggested or expected him to take on this frightening challenge. In fact, they tried to dissuade him, out of concern for his safety. King Saul, after accepting David's offer to fight Goliath, sought to prepare David in the conventional way, by equipping him with armor that was too heavy and awkward for David's small stature. Both in volunteering for the task and in the way he implemented it, David relied on his own inner or autonomous sense of who he was and what was best for him.

At the Integrated stage, a reader of this story might consider all the other levels, and also find herself pondering the paradox of God choosing a shepherd boy, small of stature, and without the paraphernalia of the organized military, to vindicate a nation in a military battle with a strong and daunting opponent. She might reflect on how this story is integrated with other themes in the history of God's people where God lifts up the humble and brings down the mighty.

This brief look at one Biblical story serves to illustrate how Scripture provides truth that can be absorbed by our minds and hearts at our present level of development, and encourage our intellectual growth. Based on the view that part of putting on the mind of Christ involves responsibility to develop our thinking complexity, those who lead us spiritually are challenged to be prayerfully and intentionally fostering such growth in the church and providing educational experiences that meet the needs of various levels of cognitive development. We need to understand more of how to look at Christian issues in ways that are true to the gospel and yet do not reduce the issue to simplistic black-and-white thinking if Scripture itself does not do this.

Such a stance does not do away with absolutes that are clearly scriptural. It does challenge us to stretch our minds and expand our hearts to their full capacity, however. Unfortunately, failure on the part of his accusers to do this was part of the reason that Jesus died. His accusers failed to grasp the paradox and complexities of the prophecies concerning the Messiah. How could someone claim to be the Messiah, and not be a conquering king who would wipe out Israel's enemies? How could such a person break the Sabbath law?

Considering issues like this is very humbling. How much divisiveness among Christians could be avoided if we were more aware of the need to ponder issues at our highest thinking capacity, combining this with prayer? Mary's pondering could be a useful example to us.

We come now to the third implication—the powerful impact that embracing the intellectual gifts of women can have for evangelism and discipleship. Recently I was in a wide-ranging, delightful conversation with an intelligent, gifted career woman. In the course of our conversation, she spoke of her upbringing within a mainline Christian church, and her undergraduate degree in philosophy of religion. We noted certain commonalities in background. She remarked that she was no longer affiliated with that or any organized church body. The gist of her remarks went like this: "I consider myself spiritual and that is an important part of my life, but somehow my spirituality and the church don't seem to fit. Yet I'm not ready to join the Unitarian church—that would be no more for me than going to the grocery store. Also, I don't fit into New Age spirituality." She seemed to feel that her spirituality had grown beyond the church as she experienced it.

Another recent conversation occurred with a charming, bright young woman on an airplane flight. She had grown up within what she was now coming to see as a very constricting but solid Christian faith. Now she was questing within the spiritual realm, reading books that wove spirituality into their themes, talking with a wide variety of people, and feeling uncertain that her spirituality fit within the Christian scope any longer. As I listened and also shared some of my ideas about God's affirmation of women within the Christian faith, I seemed to be adding new food for thought to her framework. Could it be there was a place for her within the body of Christ? Could she be herself and not be stifled? Perhaps these will be questions she explores.

As the Church aligns itself more fully and proactively with the truth of Scripture regarding women in this matter, a powerful but hidden reason for the problems of the Church may be corrected. With the advent of more education for women and expanded roles created by the work of the women's movement, large numbers of women have not been able to find an atmosphere for nurture, growth, and challenge within the Church. Some have left, taking their husbands and children with them. Some have become deeply involved with spiritual movements outside the framework of Christianity. What a loss this is to the Church—to all of us within it!

Thankfully, God in his grace desires us to redeem our lost years and gives us new opportunities. Let us provide the strong and healthy view of women that God intended, one that includes value for intellectual giftedness in the many delightful and varied ways created by him. Let us begin by seeing the gifts of women in Scripture all along, teaching and celebrating those. Let us examine the implications of this fresh look at God's truth, and discover ways to include this part of women within our body.

As we do this, both women and men whom the Church has been missing may respond in positive ways. Numbers of men share the desire of women for mutual relationships and solid guidance through the maze of how to live fully in the contemporary world. Seeing a more accurate, fuller picture for women opens the opportunity for men to be more balanced also. The

Hellenistic view we have discussed tended to foster a distorted view of men as well. Emotionality devoid of intellect was projected onto women. At the same time, men were encouraged to disown their emotional side but had the full force of intellect devoid of feelings projected onto them. Whenever reality and truth are distorted, all suffer. As both genders can embrace all aspects of themselves in more balanced ways, all can benefit. When this distortion is sensed within the Church, it can be an obstacle for all truth seekers, and an unrecognized block to full growth for some within the Church.

Yet what, a friend challenged me, are women to do in the meantime? Where do we exercise our gifts if the Church won't accept them? How do we continue in an environment that is stifling or oppressive—or should we? Where do we go to receive the spiritual instruction and nurturing required in order to learn to exercise our gifts as God has intended? "Show us the bloody wounds in the body of Christ!" regarding these issues, she implored. A full showing is beyond the scope of this book. However, I suspect that depression and eating disorders are a few of the disorders that are increased when women find no sources of encouragement for the fullness of whom they were meant to be in Christ. The wounds would likely run the gamut from contributing to serious illnesses to the loneliness and isolation experienced when a woman senses parts of her are not noticed and welcomed. Also, the "bleeding" may be internal and not even recognized by the woman herself.

Furthermore, the question of where does a woman go if she wishes to be Biblically grounded but is not being affirmed and encouraged is a difficult question, with no easy answer. In some ways, each woman or each husband/wife team must work these out prayerfully according to what is best for their situation. Women and men can actively bring these matters up as areas needing attention within their church body. Support and study groups can be formed. As church and spiritual leaders recognize this as a need, proactive remedies are called for. For example, some church bodies now may have a sound theological understanding of the issues, but may not be instructing the whole body and grounding them solidly in these understandings. There may need to be time for individuals to share their stories in relation to this topic, and for healing to take place regarding their wounds. Creative and varied ways can be found to build us all up in this area, within a context of love and understanding. Sensitivity is needed both for those who have been wounded by the negative effects of restrictive beliefs and for those who have sincerely held to more traditional beliefs they have seen as part of the very fabric of solid Biblical Christianity. Then, too, there may be women who have not experienced these stifling difficulties, even when stretched in nontraditional leadership ways. Their experiences, and those of the churches that nurtured them, need to be shared and celebrated.

Willow Creek Church, one of the largest congregations in the United States, is an evangelical church body that affirms that women may take part in any ministry in which they are called by God, as well as the idea of mutual submission within marriage. My understanding is that when the church was being formed, the early leaders diligently studied Scripture regarding these issues, because they wisely realized it was a crucial issue if all were to be encouraged to use their gifts in ways pleasing to God. They embraced full roles for women within the church and within marriage after prayerful study, and feel that it is crucial that their leadership supports and understands this stance. Otherwise, they believe they are in danger of quenching the spirit. Careful and sensitive teaching about the rationale for this Biblical stance is only one facet of their dealing with this important issue. Another is sensitivity to including women in the leadership structure.

Fourth, in our discussion of the implications of Mary's thinking abilities, we turn to the concept that both the body of Christ and the world at large will benefit as women are encouraged to use their intellectual abilities. The story told by Jesus[13] of the talents challenges us to use our gifts. In it, three servants are entrusted with talents (a form of money in the story, but a useful metaphor for us) by their master while he is away. They are given the talents in different amounts, each according to their ability. Two of the servants put their talents to work and doubled them. One servant dug a hole and buried the talent, fearing to use it. Upon the master's return, the servant who had buried the talent lost it, and was cast out, while the other servants were rewarded with more.

Though this story seems to be particularly about spiritual gifts, I believe it has some application to the use of all our gifts, in that God expects us to use our gifts for the benefit of his kingdom. As women are more and more fully encouraged to do this within the solid grounding and support of the family of God, we can probably not yet imagine the benefit this will bring to the body of Christ and to the world as a whole. We have only a few glimpses of Mary's intellectual gifts and how she used them. Yet these brief glimpses are packed with power, encouragement, and hope for women, for their loved ones, for the church, and for the world.

Chapter Five

Faithful Mary

"Blessed is she who has believed that what the Lord has said to her will be accomplished."   Luke 1:45

LIZABETH, MARY'S much older cousin, uttered these words while filled with the Holy Spirit. The occasion was the newly pregnant Mary coming for a visit with Elizabeth and Zechariah in the hill country of Judah, where they lived. This is where we are told that Mary hurried after her visit from the angel.

How would it feel to be in Mary's sandals? In order to get a fresh view of Mary at this point in her life, I let my imagination flow as to what it might have been like for her. I invite you to join me in that reflection.

IN MARY'S SANDALS

Imagine. Mary has just received the astonishing news that she will conceive and bear a child by the Holy Spirit rather than by sexual intercourse with a man. And she chooses to say *Yes*, with the words, "I am the Lord's servant. May it be to me as you have said." She consents and accepts in faith.

Mary must have had her own dreams about how her life would take shape. Young women preparing for marriage are typically full of dreams and longings. In Mary's culture, the marriage was likely arranged, yet the two had probably known each other for years in the small village.

Imagine yourself in Mary's place. You are excited about plans for the wedding festivities. You picture the house you and Joseph will live in, and how life will be, perhaps with children in a few years. You think about how Joseph's business will grow—after all, he is personable, skilled, and knows the people of the area. You imagine how the two of you will have friends over for meals and the way you will use your gifts for making simple things lovely.

THE GOD AGENDA

However simple or complex one's life agenda is, it is part of who we are, how we see ourselves. Then suddenly God intervenes, and a God agenda is before us. We could not have imagined such an agenda. It demolishes our categories, partly because we could not have conceived of such a plan for us. Even more astounding and disconcerting is that God's agenda can be more like a scroll—we see only one item, and must wait for the rest to be revealed. In some ways our puny agenda pales beside God's, and our heart may become riveted to the new plan.

Yet how many of us wait until we are in the crucible to say *Yes* to God? Running from God and his agenda for our lives is described in an old poem, "The Hound of Heaven," which describes the process that can go on for many people. Only when the person in this poem has tried to escape in every way possible and finds that he cannot hide from God, who pursues him as relentlessly as a hound pursues its prey, does he finally say *Yes*.

Mary probably did not need to be in this type of crucible. She was not in desperate need, but in a time of quiet happiness and joy, a time when she had many good things to anticipate. It was not a case of "When all else fails, read the directions." All else had not failed. Her plan, and that of her loved ones, was in place and moving forward well, from all we can tell.

Perhaps saying yes to God's plan for us when our plan seems to be going well takes a more profound faith than that of saying yes when the choice seems to be between the disaster we have clearly made of our own lives and the plan that God has for us. When we are in this position—when all else has failed—God's plan can't be much worse than the mess already created, so there is not much to be risked. This was not Mary's situation. Rather, her plan was in place, was honorable and good. No one could have faulted her for going forward with it, for choosing not to have it disrupted by some strange apparition.

Perhaps she could have easily put the angel's visit out of her consciousness—only a dream, a case of a young woman's pre-wedding jitters, even. Yet Mary believed in the reality of this most unusual of experiences. She believed in the God who sent the angel. Trusting that God's goodness and purpose for her life were sufficient, she was able to consent, "I am the Lord's servant. May it be to me as you have said."

"It is easier for a camel to go through the eye of a needle than for a rich man to enter the kingdom of God,"[1] Jesus was later to exhort. As we have seen, Mary was a rich woman, in the sense of having a full life with much to anticipate. How hard it can be to even hear "change" orders in circumstances like these, much less say yes to them! And saying yes was exactly what Mary did. She was willing to put her own plans aside, committing everything to God in faith.

Corrie ten Boom, author and missionary, who wrote about her imprisonment in a concentration camp, has noted that she frequently hears people speak of God's goodness when he answers prayers for good weather so that outings can occur. "Yes, God is good when he sends good weather. But God was also good when He allowed my sister Betsie to starve to death before my eyes in the German concentration camp," she states.[2] With her yes, Mary said yes to both kinds of God's goodness— the delight of giving birth to a very special child and the agony of seeing a loved one die before her eyes.

Mary's yes meant that she would soon be a refugee, fleeing from a government intent on killing her offspring. Her yes meant she would be seen not only as an unwed mother, but an adulteress, at the very least by the man she loved, and perhaps by the whole community, if Joseph shared his perspective. Death by stoning could be the consequence. This strange request of God's could plunge her from the happiest time of her life to a whole set of reactions and perceptions from others who could now hate her, scorn her, kill her!

And that was not all. Though she likely did not know it at the time, before it was all over, she would be seen as the mother of a madman, and then the mother of a man who betrayed his faith and his God in the most blasphemous of ways. Most probably, she herself would go through the throes of questioning his sanity and purpose. The religiously upright of her own faith were so outraged by Jesus's perceived affronts that they arranged for his painful and humiliating execution. As Simeon prophesied at the temple,[3] her soul would indeed be pierced by a sword.

THE ORGANIZING PRINCIPLE

As we look at the characteristics of Mary and of the Mary archetype, it becomes apparent that her faith is the organizing principle that permeates her life. Faith is the beginning and the end of the story. Without the faith aspect of her character and very being, her other traits, no matter how healthy, unique, and strong, would not have been used effectively by God. Faith was crucial to Mary's life purpose. Likewise, it is crucial to ours, if we seek to have Christ within us.

Ironically, in outlining the chapters for this book, I projected this to be one of the shortest chapters. This was probably due to several reasons, one of which was that faith is more related to theological training than my area of formal study, psychology. Thus I felt that, important and basic as this characteristic is in Mary, and in any believer's life, it was one where I would have less to contribute. Another reason was that this trait in Mary has been more noticed and celebrated in the traditional view of her, and therefore might have less that is new to be said about it.

Yet a third reason is that while it is true that we often teach what we most need to learn, I am in awe of Mary's faith, and greatly aware of ways in which my own faithfulness falls far short. Whereas her faith seems to me to be serene and steady, my own is more fitful and jerky. Mary's steps seem smooth and graceful even when her path is difficult, whereas mine can seem clumsy, tense, and even leaden much of the time, compared to hers. I have my moments of soaring and gliding along the path of faith, full of ecstasy and delight, but those stand out more because of their momentary glory than because of any consistency! What were Mary's faith valleys and troughs like? We are not told much about these; we simply know that whatever emotions she experienced in the hard times, Mary remained true.

While these factors remain valid, what has happened is that the beauty, mystery, and health of Mary's faith have drawn me in, and invited me to explore and reflect on this part of Mary. As we explore her faith and ours further, let us first look at what psychology believes lays the foundation for faith in the lives of children.

FOUNDATIONS OF FAITH

The psychoanalyst Erik Erikson is well known for his seminal work on psychological developmental stages that begin at birth and continue throughout the lifespan.[4] Many others have since explored the ramifications of his work. The first and crucial stage is referred to as trust and bonding, and has its foundation in the first year of life. It is during this stage, when an infant is helpless and needs near-constant care and protection, that deep bonds of trust begin to form as the child receives adequate care, comfort, and love from primary caregivers. From this foundation, the child begins to build a basic trust in both her own loveability and goodness and the loveability and goodness of the one who cares for her.

When the child receives good-enough amounts of this loving care and has the capability of taking it in, a foundation is built from which all other relationships can grow. Both the quality of the relationship and adequate amounts of loving care are important to this foundation. More recent studies indicate that the neurological capacity for many aspects of emotional and intellectual capability is formed and enhanced during this crucial time. Little neurons are literally nourished and encouraged to form by attention and loving care.

Because we do not live in a perfect world, nor do we have a perfect ability to receive what is given, we all have weaknesses in this foundational level. Fortunately, we typically have opportunities to strengthen the foundation and heal the weaknesses found there, throughout our lives, and God's healing power has been known to work miracles in even those who have great deficits in this area. Crucial to our human relationships, this foundation of trust and the ability to bond also lays the foundation for faith in God. This is one reason that God puts such a high premium on loving and on parenting.

Therefore, a key foundation for faith is the sense of being loved and lovable in our early lives. This is not to say that those who did not receive adequate amounts of such love cannot be healed by God's love and develop a strong faith. In fact, some members of this group have very strong faith, because they are most aware of the miracle of God's healing love.

Now we come to the second foundation for faith in God: receiving God's love. Just as ideally we learn to love ourselves and others because our parents first loved us, so we learn to love God because God first loved us.

Possessing a solid psychological foundation in trusting and a solid sense of God's love for us are thus two foundations for faith in the Biblical God. It is on those foundations that faith can build. While the Biblical record does not specify, we can extrapolate that Mary likely had a solid foundation for faith in these two key areas. Most probably, she had loving parents who had fostered an environment where receiving God's love could flourish. Clearly, she had a base of knowing God and being receptive to his love before the angelic visit. Her act of faith in believing that what God said to her would be accomplished was embedded in this solid foundation. As she continued to live out her decision in a variety of circumstances, this foundation would help sustain her in the days and years to come.

Let us turn now to some considerations on the content and structure of faith and how they might apply to Mary's faith and to ours.

CONTENT AND STRUCTURE OF FAITH

Just as developmental stages have been identified in psychological growth and in cognitive growth, so have stages been identified in faith development, stages that shape the structure or form of our faith. We will first look at some of the work of James Fowler, who is widely renowned for his classic contributions in this area.[5] Then something about the content of Mary's faith will be discussed. After this, another perspective on faith development, one that compares our relationship with God to the relationship of a child and parent, will be discussed.

Fowler's Stages and Mary

Fowler has proposed six stages of faith development, beginning in infancy. According to him, these stages can apply equally to many varieties of faith or theological content. His stages 3-6 correspond in significant ways with the cognitive development levels discussed in Chapter Four of this book. For example, his Stage 3 of faith development is dubbed Synthetic-Conventional Faith. At this point the person relies on structure and faith content supplied by significant others because there is not yet enough clear sense of one's own identity and ability to make independent judgements. The person conforms to the teachings of the respected authority, whoever that is deemed to be. Clearly, there are similarities to Stage 3—Conformist, of the cognitive developmental stages.[6] A number of adults remain in this stage of faith development all their lives, and function satisfactorily.

Delving into detail concerning Fowler's stages of faith development and their application to Mary is beyond the scope of this book. Instead, only a few points will be noted.

Mary appears to be in at least Stage 5—Conjunctive Faith—at the time of her Song. For example, the emergence of Stage 5 as described by Fowler is analogous to "looking at a field of flowers simultaneously through a microscope and a wide angle lens."[7] In this stage, a person comprehends the power of paradox and realizes that apparent contradictions can contain truth. Mary's Song, as described in more detail in Chapter Four, gives evidence that she was aware of paradox and the truth in apparent contradictions, and that she possessed the ability to unify opposites. Relating her specific situation and what God was doing in her life to the broader lens of the history of her people and God's relationship to the world also occurred in this song.

In his discussion of Stage 6, the highest stage in faith development, Fowler suggests that "the rare persons who may be described by this stage have a special grace that make them seem more lucid, more simple, and yet somehow more fully human than the rest of us."[8] The unusual person who reaches Stage 6 is also depicted as an individual who has somehow reconciled the paradox of the need to preserve oneself and the desire to give oneself up in order to serve the world. Having embraced this paradox, the person lives out what Jesus described as dying in order to have life.

A transforming influence on the world is the result of the lives of these individuals. Fowler cites Mother Teresa, Gandhi, and Martin Luther King Jr., in his most mature years, as examples of persons who reached Stage 6. It seems to me that in the course of her adult life Mary embodied many of the elements of Stage 6. While maintaining a strong sense of self, her fulfillment came in giving herself whole-heartedly to the very particular task of raising an individual Messianic child, with all of the implications the task held for the world. Both the particularity of her calling and the universality of its implications seem to have been grasped by her. Mary also seems to have reconciled the paradox of the need to preserve her true self and the desire to give herself up in order to serve the world. Also, does not the description of a person who possesses special grace that makes

her seem more lucid, more simple, and somehow more fully human that the rest of us also fit Mary? Surely lucidity, simplicity, and special grace are some of the reasons she has captivated the hearts of so many through the ages.

Further Considerations on Faith Development

But what about the rest of us, who may be inspired by Mary's faith but have not reached Stage 6? Is there hope for us? In considering these stages of faith development, it is important to realize that our faith can be strong and healthy at each level, just as a child can be strong and healthy at each stage of physical development. Furthermore, just as in a healthy family an infant is loved just as dearly as a child at later stage of development, and vice versa, so God loves us just as dearly at whatever faith stage we are.

Also, just as it would be unwise and even detrimental to hurry a child through a physical developmental stage, no particular wisdom lies in hurrying ourselves or others to prematurely reach a higher stage in faith development. Of course, hindering or holding back children when they are ready to go on to another physical stage is also not wise, and this is also true of faith development. With physical development, we strive to provide the nurture, training, and nourishment that will help children reach their fullest potential. Should not this also be the goal for spiritual development? Certainly the writer of Hebrews spoke of his desire to nurture the young church members with solid spiritual food, and expressed his frustration that they still needed spiritual infant's milk.[9]

From Glory to Glory Through the Muck

Periods of extreme awkwardness can occur as a child makes the major shift from childhood to adolescence on the journey to adulthood. Our faith may be like that at times. It may appear stable and graceful at one stage of our lives, only to become excruciatingly awkward and ungainly at another stage.

Wondering what has happened to our sweet and pure faith, we may long for a return to an earlier stage, just as some parents are tempted to wish their sweet and loving child would return in place of the turbulent adolescent they suddenly have.

Yet, by staying the course, we progress to more mature levels of faith. As we go from glory to glory, it is often through the muck. If we had the luxury of more detailed accounts of Mary's faith journey, we would likely find that she too endured periods of clumping through the swampy muck. Certainly her faith was able to weather many storms—rejection by her betrothed, exile to Egypt, enduring the perplexity of not understanding Jesus at times during his adult ministry, and suffering the pain of seeing him crucified.

Let us turn now to a slightly different perspective on the stages of the faith journey. Since our relationship to God is often likened to that of a parent and child, it may be useful to further examine faith development from this perspective.

Another Perspective on Faith Development

Consider a little child, well bonded to loving parents. Especially when we are newly initiated into the life of faith, we are in a position similar to that of an infant, relaxing in the ocean of God's love and care. We trust that he will provide for our every need, and in sometimes miraculous ways, he does. Our faith shines, and God's answers are proof of his goodness. Sensing God's presence with us constantly, we assume that this feeling will never go away.

As time goes on, however, the sad realization comes that this sense of God's presence is no longer with us constantly. Then may come a jarring, jolting time. Perhaps things in our life begin to go wrong. Hardships come. We are undercut unfairly in our jobs. A loved one dies or becomes ill. This time our prayers for help do not bring God's immediate answer. We may feel abandoned.

Perhaps we are convinced that we are following God's direction in some specific matter and all of a sudden, things are not

going the way we would anticipate if we had heard correctly. Have we sinned, we wonder?

Sometimes we are simply being stretched to different levels of faith maturity. We are being asked to have faith on a more complex level. To us and to our friends, it may look as if we are slipping—especially since we used to be so stable. It may take longer to make a transition than we or others could have imagined.

Now return again to the image of a young child who has enjoyed a close, bonded relationship with his parents. Then the parents leave him for a time, perhaps the day, in the care of someone else. The child feels abandoned. It is as if the parents have totally disappeared. Loving assurances by the parents that they will return mean nothing—they are not there NOW. Then, the other children are picked up, but his parents have not come for him. Again, terror sets in, and the little child begins wailing, inconsolable. Finally, the parents arrive. As this process of the parents leaving but returning continues over time, the child internalizes the loving parents and begins to have a different level of trust, aware that he is loved even when the parents are not readily available, and that the parents will return.

Parallel times in our faith development occur. God is not as "visible," not as readily available to our every need. Gradually, perhaps through a series of experiences, we begin to trust God on a new level. Our faith has deepened and matured. Our ability to internalize a loving God has grown. While we do not have much to go on regarding a considerable portion of Mary's faith journey, it is clear that the road was not always easy. Mary too had periods when she needed to trust that God was there, loving her and her family, despite outward appearances. Nevertheless, she persevered to the end, and was part of the group that prayed together after the resurrection of Jesus.

Content of Mary's Faith

Now let us turn briefly and in a more focused way to the content of Mary's faith. Examining the structure of Mary's faith does not necessarily say anything about its content. According to Fowler, the structure or stages can apply equally to many varieties of faith or theological content, as we have already stated. The scriptural record gives strong support that the content of Mary's faith was that of the Old Testament and Hebrew traditions. She enjoyed a vibrant and living relationship with the God of Abraham and Sarah, of Isaac, and of Ruth, all ancestors. With Joseph, she observed the requirements of their faith. Later in her life, after the resurrection of Jesus, she embraced the realities of what came to be known as Christianity and worshipped with the new community of believers.

Thus Mary's *Yes* to God, her act of faith, is set within the context of traditional Biblical faith in a living God of the Old Testament, and within the context of an unusually mature faith with regard to structure. It is built upon a solid foundation laid by loving care by her parents and by God.

In considering these stages for our own lives, several factors emerge. To the extent that we have learned to trust and bond during our childhood, we have been blessed with the foundation on which to accept God's love and power in our lives, in order to further build our faith foundation. If major gaps exist in this area, part of God's redemptive plan and provision for us is to help heal and repair these gaps as we make ourselves available for this process. Loving relationships with other believers can be an important facet of this healing process. God uses a variety of ways, including healing prayer, counseling, small group work, and time with him to repair these gaps in the open hearts of those who call out to him. Sometimes God provides miraculous healing, sometimes healing that occurs in more usual ways over a longer period of time.

SEVEN ASPECTS OF FAITH

Having taken a look at the faith involved in Mary's *Yes* to God, and having examined some foundations and stages of faith, let us now look more closely at what guideposts there might be for us in the area of faith. Seven aspects of faith appear in Mary's story. They are:

1. **Having Ears to Hear**
2. **Discernment—Recognizing God's Voice**
3. **Willingness to Follow**
4. **Believing What God Says Will Be Accomplished**
5. **Acting on the Basis of Our Belief**
6. **Persevering in Faith—Staying the Course**
7. **Praising God Throughout the Process**

This section examines these aspects one by one, in order to better understand how they apply to Mary's faith and how to apply them to our own lives.

1. Having Ears to Hear

Mary's ears and eyes were able to hear and see what God was revealing to her. She saw the angel and heard the angel's voice. This suggests a regular prayer life. Mary's inner ears and eyes were likely in training, with regular prayer time that involved listening and receptivity to God. This suggests regular time spent in God's word. Mary's knowledge of Scripture as exemplified in her song also indicates this time spent with God. In addition, it appears that unconfessed sin was not blocking Mary's ability to hear God.

Mary's story, like all the great faith stories of the Bible, is encouragement that it is possible for us to have ears to hear God's message to us. That God speaks to us personally and directly through the Scriptures, guiding our lives, is an amazing reality. Knowing this capability in God and ourselves as humans can help us to develop this sense. Scripture provides assurance that if we seek, we shall find when it comes to spiritual matters of searching for God. Mary's story is an example of a young woman who by developing her spiritual eyes and ears received contact with God that guided and transformed her life. This holds out the tantalizing promise, backed up by Scripture in other places, that seeking God and his plan for our lives is rewarded. The book of Proverbs, for example, is full of assurances that seeking the wisdom of God, personified as a beautiful, desirable woman, will be rewarded.

There is another facet to having ears to hear. Rev. Terry Fullam[10] stresses that it is only when we have told God that we are willing to do his will that we can count on that will being revealed. It is our job to yield, and then God's "job" to penetrate our awareness with his will. This message can be a relief. What Rev. Fullam is asserting is that we can trust God will get the message to us in whatever means necessary, once we have made it clear that we are putting ourselves in God's charge to fulfill his purposes in us. We need to keep our ears tuned in the ways described above, but we can also trust that God takes responsibility for making his will known as long as we remain committed to doing it, whatever it is.

2. Discernment—Recognizing God's Voice

Jesus assures us in Scripture that, "my sheep know me."[11] Recognizing God's voice is part of knowing. Mary knew her Lord's voice. Because we don't want to go out on a limb unless we know a message is of God, this is a vital facet of our faith. It is also important to note that when God needs us to say *Yes* to something that is off the beaten track, he usually gives us the message in a stronger, more unmistakable way. Even then, what he asks us to do will be congruent with Scripture.

As we have seen in Chapters Two and Four, Mary knew Scripture and had some keen insight into the history of her people. She most likely knew that a Messiah, born of a young woman, was promised through the ancient Scriptures. Understanding concepts at a high level was an ability she possessed. Also, Mary asked at least one key question, dialoging with God before saying yes. Thus she recognized God's voice and recognized that what she was being asked to do fit in with God's plan as revealed through his word.

This ability to discern God's voice is a vital one if we desire to follow his direction in our lives. The stories of a culture are a way of imparting the wisdom of that culture to the young. One of my favorite stories as a child was of the little kid goats whose mother left them at home alone and warned them not to open the door to anyone but herself, because she did not want them to be devoured by the wolf. When the wolf knocks at the door, pretending to be their mother, the little kids recognize that while the words are like their mother's, the voice is deep and not their mother's. Therefore, they refuse to open the door. Taking in their reply, the wolf comes back later, having sweetened the tone of his voice with honey. The little kids are about to let him in when one of them notices the gray wolf paws through the window, and exclaims that he is not their mother.

This part of the story stayed vividly with me as a little girl, and began to impress upon a naive child that all who seemed nice might not be, and that I needed to discern the nature of the person who sent the message. Somewhat like the kids in this children's story, we as God's people are described as sheep who need to recognize God's voice. We are told that there will be wolves who will try to enter the pen and deceive the sheep, just as the old wolf in the story of the little kids was up to no good. Like the little kids, we must make sure the voice is of the one who loves us and wishes us good, rather than the one who would lie to us and do us harm. Part of discernment and using our wits is to know Scripture, steeping ourselves in its instruction.

Some years ago I was enjoying lunch with a younger woman who was on a spiritual quest. Drawn to a popular guru of the time who was attracting many young people, she confided that she had obtained an audience with this leader, and was seriously considering following him. There were those who felt that he was the Messiah come again, and he had not denied this possibility. To the contrary, he even seemed to be encouraging this belief in his followers. So many had not believed in Jesus when he came to earth the first time, particularly those in established religion, the young woman reflected. What if this were a similar situation? She did not want to be one of those who refused to believe if the Messiah had indeed returned, and once again was not being recognized by the established church and culture.

In the course of our conversation, I related that I could understand her dilemma, and had wondered about the same possibility of missing out on a new expression of truth for myself. However, words of Jesus recorded in Scripture had given me guidance in this area, and put my mind at ease about the possibility of missing his return as the Messiah. In Mark 13: 21-23 Jesus says to his followers, "At that time if anyone says to you, 'Look, here is the Christ!' or, 'Look, there he is!' do not believe it. For false Christs and false prophets will appear and perform signs and miracles to deceive the elect—if that were possible. So be on your guard; I have told you everything ahead of time." Jesus adds more details and concludes that when he returns it will be in a different way. "At that time men will see the Son of Man coming in clouds with great power and glory. And he will send his angels and gather his elect from the four winds, from the ends of the earth to the ends of the heavens."[12]

These instructions of Jesus gave me peace that I did not have to search out and work through the claims of those declaring themselves to be Messiahs. Jesus has made clear that his second coming will be of a different nature than his first coming, and that all believers will be gathered by him at that time. These words of Jesus made a decisive difference to my lunch companion, she later told me, and helped her redirect her spiritual search. She accepted the Biblical Jesus as her Savior a short time later, and has remained a committed follower. Knowing that Jesus had left this prophetic direction was an important part of the discernment process in this instance.

Being open to hearing the direction, and having a heart that was searching for truth, were also important assets. This young woman could have reacted by discarding this information if she had been set upon following her own path, for example.

Another, more recent instance of the importance of discernment involves the tragic Heaven's Gate suicides. The followers of Ti and Do certainly had faith in their leaders, enough to die early deaths in the belief that they would be joining beings in the next level beyond humans, beings who were in a space ship following the tail of the Hale-Bopp comet. The leaders included portions of the Biblical record in their message, and mixed it with a generous blend of their own ideas. Had their followers known and heeded the Scriptures in Mark 13, their needless deaths could have been prevented.

When a college student, I prepared for a career in elementary education, and my first job after graduation was teaching a fourth-grade class in Ukiah, California. As a novice teacher, my principal assigned an experienced and well-liked fourth grade teacher to mentor me that first year. One of the things that this mentor did was invite me and my new husband to join his church fellowship, which he explained was lead by an extraordinarily loving and visionary man who had taken many neglected children under his wing. The leader had chosen this northern California area for the community to settle in because it was deemed less likely than other areas to be damaged by a potential nuclear attack.

My husband and I never did worship with my assigned mentor, and by not doing so we missed the opportunity to hear the Rev. Jim Jones years before he moved his group to South America, where they later committed mass suicide. I often wondered if this teacher had left the group by then, or if he died with the others by drinking the infamous cyanide-laced Kool-Aid. At what point would the followers of Jim Jones have been able to discern that their leader was no longer following Scriptural guidelines?

Mercifully, God takes on part of the responsibility for letting his children know his voice. There appears to be a dance between our search for God and God's reaching out to us. Our free will is key in this process, and is related to the next step.

3. Willingness to Follow

We have seen that Mary was willing to follow God's unexpected plan for her, even though it changed forever the course of her life. Sometimes the willingness to follow and the actual act of following come close together and are one apparently seamless act. Other times the willingness is maintained as a state over time, while the person waits for further direction as to the exact timing. For example, some who desire to go into the mission field indicate their willingness to the Lord, and then wait until God opens those doors. Mary's willingness is indicated by her words, "I am the Lord's servant. May it be to me as you have said."[13] At this point what was called for, and what Mary gave, was her receptivity to do God's will and have this child.

Her words indicate two levels of choice, which are important to note. "I am the Lord's servant." This was a statement about who Mary was, and a choice she had made, prior to the angel's visitation. She was a person already committed to her Lord, and to her Lord's purpose. Thus the angel was sent to someone who lived within a context of a close and committed relationship to God, and was prepared to do God's will. This first level of choice prepared her for the second level of choice and of faith. Mary made this first level of choice without having any idea about what God's specific life purpose for her entailed. This is demonstrated by her initial shocked surprise at the angel's announcement, and by her dialogue with him. As Rev. Fullam puts it, the decision to do the will of God is key to getting the plan.

The second level of Mary's choice is her decision to consent to this specific mission, to bear the Christ-child, indicated by her words, "May it be to me as you have said." That this second level of choice is offered says something wonderful about the nature of our relationship with God. As his servants, we could simply receive orders with no choice in the matter. We have enlisted in his service, so to speak. Yet within that context God does not obliterate us. Rather, there is the mystery of how he continues to honor and respect both our free will and the uniqueness of our personhood.

It is as if God is leading us in a dance, and desires to dance with a loving partner who responds and contributes, not with a limp rag doll. Some years ago my husband and I took several dance lessons in an attempt to compensate for the apparent lack of any rhythmic genes in our makeup. At one point the instructor surprised me by suggesting I resist more with my right hand, held in Bill's. If my hand was too pliable, leading me was more difficult and less fun.

Yielding to God's will, yet remaining active and fully ourselves in the process, is both a mystery to be pondered and a paradox to be worked out in our own lives. A joke about therapists indicates a small aspect of this reality. "How many therapists does it take to change a light bulb?" begins the joke. The answer, of course, is "Only one, but the light bulb must want to be changed!" God, too, respects our boundaries, and awaits our permission as autonomous beings to have him dwell within us. He may also await our consent before doing other growth work within us.

With regard to this willingness, Mary followed in the footsteps of some of the faithful greats. Abram and Sarai [later, God would change their names to Abraham and Sarah] were willing to follow God even though it meant leaving their homeland and stepping out to a new land, they knew not where. Moses, too, was willing to leave the comfortable lifestyle he had created for himself in the desert, when God called him to go back to Egypt. Ruth was willing to leave her own people, clinging to her mother-in-law Naomi and the God she saw in Naomi's life and people. These are just a few who were willing to have their own plans disrupted in order to follow God. We have seen how Mary was willing to follow even though it meant giving up her plan. She had already chosen a stance of saying *Yes* to God.

For while God is prepared to lead us into his plans for our lives, Rev. Fullam puts it well when he says that, "It is possible to miss your own destiny."[14] This does not occur because of being fully yielded to God and then somehow getting the message wrong. Instead, it happens when we use our own free will to decide not to follow. Or we may hold back from a commitment, asking God to show us the plan first, and then deciding whether or not to commit. Mary had done her part by living in a zone of faith where she could be approached by God with a specific task. She had enlisted, indicating a general willingness to follow before being given the opportunity for a specific mission to complete. This is an important part of how she found favor with God.[15]

Considering further the analogy of enlisting, because I have not signed up for the military, I have never received specific orders or assignments from the armed forces. Neither has training been provided by them, such as basic training or officer's training. Those who do enlist choose to give up a certain amount of control in their lives in order to serve their country. The military then takes on the responsibility to train and equip these individuals, as well as to provide certain benefits, such as a paycheck. The soldiers also await their specific orders at the proper time—the unfolding of their particular missions. In some cases, an officer might be offered an assignment rather than ordered to take it. He can then say yes or no to this particular assignment, even though he has already said yes to being in the military. This is in some ways analogous to Mary's situation with God. She had signed up in general, and was now being asked to take on a specific and unusual mission. God graciously gave her the choice of saying yes or no. However, the matter would not have even been likely to come up if she had not already given a general consent to doing God's will in her life.

4. Believing What God Says Will Be Accomplished

Here is an area where I especially admire Mary, and where she provides a particularly inspiring and needed guidepost. Somehow Mary was able to believe that what God said to her would be accomplished. This began with her believing and accepting that the Holy Spirit would overshadow her and she would conceive a son by the Holy Spirit who would be the Messiah. It continued with her maintaining that belief over time, even when it must have seemed highly improbable, if not impossible, that Jesus was the long-awaited Messiah. We can see that this part of Mary's faith was predicated on her ability to hear and know God's voice. It was embedded in a loving relationship with God. If she had been mistaken in this relationship, then she may indeed have believed, but then so do those who are in mental institutions and claim to be Christ, God's anointed one. Her ongoing relationship with God helped her to believe and rely on what God said.

Believing is stressed in the Bible as a very important aspect of faith. It is one of our jobs in working together with God. For example, once we have committed ourselves to doing God's work, whatever that might be, it is part of our job to trust that he will reveal the plan to us and equip us with everything needed to do the work he has for us.[16]

Another important aspect of faith appears to be the willingness to be radically different from others, and to live within the zone of faith. That period of time from when we believe what God says and when it is accomplished can be short or long. While Mary soon had confirmation that she was indeed pregnant, it was many years before she saw Jesus raised from the dead and ascending into heaven as the Messiah. His triumphal return as the traditional Messiah King that the Jewish people anticipated has still not occurred.

5. Acting on the Basis of Our Belief

Mary followed through on her willingness to say yes to God by acting on the basis of her belief. Faith has been described as a combination of belief and action. Someone once said that if a person dashes up and yells, "Fire! Fire!" faith is demonstrated by the hearers when they leave the building. Clearly, they would not act if they disbelieved the message, and just as clearly they would not fail to act if they believed the person yelling, "Fire!"

It is at this aspect of faith that many of us drop off in the faith journey. We say we believe, but do not change our lives in the significant ways that would indicate the reality of our belief. Several stories that occurred close to home dramatically illustrate taking action on the basis of belief.

Some twenty years ago a sudden and devastating flood occurred in the Big Thompson Canyon, the beautiful entrance to Rocky Mountain National Park, which is not very far from where we live. 132 people lost their lives in the canyon, some caught at their cabins or in motels or restaurants along the way, and others caught in their cars as they traveled down the winding canyon road, unaware that a wave of water was about to overtake them. There are many stories of courage and loss connected with this tragedy. Two of these stories especially relate to our discussion.

The first involves a bus driver with a busload of students on a trip, visiting the area from another state. Scheduled to travel down the canyon road to their next destination, the driver saw the gathering storm clouds. Something told him not to travel down the road at that time. His willingness to disrupt their travel plans while others were going forward saved the lives of a school bus full of children, who would have otherwise been swept away by the flood.

When twenty years had passed since the time of the flood, a memorial service was held for those who lost their lives. My husband and I attended, watching as a single long-stem rose was tossed solemnly into the river for each loved one lost in the flood. After the service, there was a picnic-like reception held in the canyon, and a couple we did not know joined us on the grassy area where we were eating. They had returned for the memorial service from another state to pay their respects and in hopes of learning what had happened to others who were staying in the motel that they had fled the night of the flood.

The husband related how they had just arrived and were staying at an inn built on a rock island that jutted out from the swiftly moving river, like the prow of an ocean liner. A bridge joined this island to the canyon highway. It was raining hard as they checked in, but they were assured by their innkeeper that such storms occurred and were no cause for concern. Along with their daughters, the couple settled into their room. Later, one of the daughters looked out to the patio where she had set her shoes out to dry, and shouted, "Look at where the water is!"

Her father took one look at the rapidly rising water and realized the extreme danger in which they found themselves. There was no time to even warn others at the motel, he related to us in a steady, somber voice. Leaving all their belongings, he rushed his wife and daughters to their car, which he had fortunately parked facing outwards. They made it over the bridge just moments before it was washed away by the rushing waters, and then sped down the canyon road in a race for their lives.

His wife related that her husband was driving so fast that she feared they would die in an auto crash if they did not perish in the flood. Arriving in the peaceful town at the mouth of the canyon, they found a community not yet aware that a flood was occurring just a short distance upriver.

These poignant stories sent chills down my spine. Like the person who hears "Fire!" and illustrates faith in the message by fleeing the building, these two men had each received a message that called for action. The message was conveyed by the storm clouds for the bus driver, and by the daughter seeing the rapidly rising water for the father. If the men had not known how to understand the message and had not been willing to disrupt their lives to act decisively on the message, more lives would have been lost.[17]

Mary was willing to act on the message she received. We, too, are sent messages, through Scripture, through the pattern of events in our lives, and in other ways that God may choose to communicate to us when we seek guidance in prayer. Are we prepared to act when we receive the message?

C.S. Lewis spoke of the building of character being accomplished by many small choices, which set the stage for being able to make the big choices when they come along. This applies to faith choices as well, I believe. For most of us, it is making many little choices that set the pattern of our ability to hear and then act on what we hear. The men who saw the unusualness of the weather patterns that fateful day in Big Thompson Canyon when many did not probably were experienced in reading weather patterns. They had noticed and made many choices of lesser than life-and-death importance over time.

6. Persevering in Faith—Staying the Course

After the angel's visit, Mary persevered in her faith that God was acting upon her life in a special way. She and Joseph were called upon to keep exercising their faith in the early years of Jesus's life, as they fled to Egypt and then awaited God's timing and direction for a return to their homeland. There are glimpses of Mary, which we will discuss in more detail elsewhere, as she dealt with Jesus as an adolescent, encouraged him to perform his first miracle, and traveled with him at times during his adult ministry. She is with him during the crucifixion, and with part of the faith community after his resurrection and ascension.

We know that she pondered many things in her heart, no doubt wondering at times just how God was going to carry out his plan. At times she must have found it strange that the Messiah's life was unfolding as it did. After all, most Jews understood that the Messiah would be a conqueror and rule over Israel. That certainly did not seem to be happening.

The living out of God's plan for Mary required a lifetime of persevering in faith, even when things were different than what she could have anticipated. In this Mary has the example of others who went before her. Abraham and Sarah (the name change from Sarai to Sarah mentioned earlier, as well as Abram having his name changed to Abraham, had now taken place) once again come to mind as ones who were given promises that required perseverance. At one point, Abraham was quite perplexed that he had no heir. He was an old man and Sarah was past childbearing age, yet God had promised that Abraham would be the father of a great nation. Referring to these giants of the faith, the writer of Hebrews exhorts believers to perseverance in matters of faith: " imitate those who through faith and patience inherit what has been promised."[18]

Many of us have experienced peaks where there have been great moments of faith, and then gone through the valleys where it seems nothing is happening. Persevering in the faith that we once were so in touch with is a part of the task in the valley, and in the day-to-day operation of our lives. God must help us do this; we surely cannot do it on our own.

7. Praising God Throughout the Process

Mary's next recorded words after the visitation of the angel are words of praise: "My soul glorifies the Lord and my spirit rejoices in God my Savior."[19] These are the first words in Mary's Song, of course, and the whole song is one of praise. This is both a natural response to the wonders of God, and something that demonstrates our faith as we persevere over time. Praising is interesting in that it is both an exercise of faith and a building up of faith. Praise calls us to awareness. Sometimes praise spills from our lips because we can barely help it, and other times praise is a sacrifice, done as a discipline, perhaps in one of the difficult and mysterious times when we don't see how God's goodness could allow events to take the turn they have. Thus, an important manifestation of faith is praising God throughout the process.

IN SUMMARY

As we seek to grow in these seven aspects of faith, several things can help us along the way. We can pray for ears to hear God's voice, for the gift of discernment, and for the gift of faith itself. Scripture promises that God desires to give us good gifts, and that persistence in prayer is rewarded. Studying and reflecting upon the Scriptures will help us to develop wisdom and discernment. We can also be aware that God's voice will be congruent with Scripture. Taking the steps that are available to all of us—believing the promises of Scripture and acting on those promises—is a place to begin. Also crucial is getting clear that God does indeed love us and has a specific plan for our lives, which he will reveal as we choose to do his work and trust him for his provision in equipping us. Keeping a journal of how God acts in our life can help build faith. Another important support to faith is sharing and praying with others we have carefully chosen.

Encouragement from others can help us stay the course, and can even help us praise God throughout the process. Finding someone who can mentor us, as Elizabeth likely mentored Mary, can be a source of growth and support. Remembering that "blessed is she who believes that what the Lord has said to her will be accomplished" and living consciously in that zone of blessing can encourage and strengthen us as we persevere in faith.

As we look at Mary's story, we can see that faith has much to do with reality, but it is not necessarily the reality that typically captures our focus. Faith sees through illusions. It sees a reality many of us cannot see. The nature of the universe is different because of the reality of God and who God is.

This quality of faith is reminiscent of Plato's cave story, where the cave dwellers eyes are dimmed by living in the dark. They can only make out shadowy forms within the cave. When someone whose eyes are not dimmed enters the cave and describes what he sees, he is attacked by those who cannot see because his description differs from theirs. Like the cave-dwellers, we are blind but think we see. When someone can see and tells us what the cave looks like, we "kill" him. The vision is too disconcerting to our equilibrium.

Recently, I took training in a new area of psychology. As the participants heard the presenter describe the theoretical basis of his work, our minds reeled. Accepting these new methods was one thing. Beginning to glimpse the reordering of our conceptual framework regarding the fundamental nature of the area we were dealing with was quite another. It required enlarging our world-view. Whenever people are called upon to do this, there is much resistance. Indeed, discernment is required, for if we changed too often, we would be unable to function in a stable way. Conservatism has survival value at times.

Mary was able to have radical faith. She saw a different reality, and faith was the natural consequence of this, because the reality God showed her was emblazoned with God's love and truth. Yet most of her life was lived out in a very ordinary fashion, caring for her family, conversing with friends, and observing the religious festivals. She not only had the ability and faith to see a different reality, but to graciously live in the everyday world, day in and day out. For any of us who have accepted the Biblical view of reality, we are called to join Mary in this aspect of her faith—of seeing and acting on a different reality while at the same time conducting our lives in this reality. We are to live in the world but not of the world. This is the paradox of living the life of Biblical faith. "Blessed is she who has believed that what the Lord has said to her will be accomplished!"[20]

Chapter Six

Individuated Mary—Being Close and Separate

A PUZZLING PASSAGE in the eleventh chapter of Luke had captured the attentions of the Wednesday night study group. In it, Jesus appears to invalidate a woman who tries to pay tribute to him and his mother. The woman cries out, "Blessed is the womb that bore you and the breasts that you sucked!" Jesus refuses to accept this tribute without a correction. Instead, he replies, "Blessed rather are those who hear the word of God and keep it!" What could this mean, Cynthia asked the group leader, feeling that Jesus was rejecting a compliment to his mother.

Like Cindy in the study group, I too had puzzled over this Scripture earlier in my life. Then, while reading a friend's senior honor thesis, back when I was beginning graduate school, this passage was illuminated for me.[1] My eyes fastened eagerly on the typed words of my friend's scarlet, Kinko's-bound thesis. The traditional way of viewing women in the culture of Jesus's time was in terms of their relationship to the men in their lives, the words revealed. Thus a woman's praise-worthiness was based on the accomplishments and talents of her husband and male offspring, rather than on who she was.

Jesus held to a radically different view of women, even when that woman happened to be his own mother. Jesus saw Mary as one whose worth was based not on her traditional role of producing a talented male offspring, but on her own individuated choices. She chose to hear and do the word of God. It is this attribute of hers that is praiseworthy. Jesus defines blessedness for both women and men in terms of their choices to hear and act upon God's word. Being able to make such a choice in the fullest way requires that a person be individuated.

Such news is indeed good news for women. For me as a younger Christian, one of the struggles had been the tension between the liberating spiritual news that Jesus was indeed the savior, and the sometimes gently suffocating messages that were tagged onto this, which did not fit for me as a woman. Messages that subtly or not so subtly encouraged me to set aside my own individuality if it did not fit the traditional church view of the submissive, devoted wife and mother. Messages that seemed to exclude the possibility that I could be a devoted wife and mother and blossom as a person if my talents spread beyond the tent of domesticity. For me, hearing Jesus's personal validation of his mother's individuation was a radical affirmation for women of his time and ours.

So what is individuation, and why is it important? Individuation refers to being a separate, distinct person who is able to have enough sense of her own personhood to make real choices. Thus someone who is individuated is able to be separate, to stand apart. The close link to inner-directedness becomes apparent. However, there is another important part of being individuated, and that is the ability to be a separate person while at the same time being close to others. Some people are able to be separate, and have a strong sense of making their own choices, but are unable to be emotionally close and intimate with loved ones.

Other people are seemingly able to be very close to others, but they do so without a real sense of their own identity and separateness. If the group does something, they will too. Such a person may embrace his or her spouse's ideas about where to live, or what lifestyle to adopt, mostly because it is desirable to fit in and keep the sense of closeness. To do the work of discovering what they themselves would like, and how to communicate that clearly and lovingly to the spouse, and then come to a mutual decision about what to do, would be too difficult or frightening. Simply fitting in feels much cozier, much less threatening. Thus, as we are using the term here, individuation refers to being able to be both close and separate.

In this chapter, we are going to explore individuation, and why it is vital to our lives if we desire to be all that we were created to be. We will look at differences in the typical psychological development of men and women, which affect how we individuate, and explore how this development often poses dilemmas for women in the individuation process. With the issue better defined and understood, we will then focus on how Mary models and validates the individuation process for women. This is especially important, since sometimes Mary has erroneously been used more as a model of a self-effacing person, which seems to encourage women to also be self-effacing.

A DEVELOPMENTAL PERSPECTIVE

Individuation—The Dance

It is thought that when we are first born, we do not even realize that we are separate beings from our mothers. After all, we have been literally enveloped by their bodies for nine months, with a pipeline, the umbilical cord, that supplies our every need. After birth, the attention to our needs continues, as we are held, cuddled, nursed or fed, changed, and burped. There may be moments when no one can guess what we need, and we cry in helpless rage and frustration. Then, eventually, comfort comes, and all is well again.

Bonding, the crucial first psychological developmental stage, develops with this care and love. As we saw in the previous chapter, infants who are able to bond well with their caregivers develop a sense that they (the infants) are basically good and worthy of love, and also that the people in the world are basically trustworthy. This is the foundation of all later developmental stages. This stage is so crucial that infants who do not get adequate handling and cuddling may die of something called anaclytic depression, even though they are cared for adequately with regard to basic physical needs.

At some point, a baby begins to realize that he or she is separate from the parent. This realization can cause heady excitement, as well as moments of anxiety and panic. The little one loves doing things that emphasize her individuality, and her curiosity to explore the world. She may delight in exploring, but soon wants the reassurance that Mother or Father is still there.

I recall the long-legged nut-brown colts in the pasture of the farm where I grew up. A velvet-nosed little critter would become curious, enthralled with tufts of grass and a butterfly flitting in the sunlight, slowly exploring, bit by bit, further away from the placidly grazing mother. Then all at once he would look up, realize with a start that his mother was not within a few feet, and lurch back to her, seeking safety and reassurance. Sometimes it was the mother who looked up from her serene munching, surveyed the area for her brash young one, and with a swish of the tail and a sharp whinny, called him back to her. Gradually the distance from the mother and the time spent before alarm took over increased. The dance between exploration and security was expanding.

We have seen this same dance go on between human little ones and their mothers, as the growing baby explores its expanding kingdom, periodically seeking the reassuring comfort of mother. It is important to realize that the solid bonding of the first stage allows this sense of separateness coupled with closeness in the second stage. Without the bonding, the second stage cannot occur on a healthy psychological level. Also, since we do not live in a perfect world, these stages are not accomplished in perfect ways, but in what is called a *good enough* way, which allows normal development to proceed. Children pass through other developmental stages not dealt with here. Later in life, individuation issues tend to recycle, and we move further along the path to mature individuation.

Of particular importance is the stage of individuation that occurs during adolescence. It is a crucial time in our culture for separating more completely from parents, and coming into the young person's own identity. This is a process, and requires steadfastness on the part of parents, while the adolescent lurches between independence and dependence emotionally.

As individuals, we receive varying amounts of encouragement and support while individuating. Some young people may not sense permission that they can keep their parents' love and still do this individuation work. Some are afraid, and fail to do important parts of this developmental task, while others bolt too far, too soon, not sensing that they can be their own person and still have adult bonds to parents. Both parents and young people can have intense, ambivalent feelings about this process.

Such work often continues with parents into adulthood, even when it has gone well in adolescence. Sometimes parents breathe a sigh of relief, feeling that they and their children have passed the hurdles of adolescence successfully, only to find themselves on an unexpectedly turbulent path during portions of their children's twenties, thirties, or beyond. For instance, one wise mother sought counseling to help her deal with an adult daughter's blame as the younger woman—in her forties and a parent of teens herself—worked through some delayed individuation issues.

You will perhaps remember the joke about the couple in their late nineties who went to see their attorney about a divorce. The incredulous attorney exclaimed, "But you have made it all this time, through so much. Why get a divorce now, after all these years?" The answer came through the sharp old wizened jaws: "We were waiting for the children to die." Such a story tickles our funny bones because it speaks to the intertwining of our lives and the difficulty of making individuated decisions no matter what our time in life. Thus, at various times throughout the life span, the need for further individuation work may appear. Two examples help illustrate this further.

Two Tales of Individuation Dilemmas

Debra tells about a time in her life when she was at home full-time with three small children. Dale, her husband, was making strides in his career, and could often be very preoccupied with the demands of his job. Both had jointly made the decision that Debra would put aside her work in the insurance business while the children were small, because they were both convinced of the value of a parent being at home with the children in the early years if at all possible. Also, Debra enjoyed many of the aspects of traditional homemaking, although she was beginning to realize, perhaps not in as large a dose as she was now experiencing! Without realizing it at first, Debra began to fall into old patterns she had experienced growing up, when her mother had continually sacrificed her own needs for those of the family. Dale began to accept this pattern, though he would not have agreed to it consciously—it also fit the home pattern in which he had grown up.

The day came when Debra dissolved in tears for the fifth time that week, and began to come to grips with the reality that something was wrong with her life. As she clutched a plump pillow for comfort and sipped steaming coffee with her best friend, an attentive listener, it dawned on Debra that she had merged with the lives and needs of her husband and children. She could see them as individuals, but had lost the sense of herself as a unique individual who also had needs and interests apart from her loved ones. The picture that came to her was that the shape of her own life was no longer distinct. Rather, the shapes of everyone else's lives impinged upon and obliterated the shape of hers. No wonder she was beginning to feel quite depressed. In the dance between being close and being separate, Debra had drifted, for seemingly the best of reasons, into being too close, and needed to restore the balance.

Natalie had felt several years ago that she had the best of both worlds—a loving spouse, enriching friends, and a career she loved. Her career running a shop that sold beautiful Native-American art pieces of all sorts captured her imagination and excited both her artistic and her business senses. When an opportunity arose to relocate the shop to a very desirable area a little further from her home, Natalie and Arthur agreed that she should seize the chance. The shop was bigger, and the business was brisk, as customers from a wider geographical range, with money to spend on the art Natalie sold, now frequented her store. Later, Natalie was to describe what happened as similar to the proverbial frog who sat in a pot of water that slowly heated up, never noticing the changing temperature, until at some point the water was too hot and the frog was already immobilized by the heat.

Degree by imperceptible degree, her life became more and more involved with the shop, which fulfilled her beyond her wildest expectations. Her time with her spouse and the emotional energy she used to devote to couple activities gradually dwindled. Arthur was patient and understanding at first, because he supported Natalie's work, and understood that there would be busy, involving times. However, the time came when he felt enough was enough, and confronted her with his need for more time for their relationship. Natalie began to realize how disconnected she felt from Arthur, and how she was little inclined to reconnect. She now seemed satisfied with much less emotional connection between them. The difference between Natalie's and Arthur's needs and desires brought them to a crisis, and a therapist's office.

Natalie and Arthur, for the best of reasons, had drifted into losing the ability to feel both close and separate in their relationship. Natalie felt separate, and had no real sense of how she could maintain the excitement of the business she loved and the closeness she had once enjoyed with her husband. For her, being separate had now come into conflict with being close.

For both Debra and Natalie and their spouses, it will take good will and conscious effort to find ways to restore the balance that is right for each at this stage in their lives. The basic trust and bonding between spouses built up in earlier stages of the relationship can help couples get through the anxiety of finding ways to balance and meet these needs for both healthy closeness and an individual identity. This is similar to the infant who has a solid foundation of bonding and trust, and can therefore handle the uncertainty and excitement of the next stage.

Another factor that impacts women and men in the individuation process is that each gender tends to go about it a little differently. Understanding something about these gender differences can aid us in understanding individuation.

Developmental Differences in Women and Men

There appear to be differences in men and women regarding this important concept of individuation. Studies confirm that young men typically are able to form their independent identities with less stress and more ease than young women. It is often harder for young women to feel confident making independent decisions, doing things for their own benefit rather than for the benefit of a relationship. Conversely, young men often feel less confident when dealing with emotional and relationship issues, and quite confident when dealing with decisions that have to do with independence. To put it briefly, men often have more difficulty with the closeness side of the individuation coin, while women often have more difficulty with the separateness side.

The question of course arises as to why this is. Some have said that this is the way that God created us, and therefore how we were meant to be. This view would tend to encourage women and men to stay within their separate patterns, and perhaps strive to become more like their own gender pattern if they don't fit the mold. Certainly the traditional view in most Western cultures has historically held to this perspective.

A similar view, one not necessarily connected to a creation model, holds that men and women are genetically different, and these tendencies are built into us. This perspective can have the effect of affirming men as he-men if they fit this pattern, and somehow less than truly masculine if they do not. It tends to perpetuate the gap between the sexes by defining each sex as normal and healthy when fitting the typical pattern. Thus, the implication would be that a woman who felt more comfortable being independent than the norm might somehow not be as feminine as her less independent counterpart.

Likewise, a male who was more comfortable with closeness and emotional intimacy might also be thought of as somehow less masculine than his counterpart who had little confidence with these traits, and was proud of this fact.

Another possibility is that these tendencies of each sex are due to developmental differences because of the differences in the way males and females are raised. Some very interesting work in this area points out how this occurs. It is widely accepted that our gender identity is typically firmly formed by the time we are three years of age.[2] By age three, little boys generally know that they are little boys and have begun to identify with men as their primary models. Little girls have a solid sense that they are little girls and identify with women as their primary models as to what it is to be a female.

In our culture, most children are cared for primarily by their mothers or by other female caretakers in these early years. Thus for both little boys and little girls, the first primary bond and attachment that is so crucial in our psychological development and indeed to our very survival, is with a woman. As little girls begin to realize that they are little girls, they do not need to separate their self-concept as a female from that of their primary caregiver. Thus, the experience of attachment and the formation of feminine identity both remain with the mother. Little boys, on the other hand, need to separate their identity from that of their mother in a way that girls do not, and begin identifying with someone who has not been their primary caregiver.

At the time of adolescence, the next stage of individuation occurs for both boys and girls. Because the boys have already had to make a fundamental change by separating their identity from their mothers, they have a head start in the separation process. Girls, on the other hand, typically have a stronger ability to empathize and to deal with closeness in relationships. Yet, the need to be separate can be harder for them at the adolescent stage, because they did not need to make a shift in identity with their mothers until now. Psychologist Carol Gilligan puts it this way: "Since masculinity is defined through separation while femininity is defined through attachment, male gender identity is threatened by intimacy while female gender identity is threatened by separation. Thus males tend to have difficulty with relationships, while females tend to have problems with individuation."[3]

Some have also speculated that because our culture has long valued independence in men and dependence in women, those are the traits that have tended to thrive in the gene pool over time. Persons who fit those traits tended to marry and have the most offspring, thereby boosting genetic support for those traits. Thus it is possible that our psychological development as just described and the tendency for independent men to find nurturing women who emphasize relationships over independence both work together to increase the independence of men and attachment characteristics of women.

Let us now turn to further considerations about cultural factors.

A CULTURAL PERSPECTIVE

Women's Roles, Men's Roles

In addition to ways that early psychological development has affected both males and females, most cultures have also overtly encouraged men to be independent and act upon the world, while encouraging or even forcing most women to be economically dependent on their fathers, husbands, or sons. A woman traditionally went from the home of her father to the home of her husband. Historically, women's primary role in each setting was to obey and please the men in the family, to follow where the men went, and to help the men with their work in whatever way was suitable. Of course, bearing and bringing up offspring was also typically a key part of this role.

A friend of mine, in her early seventies, remarked on how unusual her husband had been to support her working outside the home in the early years of their marriage. In those days, it could be seen as a poor reflection on the man's ability to earn an adequate living, she explained. Recently, several friends and

I were reminiscing about the messages we received coming of age in the sixties. Teaching, nursing, and secretarial work were good for women, because they could typically be used to fall back on, wherever a wife might find herself. Interestingly, these gently oppressive messages were generally passed on to us by our mothers, not our fathers. The intent was to teach us the ways of the culture, so that we would fit in and avoid the hurt and damage that can come from going against the grain.

To decide what we really wanted to do and set our hearts on doing it could all too easily break our hearts, was the message we received. Either we would then go where the opportunities for such jobs existed, thereby likely losing the chance to be with the man of our dreams, or we would marry, follow our husband to a location where no opportunity for our chosen profession existed, and wish we had trained for a more suitable woman's profession. We were told to take typing no matter what, so we would have something to fall back on.

In spite of all the turmoil of the sixties, many women took such advice, and did not go to the trouble it might have taken to find out what they might really want to do. Therefore there was no particularly sharp pain in not doing the work of their dreams. Others rebelled against such messages, setting into motion new themes that are still working themselves out in our lives and in our culture.

Those working to encourage women in different roles in the seventies and eighties often took the tack of helping women function more like men—adopting male ways of thinking, doing, and even dressing, in an effort to find a place in a man's world and to succeed there. By adopting characteristics of men and fitting into their world, women often felt forced to abandon characteristics not seen as desirable in that world. Such women sometimes felt they needed to choose between career and family—a woman could not do both justice, even though it would have been very unusual for a man to feel constrained to make such a choice.

In the last twenty years or so, many of these messages to young women have been modified, with much larger numbers of women receiving overt encouragement to pursue their dreams and to enter any field they desire. Young women are encouraged to picture themselves able to have families and a full-time career. There is much less likely to be a "uniform" necessary to succeed in business, and the unique qualities that women often bring to the workplace are becoming more valued at all levels. Thus, while the journey is far from over, women are being valued for a fuller spectrum of important characteristics, and have less need to abandon their feminine strengths in order to solely emphasize traits viewed as belonging in the masculine domain.

Having examined these developmental and cultural considerations, let us return to Mary. Her Judaic culture gave women more freedoms and respect than the surrounding cultures of that era. Nevertheless, Jewish women were typically seen in the perspective of the woman we met at the start of this chapter, who tried to compliment Mary. A woman was blessed if she had supported a successful husband or son. This is what earned God's favor and that of the community.

A TRANSCENDENT VIEW

Jesus, who had such incisive ability to see to the core of issues, saw his mother Mary, and other women as well, in a different light. It was not that he did not value and appreciate Mary's part in his upbringing, of helping form who he was. It was that he saw her essence, the core of her being, in a different light. To accept the compliment would be to limit the core essence of his mother, and of all women; to accept a definition of Mary in terms of her attachments to the traditional male loved ones in her life. He knew this was not the whole picture. Jesus realized that Mary, and all women, are not blessed in the final analysis because of the success of such attachments, but because of their ability to have a sense of self, in addition to and apart from such attachments, and to make choices based on God's will for them. Such choices can be made when one is individuated; that is, when one can be close but also separate.

Mary was able to be both close and separate. She was able to tolerate not having Joseph as her betrothed when he planned to set her quietly aside, and to accept him back when he changed that plan after his dream.[4] An unindividuated woman would have likely been unable to handle having her village and her betrothed not understand what was happening to her.

Another capability of Mary's was her capacity to stay in touch with her own personality rather than being self-effacing in the presence of the strong, talented, and charismatic Jesus. For example, she and Jesus engage in frank dialogue when Jesus is an adolescent and is reunited with her and Joseph when they find him in Jerusalem.[5] Later, she is clear about her feelings and wishes when she requests that Jesus perform what becomes his first miracle.[6] She gathers other family members and sets off to talk with Jesus when questions about his sanity arise early in his ministry.[7] She illustrates her ability to be close even in times of dire suffering when she is present as he dies on the cross.[8] The dual capacity for closeness and maintaining a strong sense of self was an essential strength that helped Mary provide guidance and love to Jesus as his mother through varying stages of his life.

This chapter is in some ways a bridge to the remainder of the book, where Mary's interactions will be examined in detail as to how she handled aspects of her relationship with Jesus and others. Here, we note that Mary spoke up with a sure sense of herself and her beliefs and feelings when she interacted with Jesus. She stayed connected to him, and yet expressed her own heart. In the second portion of the book, watch for how this theme of individuation plays itself out in Mary's life.

Individuation is a process that lays the psychological foundation for the inner-directedness that we discussed earlier. Yet it also lays the foundation for the adult capacity for closeness and intimacy in relationships. It is what allows us to be close to others without losing our sense of self. Sometimes people long for closeness to others and yet when they allow closeness they feel engulfed, as if they have no self left. This can lead to panic and sudden withdrawal from closeness. Excessive closeness can contribute to depression and resentment, because the true self has been submerged in unhealthy ways, and has suffered unnecessary damage. Those who are individuated possess the ability to set healthy, flexible boundaries. They can certainly make sacrifices for others, but they do so freely and in ways in which they feel led by God, not simply as a matter of course and at the expense of their own well-being and talents.

Jesus was setting the same standard for men and women. All were blessed based upon their choices to hear and obey the will of God. Within society at large, and in the Christian community in particular, balanced individuation is to be valued. Young men are likely to be strong concerning the ability to be separate, but they may need extra support and guidance in finding the ability to be close, particularly in our American culture. Those men who do not fit the typical pattern but have unusual capacity for empathy and closeness need to be supported in their pattern of strength. How tragic that some are shamed for a variation that is a real gift. Likewise, young women are likely, even with changing societal values, to have a more difficult time with being a separate person. They need to be encouraged that it is good and feminine for them to grow in this area, as well as to value their capacities for relationship and attachment.

Hearing the word of God and obeying it may take men and women down paths that emphasize attachment at one point and separateness at another. Those who thrive only on attachment may not be able to withstand winds of separation, as when one partner must be away for long periods of time, for example. On the other hand, if they are acquainted only with the side of separateness, they may not be able to form the kind of stable, loving relationships that both adults and children need in order to thrive.

A POTENTIAL DANGER AND AN OPPORTUNITY

Mary can be an encouragement for us to continue our own individuation work, to grow in our ability to be close to others yet develop and maintain a strong sense of self. At this point a potential danger is worth considering. It is important not to idealize Mary to the extent that we cut ourselves off from what she can offer us. As soon as we begin to idealize her too much, she may become a stumbling block. There are at least two dangers associated with idealizing Mary.

Denying our Humanity

First, because so little is said of Mary, we are not shown much about the days when she may have felt grumpy, discouraged, or tired. Noticing and celebrating the strengths in Mary is meant to help us find and claim those parts in ourselves, to encourage us to celebrate our full personhood. It is not meant to imply that we do not have our weaknesses, our frailties, and that they are not a real part of us. Full personhood beckons us to accept our human weaknesses and integrate the reality that we are not perfect—not finished yet.

Among Christians, there are those who seem to fully accept their humanity, having faced their own demons and remaining willing to face new ones as they come up. Such people allow God to transform them into what they cannot become on their own. These Christians may eventually radiate a holiness, but they are also humbly grounded in their humanity.

Another group of Christians has not faced their own weaknesses and foibles, but instead tries to ignore these parts of themselves, believing this is what victorious Christianity mandates. They forget that victory is associated with a battling, not ignoring. The consequence of not waging battle and allowing the transformation process to take place is that such Christians eventually carry the air of hypocrisy, and others pick up on this. It is likely that each of us finds we have this air at certain times or with certain aspects of our lives. Idealizing Mary or any spiritual model has the danger of causing us to ignore our own faults in our eagerness to identify with the model.

Those parts of ourselves that we tend to hide from our own awareness and from others have been called our shadow side. Some parts of our shadow actually often hold treasures that we need to integrate and embrace within a healthy context. Other times behavior patterns need to be brought to the light, confessed, forgiven, and transformed. Someone once said that the good thing about guilt is that there is a ready remedy: we confess, repent, and allow ourselves to be changed by God. We are not meant to flagellate ourselves or hang onto guilt. As a therapist, one portion of time is devoted to helping one set of patients let go of guilt, while another portion is spent trying to help another set of patients see that acknowledging their own responsibility and guilt would be a healthy thing! Thus, once again, balance is vital.

A Model Not a Mold

A second danger of idealizing Mary is perhaps a little more tricky to see. While Mary can serve as an important model to becoming our full selves, she is not intended to be another mold into which we must squeeze ourselves. We are not to trivialize who God created us to be by merging with the archetype and losing our own unique identity.

In other words, God is not in the cookie-cutter business. He created both Mary and you, and he wants two unique people, not one real Mary and one imitation Mary. You may recall the story of the man who was at heaven's gate, and confessed that he tried to be like Abraham, but failed. God's reply was that the failure was not that he couldn't be like Abraham, but that he failed to be who God meant **him** to be. To the extent that we each learn from Mary how to be more fully ourselves, as God created us to be, and to give that true self to God, we are on the right track.

The Opportunity

"Knowing who we are, celebrating who we are, is individuating the archetype," points out Jungian analyst Marion Woodman.[9] Thus Mary is a guide into ourselves, our best selves as God created us to be. This is the opportunity and the task the Mary archetype offers. This is no small task, but it is one with liberating results.

SUMMING UP

We have been looking at Mary primarily in terms of personal traits that Scripture indicates that she possessed, traits such as her inner-direction, her creativity, her complex thinking capacity, her faith, and her ability to be both close and separate. Gradually, it becomes clearer how these qualities interact, influencing one another. Mary's qualities of individuation and inner-direction allow her to develop and express her creativity and her intelligence. They allow her to be strong enough to express her faith and abide in that faith even when others don't understand. Her faith informs all the other traits and helps keep them in right relation to each other and to her creator, God. Mary's creativity and intelligence allow her to express her faith in exquisite terms in Mary's Song, which has delighted the poetic ears and hearts of many through the centuries, inspiring the faith of others.

A fuller portrait of Mary emerges as we allow more aspects of her personhood to emerge from the shadows of time, culture, and habit. Now it is time to examine more completely this Mary in relation to the other humans in her life, to learn more about how this Mary interacts and expresses herself in relationships with spouse, children, and community. A flesh-and-blood woman set in a particular time and place, whom we can learn from, not necessarily to become more like her, but to become more like our own visceral, flesh-and-blood selves, as God created us to be.

Part Two

Mary in Relationship

Chapter Seven

Words to Say It—An Assertive Mary

*T*HE FULL PORTRAIT of Mary includes the personal quality of assertiveness and the skills to implement its use
wisely. This can come as a surprise to us—we have not
generally been taught to see this quality in Mary, or even in
Jesus. The phrase "gentle Jesus, meek and mild" comes to
mind, for example. Too often we have not been taught accurate understandings of such concepts as meek and mild, and
have taken them to be a caution against assertive behavior. We
have not fully understood that one can be humble and gentle
as well as assertive and bold. For instance, the word "meek," as
used in the Sermon on the Mount, came from the Greek word
praeis, which meant "power under control." Therefore, it was
possible, if not necessary, to be both meek and assertive, for
one who is meek has to have power, and have it under control,
in order to use that power effectively when necessary. Another
difficulty is that assertiveness is usually revealed by our verbal
communication, and there are a very limited number of Mary's
words in the scriptural account. Yet those times when Scripture
does give us Mary's communications, a Mary who was able to
speak up assertively in a variety of situations is revealed. Let us
turn now to examples of what can happen when individuals do
not have this capacity.

151

OUR NEED FOR ASSERTIVENESS

In counseling, it does not take long to see how important the ability to communicate fully and clearly about questions, needs, opinions, desires, and choices is to the development of full personhood in right relationship to God. Several examples can speak to this importance.

Maura, at age nineteen, is visiting outside her homeland for the first time. She is being shown the sights of this particular city by an old friend of her uncle, whom he had urged her to contact. After an evening filled with sightseeing, the man pulls off the road, saying he wants to show her the city lights. Maura realizes, to her utter dismay, that his intentions toward her are less than honorable. As this much older man reaches out to fondle her, she shrivels, but does not protest verbally or in actions. Frozen, she allows this contact, feeling terrible. Later, her failure to speak up clearly on her own behalf will haunt her for years, affecting her self-esteem, until she works through the trauma of this abusive event and claims a new-found ability to speak up for herself.

Lynette finds herself slumped in her sofa at the end of a long week. She has just finished running the summer Bible school program for her church, and should be feeling the sweet peace of a job well done for the Lord, she chides herself. Instead, she feels exhausted and irritable. While mulling over these thoughts, the telephone rings. Now that Bible school is over, enthuses the voice at the other end, we really need you to take on the chairmanship of the mission program. Before Lynette fully comprehends what has happened, she has agreed to this request. As the receiver clicks, she feels a sinking feeling in the pit of her stomach as she contemplates this next project. Why does she feel overwhelmed when this is a good project and she can count on the Lord's help to get her through anything, she wonders forlornly.

Larry dreads going into the house. Whenever he and his wife have one of their talks, at her instigation, he finds himself unable to speak up about his true thoughts and feelings. His wife is more articulate, he feels, and somehow Larry comes out of these talks feeling guilty and resentful. Even though he knows that Sally wants him to speak up, his sense that she might disagree or be displeased by his true feelings often prevents him from even being fully aware of what he wants to say. Larry's dad had always impressed upon him the servant role, and the meekness of Jesus. He has not seen marriage partners speak up clearly and lovingly to each other.

Ann relates to the group how her idea of love in her first marriage contributed to her major depression and a long stint of feeling alienated from God and the Church. Her ex-husband was demanding and unreasonable, but Ann clung to the love passage in I Corinthians 13. Love is patient and kind, she would tell herself. It is not self-seeking, it keeps no record of wrongs. Love always hopes, always trusts. Love never fails. Her misunderstanding of this passage caused her to not set reasonable, healthy limits on unacceptable behavior. The more she failed to speak up in a healthy manner, the more her husband took free rein in domineering, emotionally unstable ways, until Ann could bear the situation no longer, and began suffering from depression.

These examples illustrate some of the harm that can occur when persons either cannot or do not believe they should exercise assertiveness in relationship to others. Detrimental effects can range from trauma and depression to chronic low self-esteem, irritability, and exhaustion.

Some Concerns about Being Assertive

On the other hand, there are often hesitations when individuals consider beginning to speak up for themselves. In one group, Marie was ready to begin speaking up for herself more. She desired to practice within the safety of the group setting, and another group member volunteered to help in the role-play. As the women practiced setting limits on casual acquaintances who ask intrusive questions, Marie finally shuddered and asked the other members, "Do I sound like a harpy?" Although assured by the members that she sounded tactful but firm, it was difficult for Marie to shake the sensation that she was being mean and rude as she began to set limits verbally.

Especially if we have learned that it is more loving or Christian to keep quiet, it can be very difficult to break this taboo. Holly remembers sitting in a Bible study led by a beloved, popular pastor years ago. He commented negatively on the assertiveness workshops that the local university was offering, and suggested that godly women would avoid them. Holly found his comments rang in her ears for years every time she considered being assertive in a difficult situation. Finally, it dawned on her that this pastor had no difficulty being assertive when he needed to be, and she began dismantling one of her prohibitions against speaking up appropriately.

Sometimes it is not so much that there are outright taboos to being assertive as that the emphasis on desirable traits has been to be loving, and the definition of loving has not included the importance of speaking up about our desires, needs, choices, beliefs, and limits. We have not seen adequate images of loving women, particularly in a Biblical context, speaking up in these ways. That is why a closer look at this trait in Mary can be so important.

Necessary for Empowerment

As women and men embrace this part of the Mary archetype, we can receive encouragement to develop assertiveness and the skills necessary to express this important quality lovingly in our own lives. Assertiveness provides a necessary component of being empowered.

In the remainder of this chapter, we will look at the definition of assertiveness, consider the foundations of assertiveness, and examine the scriptural record to learn what we can about the nature of Mary's assertiveness.

Defining Assertiveness

Let's take a closer look at the definition of assertiveness. Assertive individuals, the dictionary[1] indicates, are persons who speak confidently, who state what they have to say positively or boldly. Such persons are able to defend or maintain their positions boldly. In our society in recent decades, those regarded as assertive persons are those who are able to speak up clearly for what they want or need or think is right. They can do this on behalf of themselves or others, including God. They are able to say yes when they mean yes and no when they mean no.

The word "bold," from the definition of assertiveness, itself has several definitions. It can mean fearless and courageous or brave. It can refer to being clear and distinct, as in a bold color or bold print. It can also refer to being unduly forward and brazen in manner. This variety of definitions perhaps points further to our hesitations about daring to be assertive. It is a challenge to be courageous, but at least that can be seen as a virtue. Being seen as stepping too far and being brazen is something most of us want to avoid, and which women have historically been particularly vulnerable to, as illustrated by Marie's hesitations in the group exercise above. Assertiveness as used with Mary refers to speaking confidently and clearly, which often does take courage.

FOUNDATIONS OF ASSERTIVENESS

Assertiveness is both a trait and a skill. As such, it does not spring up out of the air, but like a plant, needs soil in which to grow. Assertiveness is built on a foundation, and typically does not appear unless that foundation is in place. That foundation includes the base of trust and bonding that is laid in the first year of life when we receive a good enough amount of love and care, so that we come to expect that our world is a generally safe and loving enough place that our needs will be met.

When that foundational block is set, another is laid upon

it—the ability to be separate. In our consideration of Mary, we have seen that she was individuated, having the capacity to be a separate person as well as to be close to others. This is a very important building block in setting the stage for assertiveness.

When the foundations of trust and individuation are strong, a third crucial trait is typically present. That trait involves the awareness and nonjudgmental acceptance of our own feelings and thoughts. If our feelings are frozen or blocked from our awareness, we do not have access to them, and key materials of assertiveness are not available to us. It has been wisely said that feelings should neither be ignored nor be in control. They have a very important part to play in our lives and our decision-making. Feelings are signals that can give us information about what we love, what we fear, and what we hate. To be unaware of our feelings is like cutting ourselves off from important input about core parts of ourselves, as well as key parts of our relationships and our world.

Most of us would not voluntarily put on a blindfold every day and miss out on not only the richness and delight of the visual world but also the crucial visual information that can guide us safely through the day. We certainly would not gouge out our eyes to keep this information from ourselves. Yet many of us blind ourselves to our feeling eyes, depriving ourselves of the rich tapestry of feelings that are key to our unique experience of the world, and that can offer important information.

Many Christians, both men and women, have confided to me that they never learned to accept the full range of their feelings. Some felt that to be angry was a sin, unless it was in direct defense of God. Some felt that a mature Christian would not be sad, because such a person would always be filled with joy and happiness. Therefore they learned to put on a happy face, and began to not only deceive others but lose touch with themselves. Their primary motivation was usually not to purposefully deceive someone, but to fulfill what they thought was God's will. As they begin to allow themselves to be in touch with their full range of feelings, they sometimes fear being overwhelmed by the feelings that have been unaccepted for so long.

Sometimes I have likened such feelings to a pet dog that has been put in the basement while the family goes out. The family is delayed, and the dog becomes ravenous and frantic, locked in the basement without adequate water or food. As the family returns, the dog makes a commotion at the basement door, and runs around out of control when he is let out. Later, after he has been fed, reassured, and rested, the dog becomes the more normal, friendly dog the family knows. Like the dog, when feelings that are meant to be accepted and to give us information are locked away in the basement of our minds without attention, they often seem overwhelming once that basement door is opened. When such feelings are accepted and worked through, they too eventually settle down and can enrich our lives.[2]

Thus, the foundations of assertiveness include the ability to bond, the ability to be separate, and the nonjudgmental awareness and acceptance of our feelings. Having noted these factors, let's return to the scriptural record and examine some of the incidents in her life that support the view of Mary as being assertive.

MARY'S WAY WITH WORDS

Speaking with Angels

In Luke, the first instance of Mary speaking at all is in the annunciation account, in response to the angel telling her that she will bear a son who will reign over the house of Jacob forever.[3] Mary asks the angel, "How will this be, since I am a virgin?" She speaks up assertively, asking clearly and distinctly what she needs to know, and says what is on her heart.

The angel answers her by giving further information that helps Mary understand, at least partially: "The Holy Spirit will come upon you, and the power of the Most High will over-shadow you. So the holy one to be born will be called the Son of God. Even Elizabeth your relative is going to have a child in her old age, and she who was said to be barren is in her sixth month. For nothing is impossible with God."

Mary then responds with a statement of who she is, and of her choice: "I am the Lord's servant. May it be to me as you have said."

The ability to ask what we need to know, as Mary did in this instance, is an important facet of being assertive. Here we begin to see how the various traits are interwoven and support each other. We have already discussed how Mary was inner-directed. We have seen also that she was individuated. Both of these traits lay an important foundation that supports the ability to be assertive in communications with others. It is much easier for inner-directed individuated persons to be aware of and speak up clearly about their needs and desires than it is for those who do not see themselves as separate from others and who need extensive approval from others. A woman who is afraid to risk disapproval may hesitate to ask difficult questions others may not wish to address, for example. Yet, being able to speak up and asking tough questions about important things that affect their lives gives important information to inner-directed persons, and strengthens their ability to be responsibly inner-directed.

One sign of a good teacher is giving permission and even encouraging students to ask questions. If someone is shamed or made to feel stupid for asking a question, learning is stifled. It is important to note that Mary's question was not out of disbelief, but out of puzzlement and a need to know.

By way of comparison, Zechariah[4] also asked a question when visited by the angel who told him that he and Elizabeth would have a son. It appears to be very similar to Mary's question. Like Mary, Zechariah is fearful when the angel appears to him. Like Mary, he is told by the angel not to fear. He is further informed that a son will be born to him and to his wife Elizabeth, a son who will have a special mission: to, "make ready a people prepared for the Lord." At this point Zechariah inquires of the angel, "How can I be sure of this? I am an old man and my wife is well along in years."

In Zechariah's case, the response of the angel to the questioner is very different. Scripture records the angel as answering, "I am Gabriel. I stand in the presence of God, and I have been sent to speak to you and to tell you this good news. And now you will be silent and not able to speak until the day this happens, because you did not believe my words, which will come true at their proper time."

This difference in the responses of the angel suggests that our motive in asking questions is an important factor in the type of response our questions bring forth. Zechariah was a mature priest who knew the stories of how God had given children to older, barren women such as Sarah and Hannah. He and Elizabeth were married, unlike Mary, so the normal means for a child to be conceived were already in place. Apparently the angel discerned that Zechariah's question was motivated by a lack of belief, a belief that Zechariah could have been expected to have, rather than by a need to know further information. Zechariah's need for a further sign was given by the silencing of his voice, which was both an answer to his question and a consequence of his unbelief with regard to this particular message from God.

One could say that it would have been better for Zechariah not to have asked his question, given the consequence he received. However, there is another possibility. It could also be said that Zechariah's question was also lovingly answered, giving him the sign that was needed to help him believe. Thus it was better for Zechariah to have asked the question, given his disbelief, so that he got the information he needed, than for him not to have asked, and to have missed out on the sign that helped him to have faith while waiting for the promised child to be conceived and born. Perhaps a profoundly awed and humbled Zechariah was able to use these months of silence to deepen his faith and relationship with his Lord, growing in spirit and being strongly prepared to be just the father that the young John would need.

Thus, while the responses to the questions of Mary and of Zechariah at first appear to be quite different, we see that both responses took into account both the motivation and the needs of the questioner. It appears that both Mary and Zechariah were better able to serve God because they asked the questions that were on their hearts. In addition, the two accounts taken together certainly hint that being assertive has its limits. Had Mary's or Zechariah's questions been defiant or mocking in spirit, for example, this would not have been acceptable. Assertiveness is not an umbrella under which all sorts of questionable motives and ways of communicating can be placed. Rather, at best, assertiveness has its own discipline and skill.

Let us now return to Mary's response to the angel once her question is answered. "I am the Lord's servant. May it be to me as you have said." With these simple, powerful words, Mary asserts something essential about who she is—the Lord's servant. Next, she states an important core choice that she owns: she gives her consent to bear the Christ-child. Both Mary's question and her answer can be seen as containing the paradox of humility and boldness. They model that assertiveness can be both humble (as opposed to arrogant), and bold. Both are required for healthy assertion.

Speaking Up During Pregnancy

Then, it appears that Mary chose to travel on her own to see her cousin Elizabeth. Scripture tells us "At that time Mary got ready and hurried to a town in the hill country of Judea, where she entered Zechariah's home and greeted Elizabeth." Although we are not told the details, the thrust of this passage is that Mary was key in this choice. Perhaps her family suggested and supported the idea, given the sensitive situation with Joseph and the community. In any case, Mary sought out a place where she would have support and encouragement from kindred spirits during the crucial early months of her pregnancy. Although Mary's words regarding this choice are not recorded in Scripture, the fact that she took the trip suggests that Mary asserted herself with regard to this decision.

Mary's next utterance in Luke's account is her Song. We

have already examined this song from the perspective of its creativity and intellectual complexity. Here, it is also important to note that praising God in song and putting forth our creative utterances are also acts of assertion. They require boldness, hopefully coupled with humility. As we take these risks of giving voice to our deepest expressions of self, we grow. We make the choice to let our light, part of the essence of who we are as created by God, shine.

Speaking Up at the Temple

Luke also records that Mary spoke up clearly to Jesus when as a young man he remained behind in the temple.[5] Jesus was twelve years old, and the family went to Jerusalem for the Feast of the Passover, as was their yearly custom. When the Feast was over, Mary and Joseph began the journey home, unaware that Jesus had stayed behind in Jerusalem. They thought he was part of the group that was traveling with them. No doubt the young people were grouped together, and since Jesus was reliable, they assumed he was part of that group. After a day, however, they began looking for him among the group of friends and relatives.

When he was nowhere to be found, they returned to Jerusalem, and discovered him in the temple courts, listening to the teachers and asking them questions. We are told that everyone who heard him was amazed at his level of understanding. However, when his parents saw him there, Scripture records they were astonished and Mary spoke up, saying, "Son, why have you treated us like this? Your father and I have been anxiously searching for you." Jesus also replied in a frank manner. "Why were you searching for me? Didn't you know I had to be in my Father's house?"

This incident illustrates that Mary and Jesus engaged in frank, clear communication. She does not appear to hold back in deference to Jesus, even though she is aware he is very special, but expresses her frustration and concern. Likewise, he is very straightforward, and frank, even though he is still a

youth under his parents' care. Both are being assertive in their conversation.

Mary's question to Jesus implies that he has treated them wrongly, disregarding them. However, she does not immediately pass judgment, but asks this question to get more information, giving Jesus a chance to explain, while at the same time conveying by the tone of the question something about what she is thinking. The eight brief words are packed with emotion and implication, as well as a request for information: "Son, why have you treated us like this?" She follows this up with a further statement that conveys the anxiety that she and Joseph have experienced as they have searched for their missing son: "Your father and I have been anxiously searching for you."

So, once again, we see that feelings are recognized and felt by Mary. She conveys the feeling content to Jesus, as well as the factual information. Mary is clear and strong in conveying her message without berating, blaming, or name-calling in any way. Jesus likewise speaks up clearly and directly. We will look at this story further and from a different perspective in the chapter on Mary as a parent.

Words at the Wedding

The next instance of Mary's recorded words occurs at the wedding of Cana.[6] John writes that Jesus, his newly chosen disciples, and his mother were all guests at a wedding at Cana in Galilee.

> When the wine was gone, Jesus' mother said to him, "They have no more wine."
> "Dear woman, why do you involve me?" Jesus replied, "My time has not yet come."
>   His mother said to the servants, "Do whatever he tells you."
> Nearby stood six stone water jars, the kind used by the Jews for ceremonial washing, each holding from twenty to thirty gallons. Jesus said to the servants, "Fill the jars with water"; so they filled them to the brim.
> Then he told them, "Now draw some out and take it to the master of the banquet."
> They did so, and the master of the banquet tasted the water that

had been turned into wine. He did not realize where it had come from, though the servants who had drawn the water knew. Then he called the bridegroom aside and said, "Everyone brings out the choice wine first and then the cheaper wine after the guests have had too much to drink; but you have saved the best till now." This, the first of the miraculous signs, Jesus performed at Cana in Galilee. He thus revealed his glory, and his disciples put their faith in him.

Numerous sermons have been preached concerning the many facets and possible interpretations of this fascinating and rather mysterious account of the first miracle. Because the story can be interpreted at several different levels, it is one of the more difficult stories to examine from the point of view of Mary's assertiveness. Mary's first statement, addressed to Jesus, is brief and to the point. "They have no more wine." It reflects a concrete reality, but also apparently has deeper levels of meaning for Jesus and possibly for Mary. His reply is also direct, if a bit inscrutable to us. "Dear woman, why do you involve me? My time has not yet come."

The interchange between the two appears to be fraught with meaning, the kind of meaning that two people who know and love each other very much and at various levels can sometimes engage in. Mary can be seen as either taking in all the levels of meaning in Jesus's reply or as responding on a more concrete level only, when she responds not to Jesus directly, but to the servants, "Do whatever he tells you."

Clearly, this communication was to both Jesus and the servants. It seems to signal to Jesus that she has heard his reply, but her remark to the servants now releases her expectation and puts the matter in the hands of Jesus as to whether he will fulfill the request or not.

Whatever perspective we take as to the meaning of the interchange between the two, it is clear regarding our issue of assertive communication that Mary did not hesitate to make the need and her implicit request known to Jesus.

It is worth noting that on other occasions Jesus also appears to challenge the one who requests a miracle. For example, there is the Syrian woman whose little daughter was possessed by an evil spirit. She begs Jesus to drive the demon from her daughter.[7] Jesus gives her this reply: "First let the children eat all they want, for it is not right to take the children's bread and toss it to their dogs." However, the woman boldly persists by replying, "Yes, Lord, but even the dogs under the table eat the children's crumbs." At this Jesus grants her request with the words, "For such a reply, you may go; the demon has left your daughter." Thus, this response of not immediately granting a request may be related to his testing the resolve of the person, rather than his own hesitancy to act. Jesus seems to reward appropriate assertiveness, and even persistence.

Perhaps Jesus was at least in part responding to the principle in Proverbs 3:27-28: "Do not withhold good from those who deserve it, when it is in your power to act. Do not say to your neighbor, 'Come back later; I'll give it tomorrow'—when you now have it with you."

It is also interesting that Jesus's miracles had the pattern of responding to a need, and typically a specific request of someone. As his mother and the one human being who knew him and his true nature most intimately at that point, Mary provided the request that got the ball rolling. She helped match up a real need with a real talent that helped not only the groom but also the ministry of her son. In this case, she used her assertiveness to speak up for someone else's need and request that it be filled. She also used it to bring forth a key talent of her son's into public view. Mary's boldness and persistence led to Jesus revealing his glory, which helped the new disciples put their faith in him. Thus assertiveness can be an important tool that helps further the work of God and meet the needs of others. Indeed, the last recorded words of Mary in Scripture are, "Do whatever he tells you."

A Troubling Time

Mary does appear to have spent time with the adult Jesus, traveling with him periodically.[8] In addition, Mark[9] relates

"Then Jesus entered a house, and again a crowd gathered, so that he and his disciples were not even able to eat. When his family heard about this, they went to take charge of him, for they said, 'He is out of his mind.'" At this same time, the teachers of the law have come down from Jerusalem to see him and are accusing him of being possessed by Beelzebub. As Jesus is defending himself from this charge by the use of parables, Mark tells us:

> Then Jesus' mother and brothers arrived. Standing outside, they sent someone in to call him. A crowd was sitting around him, and they told him, "Your mother and brothers are outside looking for you."
>
> "Who are my mother and my brothers?" he asked.
>
> Then he looked at those seated in a circle around him and said, "Here are my mother and my brothers! Whoever does God's will is my brother and sister and mother."

This account also has varying interpretations, and can initially seem very perplexing. Looking at it from the perspective of what it tells us about Mary, we see that she did not look the other way when she had a serious concern about her child, even her adult child. If someone is out of his mind, this is one of the few instances in which it may be appropriate for other family members to intervene against that person's wishes, because the loved one cannot be responsible for him- or herself. We only have a hint of what the family had heard, and do not know if what reached their ears was fully accurate.

What does seem apparent is that they were alarmed for the welfare of Jesus, and set off prepared to do whatever needed to be done, thinking Jesus was out of his mind. This phrase could have several connotations. Did they see his whole ministry as "crazy" and misguided at that point, or did they fear that the overwhelming strain of a legitimate ministry, such as the press of the crowds and the lack of food described by Mark, had pushed Jesus to some state of exhaustion where he was temporarily not in his right mind and needed care to restore him?

We are not given many details to help us with these questions. What we are told is that Jesus's brothers and his mother arrive and send someone in to call him out to them. When told they are outside looking for him, Jesus gives his somewhat startling reply, quoted above.

His statement can be taken in several possible ways. One perspective would be that this is a rebuff of his mother and brothers, disowning his family and taking on the new group as his family. Cults sometimes use this Scripture as a way of justifying the requirement that members cut off contact with family and friends. Another interpretation would be that Jesus is teaching his followers about how special they are. Rather than disowning his family, he is enlarging the circle of his family, just as he did later in his ministry, defining all who do the will of God as his brother, sister, and mother. This perspective honors his family and includes the new followers. Since Mary is one who did God's will, and since the latter interpretation appears most consistent with the nature of Jesus, it is the most likely case.

In this particular instance, we also do not know what happened after Jesus made his remarks. Did he go out, communicating with his family and alleviating their concerns about his mental condition? Were they able to be persuaded of his sanity at that time? We simply don't know. We do know that his ministry continued, and that for a period of time his brothers did not believe in him. We do not know what Mary thought during some of this time. Could she clearly see that Jesus was fulfilling his mission that the angel had foretold? Was she perplexed by the actions of her firstborn? What we do know is that whatever her views at that time, she appears to have stayed involved in some ways, and was present at his death, and at his ascension.

THE CONTEXT FOR ASSERTIVENESS

All of Mary's spoken words as recorded in Scripture are uttered in a rich context of committed love. She speaks to the angel, who is God's messenger. She speaks to her cousin Elizabeth and to God in her Song. She speaks to her beloved son. She speaks to the servants at the wedding of Cana, her hometown community. The scriptural account supports the view that Mary was assertive and gives us examples of her using assertiveness skills in her relationships with God, family, and others. They were used in love and respect for all concerned. As we have seen, there was a balance that included both humility and boldness. Speaking up assertively involves choice, and the wisdom to know when to exercise these skills. Possessing assertiveness skills does not mean that we are compelled to use them in every situation. In looking at the glimpses we have of Mary's interactions, we see that Mary spoke up assertively to:

1. Ask questions about matters that affected her well-being. She asks out of a right motive.
2. Make statements about her core self.
3. State choices that she owned.
4.. Make and exercise choices regarding what she needed for her own well-being.
5. Creatively express herself.
6. Praise God.
7. Express feelings ranging from great joy and awe to concern and anxiety.
8. Speak frankly with family members about their actions and the effects of their actions on others.
9. Point out the needs of others.
10. Bring out talents and gifts in others, to the glory of God.
11. Facilitate matching up needs with the solutions to the needs.
12. Instruct others to obey Jesus.

Seeing that Mary was assertive, as well as how she used this trait and skill for the benefit of herself and others, can give both women and men strong permission for owning this part of themselves. Mary's use of assertiveness shows us that it can be used in powerful, constructive ways that promote well-being for ourselves and others and that further the work of God. Like most powerful things, assertiveness can be used wisely or foolishly, rightly or harmfully. This chapter is not meant to be a comprehensive guide to assertiveness. However, it does seem important to briefly mention a few dangers concerning assertiveness.

Other Considerations

Assertiveness does not mean controlling others. Our being assertive does not control the outcome, or even necessarily mean that we should get our way. We can influence but we cannot control.

When people are beginning to increase their assertiveness, they may feel hurt, angry, or rebuffed if they assert themselves and others assert back, or maintain appropriate limits. Just because others may be encouraging them to speak up does not mean that those same others will say yes to their assertions. Mary and Jesus spoke frankly at the temple, but did not necessarily see the situation eye to eye, for example. Assertiveness on both sides can do much to increase clarity of communication, but does not necessarily bring forth agreement. To be assertive means that we must risk being told no or not getting our wishes granted. This puts a part of us on the line that can feel very vulnerable. It may be easier not to ask or state clearly than to do so and get turned down. Thus assertiveness can increase our feelings of vulnerability.

Assertiveness is neither entitlement nor aggression. Rather, assertiveness reveals something about ourselves, our beliefs, our desires, our choices, our feelings, and our limits. Choices about when and how to be assertive need to consider such things as our own safety, the safety of others, and whether assertiveness should be the highest priority in the situation. For example, Jesus was quite capable of assertively and brilliantly defending himself verbally, yet he did not exercise that skill at his own trial, to the scorn and consternation of many present. He did not because he was aware that his skill could have kept him from the very task that God had set before him at that time. His highest priority, doing God's will and dying for our sins, would not have been served by defending himself.

SUMMING UP

We see that Mary's assertiveness embodies a high level of caring and respect for herself, God, and others. Her ability and willingness to speak up clearly were vital to her understanding and fulfillment of the work that God called her to do. Further, this trait appears from the very beginning of God's calling, through the time when the most active phase of her parenting was complete and Jesus was called forth into adult ministry. This part of Mary and her archetype beckons us to explore and follow ways to speak up, affirming our own personhood and that of others. It shows us that assertiveness can be accomplished in the context of love and caring, as we keep company with Mary and her ways.

Chapter Eight

Mary and Joseph in Relationship

"When Joseph woke up, he did what the angel of the Lord
had commanded him and took Mary home as his wife."
Matthew 1:24

*N*OT MUCH IS SAID in Scripture about Joseph, the marriage partner of Mary, or about their relationship. As the more complete picture of Mary emerges from the shadows, the implications of these perspectives call for a fresh look at this primary relationship as well. A number of questions comes to mind.

Did their ways of relating fit the traditional patterns of the time? If Mary bursts forth from the traditional views we held of her as a woman, what implications does this have for her marriage relationship? To be blunt, can a woman who is intellectually gifted, assertive, inner-directed, and individuated relate intimately to a man in ways that are satisfying to both?

Sometimes the assumption is "no." Both women and men have sometimes been fearful that an independent, loving woman is an oxymoron. The seventies bumper sticker that proclaimed "A Woman Needs a Man Like a Fish Needs a Bicycle" testifies to the belief some women held that as they became fuller, more independent persons, the need for men became irrelevant. Other women have keenly desired both family and career, but felt they had to choose between the two.

171

Men have sometimes harbored fears that women equipped with knowledge and economic independence will not have reason to stay in relationships with them. Thus, taking the scriptural Mary out of the shadows has its risks. If Mary is assertive and strong, we need to examine the implications for the relationships between women and men.

Marriage as an institution has come under unprecedented assault in our generation. As some couples have begun to feel freed from the need to stay together for economic survival and/or to avoid scandalizing the community, the divorce rate has soared. Countless others would have nothing to do with marriage, choosing to live together without either the benefits or encumbrances of marriage. Theories of the logic of serial marriages have been touted. One article several years ago suggested something like three marriages: one to enjoy the fun years together, one to raise children during the formative years, and another to enjoy the sunset years. To expect that one partner would be suitable for all these stages in an age of extended life expectancy was unrealistic, this theory went.

When I began this work, I did not anticipate the need to deal with this question, or the degree to which there are possibilities for answers within the scriptural record. As time went on, reflections of the Biblical record and discussions with my husband led me to new perspectives regarding the relationship of Mary and Joseph. These perspectives are exciting, because they give space for the new possibilities that are emerging in couple relationships. Once again, there appears to be room to expand the borders of our tents.

In our time especially, we have seen more and more men and women yearning for couple relationships that are both devoted to the health of the relationship and to the individual growth of each couple member. Many are seeking new models for how to relate as husband and wife. The age-old custom of the wife promising to obey the husband in the wedding vows has been discarded by many. Numerous Christian couples struggle with the passages in Ephesians regarding submission and the role of husbands and wives. Others avoid the Church because they find its teachings regarding how couples should relate to be outdated and too constricting. Some try hard to fit what they feel is the Christian model for relationships, and find the fit is a strained one. "Why does it feel stifling if it is God's plan for us?" they wonder, and squirm to try to fit themselves into the space.

Many a woman, both historically and in present times, has endured emotional and/or physical abuse without setting limits because of the belief that her duty was to comply with her husband. Others have set their own dreams and talents aside in the belief that their roles were restricted to fitting in and complying with their husband's dreams and needs. Sad to say, some men are still using such beliefs to give them license to emotionally, physically, and sexually abuse members of their family.

One widow recently shared in a group how her spouse informed her early in their marriage, "There's only need for one opinion in this family, and that is mine." The gifts and talents she desired to bring to the marriage via her ideas and opinions were not wanted. Over the years, this had undermined her self-esteem, contributing to anxiety and depression. Her husband had not thrived either. Instead he became more and more isolated and rigid, living an increasingly restricted life. What a sad distortion of God's intentions for our lives. Yet if a woman has felt no permission to develop a strong sense of self, she will not have the base from which to set firm, loving limits if her husband misuses Scripture in such ways.

While many have struggled mightily or wearily with these issues, there has also been a strong thread of couples who have seemed to be deeply fond of each other and supportive of each other's work. A spark of independence flourishes in some of these women that their husbands seem to relish and support, and that does not appear to threaten or diminish either their happiness together or the man's self-esteem in any way. Such couples appear to have existed even when the prevailing culture failed to support such a view of relationships. In some of these relationships, equality between the spouses has been assumed.

Other couples have thrived within the traditional context of marriage. Some men have held to the importance of the man being the head of the family, and have nurtured and cherished their wives, as well as been humble and open to their spouse's input. Among this group of husbands, some have chosen to change the family style at a certain point, desiring to have a more equal partnership with their wives. They and their wives have seen room for this model in Scripture. One, pastor and author Donald Joy, speaks of how making this change further enriched an already good relationship.

Another, a minister and counselor, related to me how he came to desire a more equal relationship with his wife as he matured. At first, his spouse had a difficult time with this. Both were well practiced within the old groove, and she initially shrank back from the responsibility and opportunity, missing the security of his strong leadership. The common thread for each of these couples, and many others seeking to live within a Christian context, is that they were influenced by their beliefs about scriptural guidelines for marriage. The relationship of Mary and Joseph can therefore be highly relevant for putting flesh on Biblical teachings.

To examine perspectives on the relationship between Mary and Joseph, we will first look at what can be learned from the scriptural record about Joseph and his character, since our focus up to now has been on Mary. Then we will search for clues about the nature of their relationship and how what we learn can serve as a helpful model for loving contemporary relationships that seek to honor God.

GLIMPSES OF JOSEPH

If there has not been much written about Mary, there is even less written about the man who was the earthly father of Jesus.

Matthew[1] records that "Mary was pledged to be married to Joseph, but before they came together, she was found to be with child through the Holy Spirit. Because Joseph her husband was a righteous man and did not want to expose her to public disgrace, he had in mind to divorce her quietly."

These verses introduce Joseph and begin to give us insight

into the kind of person Joseph was. We are told he was a righteous man and that he did not want to expose the unwed, pregnant Mary to public disgrace, so he had in mind to divorce her quietly. The implication is that Joseph was both righteous and merciful. Based on what he knew at that time, he assumed that Mary had been unfaithful to him. In the Jewish tradition, a righteous man did not associate with an adulterous woman.

As a man scorned and wronged, he could have been righteously indignant and desirous of exposing what he believed to be the error of Mary's ways. The penalty for adultery[2] was death. He could have also been desirous of revenge. Being betrayed by the woman he loves is one of the most hurtful things that a man can experience, and has been known to be the cause of many a woman's death throughout the ages. While today we repudiate this type of action, in the Israel of Joseph's time, there were legal means to make it happen. Thus, one option for Joseph was to impose the death penalty. This could have been done out of either what would have been righteous motives under the Jewish law, or from vengeful motives.

Another possible option would have been to take Mary into his home even though she had been unfaithful to him. The Bible indicates that this was not what seemed best to Joseph. As a righteous man he was not to associate with an adulterous woman. In addition, he may have been distraught and shaken over this news about the woman he loved and intended to wed. What had he not seen about her character? How could she do this to him? He took this trespass seriously, and apparently valued virtue in his wife so much that he would have set aside his dreams to be with Mary rather than go forward under these circumstances.

So one thing we can surmise about Joseph is that he possessed healthy boundaries. He valued his own worth and his beliefs about what marriage should be, and set limits on what was unacceptable behavior. He therefore could not ignore the reality of his betrothed being unfaithful to him and go on with the marriage plans as if no wrong had been done. Joseph may also have seen Mary's pregnancy as sad evidence that their values were incompatible. Trust had been broken, and he may have felt that their relationship could never be the same.[3]

Yet, being loving and merciful, he did not wish to expose the young woman to public disgrace and even possible death by insisting on his legal rights. His righteousness was tempered with mercy. This indicates something about the maturity of Joseph's love for Mary. He did not view her as simply his possession, to be thrown away and destroyed if she was no longer suitable for him. Even in the hurt he must have felt, he valued her as a person, and did not want to bring harm to her. Her actions necessitated an end to their plans, but did not mean that he did not desire good for her. Therefore, "he had in mind to divorce her quietly." There is something both humble and noble in a man who values righteousness, but cares about the woman who wronged him. Pride does not have the last say with Joseph. Seeing how Joseph responded when he had reason to believe the worst about Mary tells us something about the man's mettle.

We also see evidence that Joseph was not a man of brash action. He considered what to do, we are told, taking time to reflect on his decision. During this time taken for consideration, God reveals new and important information: "But after he had considered this, an angel of the Lord appeared to him in a dream and said, 'Joseph son of David, do not be afraid to take Mary home as your wife, because what is conceived in her is from the Holy Spirit. She will give birth to a son, and you are to give him the name Jesus, because he will save his people from their sins.'"

This passage indicates several things about Joseph. He was open to God's input and perspective, he was a person of faith, and able to exercise discernment. A dream is something that some would disregard, and that requires careful judgment. Was this truly a message from God or just an ordinary dream, interesting as it may have been? Knowing that was a matter for discernment, and he was willing to obey God. Here was a man who had made a carefully considered decision about one of the most profound choices of life—the selection of one's life

partner. Now God was telling him to set aside that decision, based on evidence provided in a dream.

At that point, Joseph ended his decision-making process. We are told, "When Joseph woke up, he did what the angel of the Lord had commanded him and took Mary home as his wife." Joseph appears to have had a range of actions in his decision-making process; he considers carefully, but is also able to be decisive, and acts immediately when given instructions from God. Thus Joseph is not locked into one decision-making mode, but has a mature, flexible way of operating.

We see further evidence of Joseph's discernment and obedience in the fact that while taking Mary home as his wife, "he had no union with her until she gave birth to a son." God had apparently revealed that this was necessary, and Joseph responded in obedience. After their marriage and the birth of Jesus, further character traits are revealed in Joseph, such as his protectiveness of the mother and child, and his steadfastness in providing necessary care.

Thus, in summary, Joseph possessed qualities that made him a good match for Mary and a suitable earthly father for the Messiah. Here is a list of qualities found:

> Faith in God
> Obedience to God
> Discernment regarding God's Messages
> Humility
> Nobility of Spirit
> Righteousness
> Mercy
> Mature Decision-Making Capabilities
> Ability to be Decisive
> Self-Restraint
> Protective of Family
> Steadfastness

At this point, we can see that Joseph and Mary had some important character traits in common. Their shared faith, their

commitment to obey God, and their humility, coupled with a nobility of spirit, provided a solid base for their marriage. Combined with these traits, the steadfastness of each was crucial to their relationship and their mission.

Taped on the side of the file cabinet by my computer is a sheet given to me by another author. It reads:

PRESS ON!
Nothing in the world can take the place of persistence.
Talent will not: nothing is more common than unsuccessful men with talent.
Genius will not; unrewarded genius is almost a proverb.
Education alone will not: the world is full of educated derelicts.
Persistence and determination alone are omnipotent!

While I do not agree with all facets of this statement by an unknown author, as not even persistence and determination are omnipotent, the emphasis on persistence for those goals that we have determined are truly deserving of it can be crucial when we are discouraged or unsure of the worth of continuing. Joseph, once he was sure of the course God wanted him to take, was unswerving, persistent, and steadfast. I have counseled many women who yearned for this quality in their boyfriends or husbands. Those women (or men) who can rely on this trait in their spouse have a solid base not only for the security of the relationship, but for their own personal flourishing. This staying power of Joseph and Mary is a stalwart example for us in our couple and family relationships.

A SHIFT IN PERSPECTIVE

Now let us turn to another important facet of Joseph regarding his relationship with Mary. It appears that Joseph began his betrothal to Mary with a traditional view of their relationship. He likely expected that Mary would be a good and faithful wife, take care of him, and bear him children. Then came the jarring news that the traditional marriage was not to be. Mary was somehow pregnant, and he knew that he was not the father of the child. As we have just seen, Joseph therefore decided to put her quietly aside.

Then came the startling dream. The maiden he loved had work of her own—a mission given by God—and Joseph was also invited to play a key part in this mission. Mary's role was not to be limited to the traditional one of supporting her husband and his dreams, of raising his children. God had called her to conceive, bear, and raise the Messiah. Joseph now needed to embrace a different view of Mary and their life together in order to participate. This crucial shift had to do with seeing Mary as a full person in her own right, apart from her relationship to Joseph. It had to do with respecting her as an individual, one called by God to do something besides be Joseph's helpmate.

Joseph's ability to make this shift not only changed his view of Mary, but also of their relationship and of himself. By being willing to make the shift, his own horizons were opened up. Now he, too, had a life purpose and role that was different from what he could have previously envisioned. Joseph's ability to do this fully speaks well for his strong sense of personhood and masculinity. His identity did not rest on the need for Mary to fulfill the traditional marriage role. Although the relationship may have seemed the same to the outside world, the two became partners on a different level, and Joseph saw Mary in a different light. Mary's role was more than helping Joseph in his life and bearing him children. Instead, the two of them had a joint, sacred purpose given by God, in which both played vital roles. A mutual respect and a higher order of partnership were necessary.

MARY IN RELATIONSHIP TO JOSEPH

Having taken a look at Joseph, a return to Mary now reveals several important perspectives regarding her in relationship to Joseph. We have seen that Mary possesses many strong qualities that have been in the shadows of how she is typically viewed. Mary was able to act independently, yet also be part of a couple. The qualities of independence, inner-direction, and assertiveness are not mutually exclusive with being able to relate well in an intimate couple relationship. To the contrary, Mary and Joseph were able to be interdependent.

For example, just as God chose to deal directly with Mary in the annunciation, Joseph also received revelations and instructions from God. He was told to take Mary and Jesus to Egypt, where they would be safe from Herod's persecution. Mary, in addition to her own autonomy and capacity for independent action, accepted Joseph's leadership in this area. She allowed herself and the baby Jesus to be cared for and protected by Joseph. It was also Joseph who received the instructions about when it was safe to return to Israel. Mary trusted his discernment of God's leading and his decision to relocate to Nazareth.

Mary was able to both be herself and lean on Joseph. Here we may be called to stretch to the level of complex thinking that is necessary to understand the paradox and flexibility of a woman who is able to be both strong and needful of protection, both independent and yet depending at times in love and gratefulness on the care of her husband. Versatility is one of the marks of a strong, empowered person. Mary's flexibility and versatility allowed her to respond lovingly to Joseph in different ways at different times.

MARY AND JOSEPH TOGETHER

Right Priorities

The relationship of Mary and Joseph underwent an extraordinary testing before they became husband and wife. Mary endured a period when Joseph did not understand the reason for her pregnancy and was planning to set her aside. Assuming she knew this was going on, she had to come to terms with the idea that her *Yes* to God was likely to mean Joseph's *No* to her. She had to deal with the fact that what had happened to her could have shattered Joseph's trust in her. We do not know for certain whether Mary told him about the angel's visit and that she had conceived by the Holy Spirit. All we know is that he did not initially believe the story if he did hear of it.

We also don't know if Mary was at her cousin Elizabeth's during this time, or whether someone else, such as her parents, was doing the communicating with Joseph. Had God assured her all would be well with Joseph, or did she not know the outcome of the development? What is indicated is that, as important as Joseph may have been to her, she was willing to accept this consequence of her saying *Yes* to God. She also accepted Joseph back into her life after his dream instructed him to go forward with the marriage.

Joseph endured a period when Mary seemed to have betrayed him. Much as he may have loved her, he was not willing to go on with the relationship at any cost. His beliefs about the importance of trust and faithfulness in a marriage may have been vital to his decision not to go forward with the marriage. Thus, strong as their desire to be married may have been, both were willing to sacrifice that desire for other values. Both saw the importance of marriage as being embedded in faith and a relationship to God.

In *Beyond Companionship*,[4] Christian authors Diana and David Garland assert that it is a widely held myth that marriage is the most important relationship in life. They contend that marriage needs to be put in its proper place as secondary to the most important relationship in life, that of our relationship with God. The crisis that Mary and Joseph went through tested the priority of each one's relationship to God. Both demonstrated that they put their relationship to God first, even before marriage and each other. We have seen how Mary did this. Joseph was willing first to set the marriage aside and then to go forward with it in obedience. This fact of having one's priorities right actually strengthens marriage by putting it in right relationship to God.

Flexible Roles

Both Mary and Joseph were able to be flexible in their roles, which strengthened their union and increased their effectiveness in their work. We have seen how Joseph ultimately accepted that Mary had received a calling from God and responded with a yes without consulting Joseph first. We see that Mary was a strong person with a capacity for inner-direction and independent action. Her full personhood and God's call on her life could not be fulfilled by her simply relying on Joseph for decision-making in the traditional hierarchical model of couple relationships. Yet Mary's independence and Joseph's acceptance of this independence was not the full portrait of their relationship. Joseph was able to accept this very real part of Mary and to exercise leadership as well. The two were able to be flexible in their roles, which strengthened their union and increased their effectiveness in their work. Like trees that are firmly rooted but able to sway in the winds of the storm, a marriage that has this type of flexibility can provide a very stable environment for growth over time.

Room for Mystery

Paul alludes to the mystery of the marriage relationship, comparing it to the profound mystery of the relationship of Christ to the church.[5] By responding to God and each other even when they could not understand, Joseph and Mary allowed room for the mystery in their marriage relationship, and in each other. In *Flowers in the Desert*,[6] Demetrius Dumm speaks of the mystery of God and how some of that divine mystery is part of every creature created by God. This mystery, which by definition cannot be fully understood or controlled, is part of what we are called upon to cherish in each other.

IMPLICATIONS FOR CONTEMPORARY RELATIONSHIPS

In order to consider the implications of this perspective for contemporary relationships, we will touch briefly on some general historical considerations. Then we will look at the four styles of marriage relationships proposed by the Garlands.

Historically, there has been a strong trend within Christianity, as well as other major religions, to emphasize the hierarchical view of marriage where the husband is head of the family, including the wife. Rather than being seen as an equal partner, the wife has been viewed as a godly woman if she were obedient and oriented to pleasing her husband. Paul's comments on marriage in Ephesians 5 have often been interpreted to emphasize that the wife is to be submissive to the husband and to underemphasize the call for mutual submission that precedes in verse 21.

In fact, translators have often divided the passage segments so that the general instruction of verse 21, "Submit to one another out of reverence for Christ," is under a different heading and not included in the other comments about the marriage relationship. For example, the New International Version entitles verses 22-33 "Wives and Husbands," placing verse 21 at the end of the previous segment of instructions to believers in general. This tends to separate it from the portion where it would fit most naturally if not for the long tradition of emphasizing the submission of women over mutual submission.

Within the last half-century, views of couple relationships have become more varied within the general culture, as well as within Christendom. There remains a sizable group of couples who rely on the traditional view of marriage to guide their relationship. Some of the couples within this group hold to the pattern primarily because they believe it is the model that is sanctioned by Scripture, but would welcome a more flexible model if they believed it was congruent with Biblical principles. Others may have already explored a more flexible model, and would benefit from further encouragement and affirmation regarding the model they follow.

The perspective that Mary and Joseph's relationship may model much more possibility for a flexible, mutual relationship, one that embraces the mystery of marriage and allows for two strong persons united under God, can send a further welcome message of encouragement to couples who seek newer ways of relating. Those Christians who have had only one model, a traditional hierarchical one, presented to them as the way to please God, will have another Biblically sound choice.

Viewing the relationship of Mary and Joseph in this light has encouraging implications for contemporary couples who may desire something different than certain traditional Christian views of the marriage relationship. The Garlands[7] write that Scripture does not prescribe only one pattern of marriage that is right for all time and people. Faculty members of Southern Baptist Theological Seminary,[8] they explored traits of the traditional Biblical view of marriage that they label *hierarchical,* as well as an alternative Biblical model, which they label *mutual submission.* The hierarchical view has largely influenced the traditional cultural pattern of marriage, while the mutual submission model corresponds to the companionship cultural pattern of marriage, they report.

The Garlands contrast the motto of the hierarchical view as "Wives, be subject," from Ephesians 5:22 with the mutual submission view as "Be subject to one another out of reverence for Christ," from Ephesians 5:21. In the hierarchical model, roles for men and women are clearly assigned, and the line of authority goes from God to man to woman. In contrast, the mutual submission and companionship models have flexible roles, which can change according to circumstance and the couple's needs and desires. The authority or power in the relationship is shared in the latter two patterns, with God having ultimate authority for Christian couples.

It needs to be stated that the hierarchical model can work well when the partners, particularly the husband, are mature and loving. Many spouses have believed in this pattern in an enlightened way, and both spouses have flourished. However, there are several problems associated with the hierarchical view. Some Christians see this model as the only possible Biblically correct model for marriage, and tend to be judgmental towards those who see other Biblical possibilities. Thus, there can be real pressure to conform to this pattern, and a lack of needed support if other Biblical alternatives are desired by a couple.

In addition, for those who subscribe to this model, the wife often has less power and permission to deal with problems that arise. "How can I be submissive *and* tell my husband he's being unfairly domineering and unresponsive to my needs?" lamented one Christian wife who had felt stuck with this dilemma for years. Only when her health began to give out and the doctors suggested that she was holding in a great deal of stress did she begin to realize the pervasive toll this bind was taking on her body and soul. When she began to hold her husband accountable in assertive, firm, and loving ways, new possibilities began to open up for both.

When this model is not implemented in an enlightened way, who holds the husband accountable? Unfortunately, this traditional pattern can encourage narcissism[9] in men and depression in women. Studies have reported that women in traditional marriages have more depression and other mental health difficulties than either their unmarried or working married cohorts or men.[10] Neither of these conditions encourages healthy growth in ways that please God. It can be said the body of Christ is to mediate and help make this model work, but that is seldom the case in reality. The relationship of Mary and Joseph can be seen as giving couples space to try ways of relating other than the traditional hierarchical one.

Distinguishing between the Biblical model of a mutually submissive marriage and the cultural model of the companionship marriage is also important. As demonstrated by Mary and Joseph, the goal in the Biblical model is to honor God in the relationship and fulfill God's purpose for the couple and individuals involved. Love and comfort are mutually provided within this context. The paradox is that this will also ultimately be most fulfilling for the individuals and the marriage. The goal of the companionship marriage is more focused on autonomy and self-actualization, according to the Garlands. In contemporary times, the advent of the companionship model in our culture has paved the way for the mutual submission model to flourish.

A variety of scholars and writers, including the Garlands, feel that the hierarchical and traditional models are fading away, and that Scripture supports the mutual submission model. "We conclude from our study of the Biblical evidence that man and wife were created by God to be equal partners in marriage. A hierarchical relationship in which the husband rules is not the will of God but a distortion of the relationship between man and woman."[11]

Because gender roles have been and continue to be such an issue in our culture as patterns begin to shift, it is important to note that flexibility of roles and the mutual submission model do not emphasize specific role tasks. Spouses might choose to divide tasks in a rather traditional way, but this does not mean that the traditional model of marriage is operative in their relationship, if these tasks are fulfilling the purpose and meaning of the mutual submission model. The relationship of Mary and Joseph may well have often had the outward form of a traditional relationship. Yet the key crisis in their relationship and their resolution of that crisis set the tone for inward realities that transformed their interactions.

Stages in Couple Relationships

The stages in Mary and Joseph's relationship can be seen to correspond at least loosely to the three stages that couple relationships typically undergo. In the romantic or dependent stage, the new lovers are starry-eyed and feel that their every need is gratified by the loving other. It is a wonderful, idealized time for many couples. The world is suddenly seen in vivid colors, thanks to the way this new relationship has awakened the senses. Hearts overflow with love and trust. Life feels complete when with the beloved.

Another facet of this stage is that each person is not only loved for their more obvious endearing qualities, but also because he or she is meeting the deeply felt need of the partner for love and fulfillment. The unconscious conviction is usually that the beloved will meet our needs and heal our wounds. The wonderful feelings that flood our bodies and emotions attest to the sense that this person is good for us. It is in this stage that Joseph likely saw Mary as meeting his need for a good and loving wife who would fit in well with his life and plans, making him happy and providing him with children.

The second stage in relationships is often dubbed the power

struggle or independent stage. It is in this stage that the couple begins to realize that the partner has an agenda of his or her own that perhaps neither had been aware of before. Harville Hendrix[12] has described this as each person suddenly realizing that they have been cast as a star in their partner's play, and all the while they had believed the partner was a cast member of *their* play. To make this example more concrete, imagine the wife believing that she has found the perfect Spencer Tracy to play to her Doris Day, while the husband was convinced that he had found the perfect Marilyn Monroe to play to his John Wayne! The sense of confusion and even betrayal is understandable when seen this way.

In this stage, the expectations we have had that our beloved will make our lives complete and that life together will be unending bliss get a rude awakening. Our beloved cannot be with us all the time. Even worse, when they are with us, they can irritate us in ways we never noticed in the romantic stage. Failings stand out in bold relief. The silence seen as thoughtful and wise in the romantic stage now seems distant and withholding. Or the bubbliness that was so engaging now appears shallow and unsympathetic. Each person in the relationship now sees the other in a harsher light.

This corresponds to the stage where Joseph realizes that Mary is not the girl he thought she was, and feels no doubt confused and betrayed. Even when the truth of the situation is revealed to him in a dream, he must continue to cope with the realization that this will not be the simple, traditional relationship that he had expected, as we have discussed above. Had Joseph held to his original concepts, he might still have decided he would prefer a different wife. Contemporary couples sometimes experience this stage as one of "when the honeymoon is over," and one or both feel the need for more space. Since one person often enters this stage before the other, one spouse may feel abandoned when this stage occurs, and may wonder if love is fading.

When we persevere in our marriages, with the right tools, we can arrive at the conscious or interdependent stage of the relationship. In this stage, we are able to grow and flourish as individuals, as well as be close as a couple. The idealized view of our loved one is gone, but real appreciation for his or her true self is possible. We learn to accept the negative feelings our mates have, as well as the positive, loving feelings. This can be deeply healing. We know that sometimes we will not be in their presence but that we are loved and cared for even when we are apart.

Couples in this stage are often able to be more flexible, being there for each other when that is called for, and allowing space when work schedules, other demands, or personal needs indicate that this is appropriate. Aware of each other's strengths and weaknesses, couples have learned ways to communicate that foster growth and healing rather than allowing vulnerabilities to be the source of more wounding and strife. When Joseph accepted Mary and the life work God was giving to both of them, the couple began to demonstrate aspects of this developmental stage, appreciating the uniqueness of each one even though preconceived ideas were not fulfilled.

A Paradox of Autonomy and Self-Sacrifice

The companionship model seeks self-fulfillment and autonomy. The Christian model within the mystery of paradox fulfills those goals in the fullest and truest way possible. It is the full, autonomous life, laid down before God and the spouse, that is the strongest gift of a truly free person. Jesus is the supreme example of such a gift freely given to God.

Such was the gift that Mary and Joseph gave to God and to each other. Such is the gift that God desires from each of us, and which he treats as treasure. Out of that gift, and the crisis of their couple relationship, came a shared spiritual purpose and awe at the wonders of a God at work fulfilling longed-for promises. Luke 2:33 tells how "The child's father and mother marveled at what was said about him." Joseph's act of obedience in taking Mary as his wife was confirmed by the shepherds' visit and the prophetic words at the temple. The shared spiritual purpose and this profound sense of wonder are the stuff of deep and permanent bonding. Couples who share in this type of relationship enjoy an inward reality that can sustain them through many difficult times.

As we return to the questions posed at the chapter's beginnings, it appears that this spiritual shared purpose and the mutual submission to God that are integral parts of Christianity serve as the glue meant to hold together and transform the union of a strong, individuated woman and man. All the ingredients are necessary in order to have the union be what it was meant to be. What Joseph and Mary offer us in terms of a model can support contemporary couples in their search for healthy, loving ways that honor God and themselves. However exciting this model is, it is a tall order that requires the good will and commitment of both human parties, as well as the grace of God. The mysteries of marriage propel us back into the mysteries of God's grace.

Chapter Nine

Maternal Mary

"And the child grew and became strong; he was filled with wisdom, and the grace of God was upon him."   Luke 2:40

"And Jesus grew in wisdom and stature, and in favor with God and men."   Luke 2:52

*T*HE TWO BRIEF STATEMENTS from Luke quoted above are the only commentary we have in Scripture about the growth and development of Jesus from infancy to young adulthood. The first is recorded just after Mary and Joseph have fulfilled everything required by the Law of the Lord, circumcising Jesus and presenting the infant at the temple in Jerusalem for consecration to the Lord as the first-born male. The second statement occurs after the trip to Jerusalem, when Jesus is a youth of twelve years.

Psychodynamic psychology has long looked at the adult to form theories about how the child develops. Luke's words suggest Jesus was parented in ways that fostered his full development psychologically, spiritually, physically, and intellectually. What can we glean from the scriptural account that can help us understand how the parenting of Mary and Joseph encouraged this healthy development?

Scripture tells us that Jesus was divine and human. Was the

191

divine in him enough to cause this healthy growth and development in the young child as he grew to adulthood? It seems clear that parenting had a key role in this process. God carefully chose parents for Jesus who had the qualities and the commitment to bring him up in ways that would foster his strong physical, intellectual, social, and spiritual development. In this chapter, we will further examine Mary's role as a mother, and the parenting that she and Joseph did to bring Jesus to the threshold of adulthood, ready to go forward with his unique ministry. We will also consider her role as he entered that ministry. Gleaning principles from Scripture that show how Mary handled this part of her life, we will consider how she and her archetype can help serve as guideposts to parenting issues today.

Mary's role as mother of Jesus was crucial in her life purpose. What can prepare a young woman for such a momentous task? What are the foundations of good parenting that allowed Mary to parent in ways that prepared Jesus for adulthood? First, we will look at the parenting task. What are the goals of the kind of parenting God desires in order to produce children who will grow up to fulfill their life purpose and serve God well? We will then look at the foundations of good parenting abilities. Finally, we will examine the principles that we can gain from observing how Mary and Joseph parented.

THE PARENTING TASK

Goals for the kind of parenting that God desires are indicated by the commentary on how Jesus grew.

Growing in Stature—Raising physically healthy children.

Providing care that promotes the physical health and well-being of children is a primary task of parenthood. This part of the parenting task is important for the very survival of the child. Parents need to provide adequate shelter, nutrition, and clothing for their offspring, as well as any medical treatment that is needed. This is a time-consuming task for all parents, and can become momentous at times for those striving to provide for children with special medical conditions and needs.

As with many things, the key is moderation. Though Jesus was a king, God did not provide him with a set of parents complete with palace. The physical setting of his birth was humble, and the trip to Egypt was not in a Cadillac or even on the back of an elaborately decked-out camel. Yet Joseph and Mary provided the best that was available to them under the circumstances they were in. Their child's physical welfare was of paramount importance to them, as is demonstrated by their willingness to completely leave their country, uprooting themselves, when that environment was no longer safe for their infant.

There are many parents struggling economically who exemplify this priority today. Though their resources are small, they make it a priority and a joy to provide their children what is needed, without indulging them, for indulgence is not only the prerogative of the wealthy. I recall a situation where a couple who had probably emigrated from Europe labored tirelessly and cheerfully in their small leather-working shop. Their only daughter was their treasure, and was dressed like a princess, apparently never helping out in the shop as she reached the adolescent years, but devoting herself entirely to the extracurricular activities of a popular teen. Most of this young woman's contemporaries from middle-class backgrounds were expected to contribute to their families' well-being, but she was apparently exempt. Yet her parents' devotion did not appear to be endearing them to her, or to be helping her develop the important traits of competency, responsibility, and gratitude.

For those with abundant financial resources, the task is to provide adequately and lovingly without crossing the fine line of indulgence.

Growing in Wisdom—Intellectual and Skill Development

It is a theme throughout Scripture that knowledge alone is not enough to equip people for dealing with the realities of life. While intellectual development is valued, it is to be a facet of wisdom. In the Bible, wisdom is inextricably linked to reverence for God. For example, Proverbs 1:7 informs us that "The fear of the Lord is the beginning of knowledge, but fools despise wisdom and discipline." Helping children grow in wisdom and discipline is a basic task of parents desiring to raise their children in ways pleasing to God.

Wisdom is defined in the dictionary as the understanding of that which is true, right, or lasting, as well as having common sense and good judgment. It can also have to do with learning and erudition.[1] Within the broad category under wisdom would also come intellectual and skill development. This part of raising children presents a significant responsibility for parents. It also comes with a catch.

Working Ourselves Out of a Job

Part of our task in this area is getting really good at all this, and then letting go appropriately, while still keeping important bonds with our now grown children. Years ago, as a young parent, I attended a seminar lead by the now internationally known child psychiatrist Dr. Foster Cline. I remember being struck by his statement that as parents of infants, fulfilling our role as parents meant meeting 99 percent of our little ones' needs. By the time this same individual was 18 or 21, fulfilling our role meant meeting only about 1 percent of their basic needs! This meant that we were to be steadily equipping our children to take over responsibility for their own lives, in effect working ourselves out of a job. The very caring acts that meant excellent parenting of the infant spelled disaster for the young adolescent. Without this process of continually letting go at the appropriate time, our children do not have sufficient opportunities to develop the practical side of wisdom, part of which involves making choices and experiencing the consequences of those choices.

Thus one important aim of parenting is raising children who are increasingly able to take responsibility for their own lives, both in a myriad of practical living skills, in making major life decisions, and have the moral and spiritual fortitude to go forward with their lives. This involves not only helping our children acquire skills but also giving them the space to increasingly use the skills. The backing-off process may be one of the most difficult for deeply loving, bonded parents.

For Christian parents, a crucial priority is to raise children who will of their own free will choose to be in right relationship with God and be steadfast in this area. Instructions from the Old Testament that likely guided Mary and Joseph include Deuteronomy 4:9: "Only be careful, and watch yourselves closely so that you do not forget the things your eyes have seen or let them slip from your heart as long as you live. Teach them to your children and to their children after them." In referring to "the things your eyes have seen," the people are reminded to tell of God's loving and miraculous acts in their lives. Such accounts, both from the stories told in the Scripture and our own individual and family histories, help form the realization of God's profound love, which lays the foundation of trust.

A little later, in Deuteronomy 6:6-7, the Israelites are told, "These commandments that I give you today are to be upon your hearts. Impress them on your children. Talk about them when you sit at home and when you walk along the road, when you lie down and when you get up." This follows the command to "Love the Lord your God with all your heart and with all your soul and with all your strength."[2] In fact, God considers this dialogue and instruction of children to be so important that it is repeated in Deuteronomy 11:19. A sequence is seen: First is the telling of the stories that build the foundation of trust in a loving, powerful God who acts on our behalf, as a loving parent. Children need to have this foundation before commandments are introduced; Second is teaching the children the response to this love and care, which involves following God's command to love him with all one's heart, soul, and strength.

Proverbs 22:6 carries both instructions and a promise: "Train a child in the way he should go, and when he is old he will not turn from it."

That Mary and Joseph followed these instructions is evident from the reactions of those who heard the twelve-year-old Jesus in the temple courts, interacting with the teachers there: "Everyone who heard him was amazed at his understanding and his answers."[3] Thus, before he reached adulthood, Jesus had a solid grounding in Scripture and had developed wisdom that astounded the best teachers of the day. This was likely a blend of the influence of the parental teaching about God and Scripture and God's interaction with the young Jesus. It was crucial that the parents do their part, leaving the rest to God the Father and Jesus the Son.

In Favor with Men—Emotional and Relational Development

Jesus grew "in favor with men," which indicates he was looked upon favorably by others, and had the ability to relate well to others. Our emotional development lays the groundwork for our relational abilities, and thus the two are intertwined.

The Ability to be Close and Separate.

The ability to be close to others as well as have a sense of self apart from others is a key part of emotional development. Parents need to provide the basis for bonding and attachment in their children. We have seen how this foundation is laid in the first year of life, when the infant receives both the basic care needed as well as liberal amounts of love, cuddling, comfort, and attention.

Then, as the child grows and begins to explore his world, the parent needs to be able to continue the consistent loving and care, while at the same time supporting the young child in going out, step by step, to explore the world. The child needs to return often for reassurance, as he toddles off to explore, and then be free to go off again, experiencing the heady feeling of his own new-found ability to learn about the world on his own.

The Ability to Communicate Clearly

Jesus, with his profound and pithy sayings and parables, was the greatest communicator the world has ever known. This can be said both due to his communication ability and the content of his message. Some of this was undoubtedly a product of the divine part of him, and some was undoubtedly due to his genetic endowment as a human, in the way of a gift or God-given talent. Yet this gift was developed and honed at least in part at the feet of his parents. The stories of his birth and of the history of God interacting with his people must have helped lay the foundation for Jesus's later teachings. Mary's ability to speak up clearly, as discussed in Chapter Seven, was probably a model for him.

Quality and Quantity Time

The May 12, 1997 cover of *Newsweek* featured a story entitled "The Myth of Quality Time: How We're Cheating Our Kids." The article documented and lamented the hectic schedules that so many American parents live with and the detrimental effect that this can have upon children, who need large amounts of quantity time as well as quality time. In Mary's time, it was much more the norm for the average mother to have time to devote to her children. The mothers would be occupied with many tasks, with the children around, being tended to as needed, and learning about activities as they grew.

The basis for many of the parables Jesus told were probably learned as he spent time with one or the other of his parents going about their activities. The situation of the flight to Egypt probably provided even more of such quality time lavished on the small Jesus. Joseph's work as a carpenter probably meant that he worked in a shop that was part of the home, so when he was older, Jesus may have spent much more time with his dad than the average child of today, who may have both parents leave for work outside the home at an early hour and return for her at the end of the day. It is likely that parenting, for Mary and Joseph, provided opportunity for large amounts of time with Jesus, as well as times that were devoted especially to tending him, and teaching him.

FOUNDATIONS FOR QUALITY PARENTING

We have been looking at the full personhood of Mary in this book. The characteristics we have discovered—Mary's inner-directedness, her faith, her assertiveness, and her creativity and intellectual giftedness—all form an important part of who Mary was as a parent. The tone and quality of her parenting was in large part a product of these traits in Mary. In Erikson's writing concerning the stages of psychological development, he stresses that the quality of the relationship between a mother and child is greatly effected by the richness and stability of the mother. The qualities that we have been noticing in Mary helped make up the "richness" to which Erikson referred. So while loving and putting in time are important factors, they are enriched by the unique qualities and strengths that make up the individual personhood of the caregiving parent. The infant/child is absorbing all sorts of things, on many levels, from the person who cares for her and interacts with her. Recent research has taken this even further with discoveries as to how the brain develops according to the nature and quality of the stimulation the child receives.

Furthermore, Erikson was also convinced that the basis for faith emerges from the bonding and trust that is developed in the young child. As we discussed earlier, a child who learns to trust that care will come from loving, reliable parents comes to believe that others are good and trustworthy, and that they can expect good things not only because of the trustworthiness of the other, but because the child herself is basically lovable. Thus confidence in self and in others is formed at this time.

This basic trust allows the child, and eventually the adult, to be predisposed to have faith in a loving God, and to be able to believe that someone they cannot see loves them and cares for them. Children who have not had enough of this type of basic trust development have a much more difficult time conceiving of the idea that a God might love them and be able to keep promises.

All this goes to affirm what many parents have intuitively known: caregivers are not interchangeable. That Jesus had parenting by an intelligent, creative, inner-directed mother helped him develop into such a person himself. Likewise, the qualities of faith, obedience, willingness to act decisively, righteousness, and mercy that we have seen earlier that Joseph possessed also affected the quality of parenting that Jesus received from him.

The quality of Joseph and Mary's interactions with him as the young Jesus asked the myriad of questions that growing minds need to know no doubt nourished his intellectual development. The strong sense of poise and confidence coupled with humility that Jesus exuded in his ministry probably had at least some of its roots in his interactions with his mother.

The mutuality that Mary and Joseph enjoyed in their relationship, as discussed in the previous chapter, would have also affected the quality of parenting in positive ways. It no doubt provided Jesus with important modeling as to the worth and dignity of women in relationships. Throughout his ministry Jesus demonstrated an uncommon sensitivity toward women. He did not patronize women, and several excellent studies have noted that Jesus had a radically egalitarian stance toward women, particularly for his day.

There is evidence of shared and involved parenting between Mary and Joseph. Since the two were traveling at the time of the birth, it is certainly possible that the new little family had a chance to bond together in a way that might not have occurred if they had been surrounded by friends and family in their hometown. The flight into Egypt as recorded in Matthew also likely meant that the new family had more time together than if Joseph had been doing his usual carpenter work during that time.

In summary, the traits discussed in section one of this book regarding Mary, and those discussed in Chapter Nine regarding

Joseph, make up the foundation of the quality parenting that Jesus received. As we make it our business to develop into mature, creative, appropriately assertive, faithful persons, we build the foundations for providing the kind of quality parenting that delights God.

PRINCIPLES OF PARENTING

Having considered both the parenting task and some important foundations of good parenting, we now turn to principles of parenting revealed in the scriptural account of how Mary and Joseph raised Jesus. Since we are seeking to discover these principles from the Biblical data, it is not necessarily a complete list of either what Mary and Joseph did or what God would have us do. Mary and Joseph obviously did much as parents that is not touched upon in the record. Nevertheless, what is found can encourage us, comfort us, and guide us.

Bringing up Jesus within the Context of Faith

Luke tells us that on the eighth day Jesus was circumcised and given the name that had been revealed to the parents before he had been conceived. Then, after the time of their purification, "according to the Law of Moses had been completed, Joseph and Mary took him to Jerusalem to present him to the Lord (as it is written in the Law of the Lord, 'Every firstborn male is to be consecrated to the Lord'), and to offer a sacrifice in keeping with what is said in the Law of the Lord: 'a pair of doves or two young pigeons.'"[4]

Luke also records that the family went to Jerusalem regularly for the Feast of the Passover. These events all indicate that Joseph and Mary together observed the traditions of their faith. Jesus was bathed in these traditions from infancy to adulthood. In addition, we have seen that the traits of faithfulness, obedience, and joyfully doing God's will were ones that Mary and Joseph developed and that they no doubt modeled for Jesus. This combination of observing religious traditions and a living, trusting faith is a powerful one, and sets the stage for the child to grow strong in his or her own faith.

Nurturing and Protecting in Diverse Circumstances

Ways to nurture and protect their child in diverse circumstances were an obvious priority in the lives of Mary and Joseph. Their use of a manger in which to place the newborn also represents resourcefulness in meeting their infant's needs for a sleeping place.

Soon after this, Scripture records that the new parents faced a major crisis. Their newborn's life was endangered by King Herod, who is upset by the visit of the Magi to his kingdom as they searched for the king of the Jews. After the wise men have visited, presented their gifts, and left, "an angel of the Lord appeared to Joseph in a dream. 'Get up,' he said, 'take the child and his mother and escape to Egypt. Stay there until I tell you, for Herod is going to search for the child to kill him.'"[5]

The next verse indicates that Joseph got up, and that very night left with Jesus and Mary to flee into Egypt. It is hard to imagine what it would be like to receive a dream in the middle of the night that commands one to leave one's native land and abruptly flee with an infant. This sudden and decisive action taken on behalf of their child's safety indicates the willingness of both parents to disrupt their lives radically to protect their child. It is also yet another indication of their sensitivity to God's guidance, and their willingness to put their faith in his instructions.

Most of us have never had to face such dire circumstances with regard to our child's life. Yet multitudes of refugees can identify with the wrenching and urgent decisions that must be made in times of civil unrest. It has often been the love of children that has motivated parents to uproot themselves, leaving all that they have built in their life in order to reduce risk to their children.

There are also parents in such areas as inner cities who take extraordinary measures to make some change for the better for their children. I am reminded of a story psychologist James Dobson told regarding his own growing-up years. At some point his parents decided that the particular setting their son was in was having a poor influence on the young man. So important was this matter to them that they relocated the family, at great personal cost to themselves. Thus in a variety of circumstances parents may feel called to make major sacrifices and life changes for the welfare of their children. Mary and Joseph model making this a priority when led by God to do so. They also model trusting God as a guide in parenting decisions. There was probably no way that the two of them would have been able to determine the nature and extent of the danger in time to take decisive action. Their openness to God's guidance and willingness to obey with alacrity without gathering more information was crucial in this instance.

The warning made to Joseph to flee to Egypt may well have had other profound effects on the young family. If Joseph had felt at all left out by this amazing conception and pregnancy, God brings home his vital importance as father in this instance. Joseph acts decisively to care for and protect the mother and baby without regard for his own other interests.

A nursing mother and a young child are at a vulnerable time, one where protection and care are needed for both emotional and physical reasons. In wartime, for example, it is harder for a mother and young child to flee or protect themselves than it is for most others. The hormonal changes going on after birth within the mother and the intense bonding with and caring for the infant can be taxing for the mother emotionally. The strong, caring, protective presence of a male can be especially crucial at such a time. Joseph's ability to take charge, and God's validation of his worth as an integral part of the family unit, could well have been an important bonding experience that helped cement the unity of the family. As has been alluded to earlier, Mary learns that she can rely on Joseph both spiritually and physically as her husband and Jesus's earthly father. Joseph clearly demonstrates that he has moved fully into the role of father for Jesus.

Joseph also demonstrates staying power with regard to his

parenting commitment. The family stays in Egypt until Joseph receives another dream instructing him that the way is clear to return to Israel. Even upon return, Joseph remains sensitive to God's guidance as to where to relocate.

This total commitment to the care of his child can be a heartening encouragement and model for not only birth and adoptive fathers but also men who find themselves in the fathering position as stepfathers. The love that a child senses from such a father is an invaluable gift.

Relying on God's Guidance

As we have just seen, reliance on God's guidance was crucial to Mary and Joseph's parenting style. They were willing to obey, at whatever cost. It was a priority to follow both scriptural guidelines given to all and God's personal direction about their particular situation.

Balancing Commitment with Space

Luke 2:41-51 relates an important incident in the life of the young Jesus and his family. We are told that when Jesus was twelve, he and his parents went to Jerusalem for the Feast of the Passover, as was their yearly custom. When the feast was over, Jesus stayed behind in Jerusalem and his parents began the journey home, unaware that he was not with the gathering of people who had probably traveled together from their town. After traveling for a day, they began looking for Jesus among this group of friends and relatives. Not finding him there, they left the group to return to Jerusalem, and found him after three days:

> in the temple courts, sitting among the teachers, listening to them and asking them questions. Everyone who heard him was amazed at his understanding and his answers. When his parents saw him, they were astonished. His mother said to him, 'Son, why have you treated us like this? Your father and I have been anxiously searching for you.' 'Why were you searching for me?' he asked. 'Didn't you know I had to be in my Father's house?' But they did not understand what he was saying to them. Then he went down to Nazareth with them and was obedient to them. But his mother treasured all these things in her heart.

Our reactions to this story, as with most Bible stories, can be quite varied. I have heard parents criticize Mary and Joseph for not keeping better track of their son's whereabouts. Others tend to feel that Jesus was lacking consideration, yet are puzzled, because they know he was without sin. This incident occurs at a very important time in the life of Jesus. He is on the threshold that leaves childhood and leads into adulthood, with all its responsibilities and freedoms.

In Judaism, Jewish males are considered adults responsible for their moral and religious duties at the age of thirteen. The bar mitzvah, a special religious ceremony, marks this important initiation into adult responsibilities. Usually this involves an intense period of study for the young man, in preparation for his first public reading of the Hebrew scriptures. In other words, a ceremony taking note of the importance of this rite of passage was built into the faith structure of Judaism.

This is a time of rapid change in physical and hormonal development for young people, as well as maturing processes in the brain that allow for more complex and abstract thinking. It is a time of disequilibrium rather than of equilibrium in child development, as many a parent and child can fervently testify. Not only are the children facing the challenges of how to navigate this passage, but parents are often struggling to reach the right balance of providing needed structure and safety and yet allowing for the young person to stretch his wings and begin to fly. Many will take comfort that not even the family of Jesus escaped a few ruffled feathers in this process. Part of the difficulty is that, while the child has and needs more independence, at the same time he still needs to follow parental guidance.

Recently we were visiting a ranch near our city, and inquired whether eagles nested along the cliff that bordered part of the ranch. This led the rancher's wife to reminisce about a high drama she had witnessed involving a young eagle's first attempt to leave the nest. For the young eagles this is a very dangerous time, since they do not yet know how fast they are capable of flying, she told us. Because of this, the young eagle may fly too fast and fatally collide into the ground or another cliff. The eagle whose departure from the nest she was privileged to witness had zoomed from his perch on the nest to a swift and forceful landing on the ground. Apparently, he was so stunned and terrified by the effects of this hard but relatively safe landing that he was too traumatized to try flying again just yet. Instead, while his concerned parents hovered and shrieked above him, he waddled and skulked his way back to the nest. From there he would rest up to try again another day.

It had not occurred to me before this story that young eagles, among the most magnificent and powerful of all birds, would encounter special dangers while learning to fly. Their very gifts held special perils. Harnessing the power of those gifts with discipline and practice is crucial in order for the eagles to use them with precision. Could this have been true of the young and gifted Jesus as well? Certainly it appears that when he began his adult ministry he faced the perils of extraordinary temptation.[6] We do not know specifically what perils and temptations the twelve-year-old Jesus faced, but there are indications in this story that Mary and Joseph were not spared anxiety about getting their first-born through this passage.

When the child becomes a full adult, at around eighteen or twenty-one in our culture, another step in letting go for the parents, and moving forward for the young adult, takes place. At that time, obedience to parents is no longer the order of the day.

Recently, I was speaking with a mother whose eldest son was on the eve of leaving for a large university. Amidst describing the last-minute preparations and the anticipated good-byes, she related that she and her husband would probably do pretty well, because their son had been given a lot of independence his senior year in high school and so they had not seen much of him for awhile! She went on to explain that in preparation for his leaving home, they had intentionally given him a high degree of freedom his last year of high school, so that he could experience that freedom and the responsibility that went with it, while still within the relative shelter of the family setting.

While this tactic does not guarantee that her son will handle the heady freedom of being away from home at his chosen university well, it greatly increases the chances that he will. In contrast, some of the students who have been sheltered and heavily monitored by well-intentioned parents right up to the moment before leaving for college or other endeavors are the ones who "go wild" and do not have the built-in internal controls to handle the lack of supervision and structure they find in new settings. Parents who have gradually given more and more responsibilities and freedoms to their children over the years have the opportunity to fine-tune and guide along the way, while they still have influence. If children do not feel the need to spend all their energy resisting what they feel is the constricting hold of parents, they are more free to use that energy to assess what they need to do to keep themselves safe and follow their own life purpose.

In fact, some of the cases that end up in therapist's offices are the ones where loving Christian parents have been so protective of children, especially daughters, that their children feel untrusted and constricted. The child then begins to rebel, acting out in ways that even they may not feel good about, but gasping for the air of freedom that is needed for the growing young person to thrive. A sad negative cycle can set in, with the parents now having "evidence" that their child cannot be trusted, and the child feeling wounded that parents have no confidence in them. The space that Mary and Joseph gave the adolescent Jesus, which allowed him to frighten them, can be a good model for us during this exciting but challenging time. Even when the child has been prepared well during the adolescent time, with ever-increasing freedom and responsibility, it can nonetheless be a big step into the full arena of adulthood.

Mary as Mentor

The wedding at Cana has also been examined in Chapter Seven. It is worth noting several further points regarding parenting here. At this point the boundaries between Mary and

Jesus have changed. Jesus is no longer under her authority as a parent, and does not need to obey her instructions in that kind of way. Neither is he under her care, protection, or instruction. Yet even when the job of parenting is done with regard to those tasks that are so crucial to the younger child, an important relationship exists. Both parent and child have the developmental task of transforming their relationship into that of two adults, albeit adult child and adult parent. The challenge here is to honor and even strengthen bonds of love, while at the same time allowing autonomy and mutual respect. Figuring out how to do this is unique to each parent and child.

Mary played an important role in helping Jesus begin his adult ministry by calling forth his gift of performing miracles to meet a real need. There is another interesting facet about this first miracle that has application for this phase of parenting. Mary's request for this miracle was relatively low-risk and low-exposure for Jesus. Everyone at the party was already having a merry old time—after all, the wine was used up! If Jesus refused, or tried and failed, not much would have been lost, and no one would have likely remembered or noticed. No lives would be ruined, no hopes to be healed dashed, no anticipating crowds disappointed.

While Jesus may have needed none of these precautions or cushions, all this makes good developmental sense in terms of exercising new gifts or trying out new skills. It is an important part of being a mentor or a guide, in that we set people up to succeed where the cost of failing is fairly negligible. Mary may well have been acting in a mentoring capacity here, and she exercised wisdom in gently nudging Jesus to begin this phase of his adult ministry in a safe setting where the stakes were low. Believing in him enough to create the opportunity and nudge, she also did it in a discreet manner, without fanfare. This miracle had its profound impact, but was not done in a circus-like atmosphere.

The first miracle at the wedding of Cana therefore suggests that Mary played a mentoring role for the young adult Jesus, at least in the beginning of his work. After the wedding, Mary

accompanied Jesus, his new disciples, and others to Capernaum, where they stayed for a few days.[7] Was this a time of getting to know his disciples, and them getting to know Jesus? What role might Mary have played in this tender and crucial time at the beginning of Jesus's ministry? Certainly any of the disciples who saw her quiet but decisive role in the first miracle were given a glimpse of the mettle of Mary. During this time, relationships probably began to be forged that may have continued in some ways throughout the ministry of Jesus or were reestablished at the time of his death and after the resurrection, when Mary worshipped with the other disciples.

This story also illustrates that Mary did not shrink back from Jesus beginning the adult ministry phase of his life. Since she had been told by Simeon that her own soul would be pierced by a sword in relation to Jesus's life work, it is particularly mature and noble of her to be the one to help initiate what would surely lead to pain for her. Perhaps one reason God chose Mary was her ability to take this kind of attitude toward the work of Jesus. It is perhaps similar to those whose loved ones are called to high-risk work as police officers, military personnel, or even astronauts.

I was discussing the feelings of mothers regarding such issues with a neighbor who was selected as an astronaut[8] to do research on space missions. Acknowledging the double-edged sword this can pose for mothers, he chuckled as he told this story: "When I was selected as an astronaut, one of my mother's friends said to her in all sincerity, 'Are you going to let him go?' I was 54 years old at the time!"

As the mother of a son who also feels called to some high-risk endeavors, I chuckle, too, and I understand. There is a part of me that cheers my son on, and would not stop him for anything in the world from doing what he loves and what he feels led by God to do. There is also a part of me that is protective, and wants to continue doing what was so important for so long in his earlier life—keeping him from harm's way. It's as if as parents our first set of instructions is *Do all you can to keep your child from harm.* That is a crucial part of our job description.

Then one fine day, our orders suddenly change. *Let them meet their destiny, and cheer them on, even if it propels them into harm's way.* What a wrenching shift this can be. Mary was called upon, like so many, to make this shift.

If we eliminate the high danger factor, it still remains a developmental task to let go of the previous role we have had with our children. Sometimes parents and children alike collude in keeping this from happening. Some children only seem to leave the nest—there is a long tether that keeps them from truly going off to their own lives. The existence and strength of this tether is not necessarily determined by the number of miles that the adult child travels from home, or the frequency and depth of contact with parents. Some children live close to home and have frequent contact yet are not tethered in this way. Others may have fled across continents and seldom have contact and yet may not be free to truly commence with their own lives.

For parents to do their part in preparing the child for true adulthood, for making their own decisions and following their own life path given by God without guilt or condemnation, requires grace and maturity. The full personhood of Mary as we have been studying it, the priority of her relationship with God, and the mutuality she shared with Joseph, would have all laid the foundation for her to be able to perform this important part of parenting.

Mary in Crisis Intervention

Sometimes a parent does this work and then life intrudes with a very different kind of task. Parents find themselves needing to help or intervene with an adult child who has had some unusual circumstance where a more active parenting role is once again indicated or even mandated. For example, parents of an adult child who suffers a life-threatening illness, injury, or a serious mental condition may find themselves in the position of needing for a time to take on the care and responsibility for that child, particularly if the child is single.

Mary, as discussed in Chapter Seven, appears to have felt she might need to intervene in this way at a certain point in the adult life of Jesus. Mark[9] relates "Then Jesus entered a house, and again a crowd gathered, so that he and his disciples were not even able to eat. When his family heard about this, they went to take charge of him, for they said, 'He is out of his mind.'" Let us focus here on what this passage may reveal about Mary in her role of parent to the adult Jesus.

Mary has allowed Jesus to individuate, she has encouraged him to launch his adult ministry, and he has left the nest and gone on his way, off to a good start. Now comes some alarming news that indicates to the family that Jesus "is out of his mind." In spite of the fact that Mary has done all she could to release Jesus and encourage him as an adult, she apparently does not hesitate to intervene or at least check up on him when she has a concern of this magnitude. Off she goes, accompanied by Jesus's brothers, to take charge of him.

It seems that the principle of parenting indicated here is that there may be times when a parent needs once again to at least temporarily take a more active role in their adult children's lives. The fact that Jesus was **not** "out of his mind" does not take away from the reality of this principle. Had he truly been out of his mind, a loving parent was ready to take on the responsibility within the framework of her culture to help him at a time when he could not be responsible for himself. Parents who find themselves in this position can perhaps find comfort and support from the realization that Mary was prepared to take on such responsibility with a gifted and promising son.

Another principle that is indicated by this account, as well as the account of young Jesus at the temple, is how hard it can be for parents to discern when intervention is needed and at what time. By all that we can tell, Mary was wrong at this point of would-be intervention. Jesus was in fact not out of his mind. Mary, even as a woman of faith, prayer, and wisdom, was apparently mistaken. Her action may have made things even more difficult for Jesus at that point in his work—now people might

have said, "See, even his own family thinks he's crazy."

What appears certain is that if Jesus had been following a more ordinary life purpose, the role of adult parenting would have been easier. If Jesus had taken over the carpentry work of Joseph, settled in the village, and married, Mary's relationship to the adult Jesus would have been less unsettling, we can be sure. Being the parent of a prophet, to say nothing of the Messiah, is not easy.

Most all of us can say with heartfelt conviction that being a parent, even of wonderful children, is not always easy. These instances in the life of Mary and Jesus assure us that even when the child is perfect, parenting is not always clear-cut or simple. We are in good company in our humanness and sometimes perplexity as parents! There may be major misunderstandings between parent and child, perhaps even when sin is not involved. For example, there is not clear evidence that Mary sinned in either the temple incident or in her attempt to take charge of Jesus. Furthermore, we know that Jesus, being perfect, did not sin in either of these instances.

Sometimes we think that if only sin were not a part of our relationships, everything would be harmonious. These stories indicate that serious misunderstandings can occur in our humanness without sin necessarily being a component, especially when parenting is involved. There are times when one generation simply cannot fathom the other. Perhaps precisely because loving parents have been very involved in their children's lives up until the threshold of adulthood, the independent shaping of unexpected eddies in the stream of their lives can take us by surprise. Inability to understand may be even more likely in cases where God's hand of destiny is on a person in an unusual way. Just as Joseph could not at first fathom Mary's pregnancy, Mary was not able to fathom aspects of Jesus's life and ministry. It defied what her mind could grasp. Nonetheless, she remained steadfast as a mother, weathering the various stages of parenting as best she could, no doubt continuing to ponder many things in her heart.

SUMMING UP

It was Mary's job, with Joseph, to raise a king. One who was humble and able to walk among his people, touching them as they had never been touched before, and yet regal enough to sit at the right hand of God. One who would love her and be obedient to her as a child, and yet not swerve from his adult mission, whether she approved or not. One who would have the strength of character and trueness of heart to follow wherever God guided. This Mary did.

Someone has pointed out that fairy tales that captivate our children are typically about royalty. A young prince goes off to seek his fortune and must complete daunting tasks, risking his very life, before he wins the prize—usually a princess. These tales symbolically speak to us and to our children of the need to individuate, to strike out on one's own and complete the tasks that make us full persons. Each of us is to be a sovereign of our own personhood or kingdom. Within the Christian belief system, each of us is to then willingly surrender that sovereignty to God. The giving of the kingdom to God is all the more significant because it is territory that is ours to give. As we do this, we are adopted by God, becoming royal sons and daughters. In this sense, each parent is called to the task of raising a future king or queen.

Mary's story as a parent confirms the importance God puts on the care, protection, and nurture of these children whom God would have be royalty in his kingdom. It confirms the importance God puts on a loving partnership of parents, and the raising of children within the traditions of a Biblical faith. It confirms the vital impact of a strong, psychologically healthy parent to the development of children. Her parenting story confirms that for all things there is a season, a time for holding close and a time for letting go, even when we hold the loved ones in our hearts as closely as ever. Her story confirms that none of us will do this perfectly, but that God can use us when we entrust him with our children. Counting on his help, we commit to raising our children to grow in wisdom, in stature, and in favor with God and humanity.

Chapter Ten

The Power and Virtue of
Sexual Mary

"*T*HERE WE WERE, married at last. Finally, the moment we had been waiting for, when our love could find full physical expression. My new bride knew this in her head, but not in the rest of her body. Sex still seemed 'bad' to her, though she tried to keep this disturbing fact from me during the first honeymoon nights." (Paraphrase of statement by a Christian Protestant married man.)

How many have faced some aspect of this couple's dilemma? A young woman with a Roman Catholic background also stated confusion about messages she'd received about expression of sexuality in married women. "I realized all the images I'd seen of Mary were of the Virgin Mary. These were associated with innocence, purity, and virtue. What did that say about being married?" (Paraphrase.)

These statements point to a central theme of Christianity and Western thought concerning sexuality. For many, the theme is like an unnoticed vapor that wafts through their lives, exerting an influence without their awareness of its source or even, perhaps, how to give it a name. This theme has to do with our ambivalence about the healthy expression of sexuality, even within the framework of Christian marriage. The roots of this ambivalence go back at least to the early Christian church.

Because of its subtle but pervasive influence, as well as its relevance to Mary and to ourselves, we will examine certain aspects of this ambivalence in some detail.

The theme touches both sexes. It begins with ambivalence about the development of sexual hormones and their resulting changes in the adolescent. Will the young person be willing to welcome and embrace these changes as part of how he or she is created, or will there be shame, embarrassment, and guilt associated with the changes and the drives that accompany them? In *The Ragamuffin Gospel: Embracing the Unconditional Love of God,* author Brennan Manning describes how he felt in the shower as a young man, when for the first time he was exploring his body and felt a sexual response. "I masturbated, panicked, threw on my clothes without drying off, raced to the local church, and confessed my sin. The priest thundered: 'You did what? Do you know you could go to hell for that?'"[1] To make matters even worse, this loud voice carried to others in the church, further shaming the terrified adolescent.

A professor described the type of messages she received about her developing breasts as a young woman. Her priest maintained that such things were evil, and it would be better if they could be cut off, like slices of bologna.

Furthermore, many a young woman, myself included, has tales from when we were coming of age about the young men from very conservative church backgrounds who were the hardest to handle on a date. Obviously, uneasiness about sexuality and its place in the life of a Christian crosses denominational backgrounds, though some branches seem to provide more healthy guidance than others.

Where does Mary fit into all of this? She is right in the thick of the issue, because of how she and her story have been viewed. Was she a virgin at the time of Jesus's conception and birth? If so, what was the purpose of this? After the birth of Jesus, did she and Joseph enjoy a sexually intimate relationship together? I believe that it is vital to see how the Scriptures portray Mary in this core aspect of her personhood.

After discussing these issues, we will turn our attention to influences that may have distorted the Biblical view. By increasing our understanding of this area, we can begin to identify the vapor that has entangled many throughout generations, and that has often been part of our "invisible" heritage.

THE SCRIPTURAL RECORD

> But the angel said to her, "Do not be afraid, Mary, you have found favor with God. You will be with child and give birth to a son, and you are to give him the name Jesus. He will be great and will be called the Son of the Most High. The Lord God will give him the throne of his father David, and he will reign over the house of Jacob forever; his kingdom will never end."
>
> "How will this be," Mary asked the angel, "since I am a virgin?"
>
> The angel answered, "The Holy Spirit will come upon you, and the power of the Most High will overshadow you. So the holy one to be born will be called the Son of God. Even Elizabeth your relative is going to have a child in her old age, and she who was said to be barren is in her sixth month. For nothing is impossible with God."
>
> Luke 1: 30-37

When told by the angel that she will conceive and bear a son, Mary responds with a very important question: "How can this be since I am a virgin?" It is clear from this question that Mary is not only thinking of the term virgin as meaning a young woman, since that would not hinder her getting pregnant. Rather, she is asking the angel, "How can this be, since I have not had sexual intercourse?" Indeed, *The Message* translates this as "But how? I've never slept with a man?"

The angel also replies in a forthright way, explaining that it is the Holy Spirit who will be the partner in conceiving this child, rather than a human father: "The Holy Spirit will come upon you, and the power of the Most High will overshadow you. So the holy one to be born will be called the Son of God."

Thus the scriptural record clearly indicates that Mary was a virgin who had not known a man sexually at the time of the conception of Jesus. Matthew further corroborates this, describing how Joseph planned to divorce Mary quietly when he realized she was with child. He knew that he was not the father, and supposed that it must be some other man. However, an angel appears to him in a dream, and says, "Joseph son of David, do not be afraid to take Mary home as your wife, because what is conceived in her is from the Holy Spirit."[2]

Matthew then records that Joseph obeyed, taking Mary home as his wife, and adds, "But he had no union with her until she gave birth to a son."[3] The scriptural record makes it clear that Mary did not have sexual intercourse with any man, including her husband Joseph, until after the birth of the tiny Messiah.

The Purpose of Mary's Virginity

What, if anything, was the purpose of Mary's virginity? Why does it matter? The primary purpose of establishing her virginity is that it makes clear the unique role that God played in this conception, and therefore the fact that Jesus was conceived with a heavenly parent and an earthly parent. This parentage is central to the Biblical understanding of the uniqueness of Jesus as the Son of God.

Thus, while it was indeed virtuous to be a virgin before marriage, this is not the primary purpose of stressing Mary's virginity. The primary purpose is to make clear the unique parentage of Jesus.

Mary as a Virtuous Married Woman

Once Jesus was born, what was the relationship between Mary and Joseph? It appears that she was free to enjoy a full sexual relationship with her husband. Matthew 1:25, as we have seen, states "But he had no union with her until she gave birth to a son." The word "until" strongly implies that after Mary gave birth, Mary and Joseph enjoyed sexual union. There is nothing in the Biblical record to indicate that they did not.

Further, Scripture indicates that Mary and Joseph went on to have other children, and that Jesus was the eldest of a rather large family. For example, Mark 3:31 reads: "Then Jesus' mother and brothers arrived. Standing outside, they sent someone in to call him. A crowd was sitting around him, and they told him, 'Your mother and brothers are outside looking for you.'"

In Mark 6, Jesus goes to preach in his hometown, and begins to preach in the synagogue on the Sabbath. The locals, who knew him and his family, are amazed, and take offense at him. "'Where did this man get these things?' they asked. 'What's this wisdom that has been given him, that he even does miracles! Isn't this the carpenter? Isn't this Mary's son and the brother of James, Joseph, Judas and Simon? Aren't his sisters here with us?'"[4] This Scripture indicates that Jesus had at least four brothers and at least two if not more sisters, although of course these were half-siblings in the sense that Joseph was the one who begat them, not the Holy Spirit.

While Protestants accept that Jesus had brothers and sisters, during at least much of the Roman Catholic Church's history, it has been the tradition that Mary and Joseph remained sexually chaste; that is, did not engage in sexual intercourse with each other, ever. This tradition has interpreted the terms used for brothers and sisters in various ways, including extended family members such as cousins. Recently, however, there is more movement within the Catholic Church to acknowledge that the meaning of brothers and sisters within the context it is used is much more likely to refer to actual siblings than to cousins.

Among lay Catholics, there appears to be openness to the idea that Mary and Joseph had other children together. For example, one colleague and friend, a Catholic who holds Mary in deep respect, concurs with the belief that Mary was free to enjoy sexual relations with Joseph after the birth of Jesus, and that this does not affect her purity, her virtue, or her spirituality.

Another friend, who studied at one time in the Vatican, passionately held to a different view. Mary and Joseph, he explained to me, were the prototype for those who took vows of chastity in order to serve God. They both willingly devoted their lives to the task of raising the Messiah, and were completely fulfilled by this work, thus being the model for all those priests, nuns, and monks who have followed in their stead. As we discussed this several years ago atop a red hill in New Mexico, the setting sun in glorious splendor all around us,

I deeply sensed his sincerity. He seemed to further believe that this view of Mary and Joseph was a lynchpin in the underpinnings of the logic for vows of chastity, and that therefore it must be firmly kept in place. Interestingly, some other Catholics to whom I have spoken, while aware of the idea of perpetual virginity for Mary, were not aware that Mary and Joseph were seen as prototypes for taking vows of chastity.

So, we begin to see that there are strong and differing views about Mary's sexual expression.

This work, as stated, takes the view that the Scripture most strongly indicates that Mary was a virgin at the time of the conception and birth of Jesus, and that after the birth, she and Joseph enjoyed a sexual relationship that bore the fruit of other children who were siblings of Jesus.

Mary's healthy sexuality and its expression have important implications for both sexes, but particularly for women. Because the virginity of the betrothed Mary has been emphasized by the church, while the later full sexuality of the married woman was ignored, being sexually uninitiated or innocent became associated with being virtuous, blessed, and pure. The strong implication, if not the outright assertion at times, became that being virginal and sexually innocent was virtuous, while being sexual was somehow less holy, even when married. We will now turn to examine some of the roots of this belief, because of its pervasiveness in our Western tradition.

Looking at Our Western Roots Regarding Sexuality

It was some years ago that I first consciously encountered some of our Western roots regarding attitudes towards sexuality and virtue. It seems that the Greek view during New Testament times, and for several centuries after, was that certain human traits were higher than others. The ancient Greeks are known for their valuing of reason and the power of the will. This was a major contribution of the golden age of Greece. What is perhaps not as widely known is that while elevating the faculties of reason and conscious will, many in the

Platonic Greek tradition devalued greatly certain other aspects of human personhood. Such aspects included the emotional and the sexual. These intrinsic parts of ourselves were seen as baser, and less valued. Because of the great influence of Greek ideas, when Christianity began spreading, many synthesized the Biblical perspective with the Greek perspective.

The traditional Hebrew world-view did not share this perspective of human makeup. Instead, it saw all of the created human as good, but flawed by the fall. Thus, intellect, will, emotions, sexuality, and the physical body were all created by God and therefore good. All were also flawed due to the fall. For the Hebrew, there was no schism between intellect and sexuality, for example. For the classical Greek, influenced by the Platonic tradition of Greek philosophy, there was.

One person in particular, a remarkable, sensitive and brilliant man, was able to leverage these ideas from his position in the fifth century far into the twentieth century. That man was St. Augustine, bishop of Hippo. Of him, scholars generally agree that he was "the dominant personality of the Western Church of his time, [and] is generally recognized as having been the greatest thinker of Christian antiquity. His mind was the crucible in which the religion of the New Testament was most completely fused with the Platonic tradition of Greek philosophy: and it was also the means by which the product of this fusion was transmitted to the Christendoms of medieval Roman Catholicism and Renaissance Protestantism."[5]

When we love and respect someone greatly, it is far easier to transmit their errors as well as their brilliance. Perhaps Augustine would have been among the first, had he appeared in a later time, to critique and correct his own thoughts from an earlier age, or to encourage us to do so. It is in a spirit of respect and humility that I critique him now. While doing research for my dissertation in the late eighties, I read some of Augustine's works and discovered for myself some interesting things about his views on sexuality. Basically, Augustine believed that before the fall, "lust was not experienced but that physical sexual arousal took place totally under the conscious control of the man's will, informed by reason."[6] In other words, Augustine believed that when humans were perfect, before the fall, sexual arousal did not occur unless the man considered the situation and consciously decided, "This will honor God if I become sexually aroused." Erections would therefore not have occurred, according to Augustine, for any other reason.

The fact that we are not able to will sexual arousal to occur or not to occur on any reliable basis led to the shame that Adam and Eve experienced after the fall, according to Augustine. It was this that led them to cover themselves with fig leaves, he believed: "And therefore, being ashamed of the disobedience of their own flesh, which witnessed to their disobedience while it punished it, 'they sewed fig leaves together, and made themselves aprons,' that is, cinctures for their privy parts."[7]

Augustine also believed that this shame of not being able to willfully control sexual arousal was felt even in the marriage bed, and that this was why even sexual acts within marriage were done in private. Augustine experienced a mighty uneasiness with any sexual response, because its existence could not be willfully controlled. This uneasiness comes from his having accepted the Greek view that the will was virtuous but that physical, emotional, and sexual things were base, and should therefore be controlled by the will and intellect. Because this difference is so crucial, a diagram is presented to illustrate the difference between Augustine's understanding and the contemporary psychological understanding.

The diagram on the next page illustrates that in Augustine's view a potentially arousing situation occurs. The person's body and feelings do not yet respond because the person can consciously control this. Moral responsibility occurs at this point, and the person has failed before God if physiological and emotional sexual arousal occurs before the person has concluded that such arousal would honor God. The individual then uses reason to decide if arousal would honor God. If reason decides the answer is yes, the conscious will then signals that arousal can occur, and it does. If the decision is no, arousal does not occur, because arousal is under the control of the conscious will.

TWO VIEWS OF MORAL RESPONSIBILITY FOR SEXUAL DECISIONS

CONTEMPORARY VIEW   AUGUSTINE'S VIEW

Point of beginning arousal   **A**   Point of Moral Responsibility
and/ or interest   begins before sexual arousal
occurs—therefore potential for
guilt begins with occurrence of
sexual arousal, because this
should be controlled by the will

Point of Moral Responsibility   **B**   Point of Action
begins at the point of action—
sexual arousal is neither right
nor wrong in itself, (and is not
controlled by the will) but we
are responsible for the
decisions we make concerning
it. It is here that the will and
reason come to bear

> **A** represents the point where arousal begins in the Contemporary View and where it can begin in Augustine's View. **B** represents the point where a person makes a decision in response to the arousal in the Contemporary View, or in response to the potential arousal in Augustine's view. The space/time between point **A** and point **B** is where unnecessary guilt can occur under Augustine's system. Arousal may be experienced in various durations.

Under this view, if any arousal occurs spontaneously, before such a conscious decision, the person is guilty of sin. Since our bodies are made to have arousal occur spontaneously, before a conscious decision occurs, we find ourselves in a guilt-inducing double bind with this view. No wonder some felt that adult sexual development was a spiritual cross to bear or a force to be conquered and eliminated! Try as we might, we cannot stop arousal from occurring solely by a conscious act of the will. In fact, this can lead to obsession about sexual feelings, rather than freedom from them, or a healthy acceptance of them.

As if this situation were not difficult enough, Augustine also held views about the feelings of sexual arousal themselves. To copulate when married was good, he held, because the human race did need to continue. However, the passion felt in the marriage bed was tainted with sin. Thus children were conceived in sin, because the sexual act necessarily contains passion. Thus, in Augustine's view, there does not appear to be any condition in which a man and woman can enjoy the pleasures of sexual love without the guilt of sin. Feeling guilty and being guilty appears to be a given, if one accepts Augustine's views, or is under their influence without full understanding of them. It is no wonder that many were drawn to a reclusive life without much contact with members of the opposite sex. In a monastery or nunnery many believed they might find some relief from this difficult bind, and ensuing feelings of unworthiness and guilt.

Most of us have probably not been exposed to the conscious expression of Augustine's ideas. Yet they are the source of the vapor that has permeated so much of our culture for hundreds of years. Being under the influence of these ideas without understanding them is like the woman who was preparing the family's traditional Easter ham. Before placing the ham in the pan, she carefully cut off the end of the ham and discarded it. One year, a guest asked why she did that. "I'm not sure," the woman replied, "but this is the way my mother always prepared the ham." Later, the woman asked her mother about this family custom. She had to ask her mother, who explained, "Why, I did that because the pan and oven weren't big enough, so I had to cut off the end to fit the ham in the pan." In a similar way, we may no longer accept Augustine's logic, but many are still feeling the lingering effects of guilt and uneasiness about sexuality, even when expressed in ways that Scripture clearly condones.

In the contemporary view, the potentially arousing situation occurs, and with it a spontaneous physiological and emotional response may occur, one that is not under the control of the conscious will. The person acknowledges without self-judgment that the response has occurred. Using conscious will and reason, the person decides if the response should be paid attention to and/or acted upon. It is at this point that moral responsibility enters in, not at the point of the spontaneous arousal itself. If the person decides it is not appropriate to act on the feelings, he or she can use conscious will at that point to choose to dwell on something else, leave the situation, or whatever action is appropriate.

Because this is so important, let's look at how this might play itself out in the lives of contemporary people. First, we will look at how someone might react under Augustine's belief system.

Nathan was single and wanted to marry when the timing was right and he had found the right person. He began to notice Stephanie, enjoyed conversing with her after the graduate school class they shared, and eventually they began dating.

As their relationship progressed, Nathan became conflicted and confused about his sexual feelings toward Stephanie. At the time he enjoyed the sensations he felt when hugging and kissing her, but afterwards he became overcome with uneasy, guilty feelings. She was a nice, respectable young woman—he should be feeling love towards her, but not these strong desires, he believed. Sometimes the strength of his shameful feelings after an enjoyable date meant that he avoided Stephanie, rather than having to deal with the backlash of self-reproach that he heaped upon himself afterwards. This began to cause conflict in their relationship, as Stephanie did not understand why Nathan would avoid her at times.

About this time Nathan went for pastoral counseling, and when his pastor heard about Nathan's difficulties, he was able to clear up some of Nathan's misconceptions. In fact, the pastor met with Nathan several times to explain how understandings had changed, and to help Nathan fully understand that his sexual feelings toward Stephanie were a God-given part of himself. Eventually, Nathan and Stephanie were married, and began to enjoy the full expression of these feelings without guilt on Nathan's part.

Alexander shared the same belief system as Nathan, but handled it in a different way. He idolized his girlfriend Maria, and treated her with utmost respect and tenderness, as was the tradition in his family. Another, less spoken-of tradition in his family was that the men handled their sexual urges not with their girlfriends, but with prostitutes or women they considered sexual but unvirtuous. Thus Alexander was able to keep his relationship with Maria "pure," and deal with his sexual feelings outside that relationship. He did not experience much guilt about this, both because it was the family tradition, and because he projected any negative feelings about this onto the women he engaged sexually.

After Maria and Alexander married, they enjoyed a brief time of pleasurable sex between them, but Alexander soon began to seek his old sources of sexual outlet—he thought of Maria as the mother of his children and someone who was above enjoying sexuality in the way that he desired with the women he considered bad. In fact, if Maria seemed too eager, it made him uncomfortable, because it did not fit his image of the good woman who was his wife. Since Maria had come from a similar family tradition, she had her own conflicted feelings, and settled for this arrangement, even though a part of her ached for more, and resented this unspoken setup.

Drew, on the other hand, was a young man who became very attracted to Lucia, and began dating her. Because both Lucia and Drew had decided to wait until marriage to begin a relationship that included sexual intercourse, they had to deal with the sexual arousal that occurred as their relationship progressed. They accepted and enjoyed these feelings without guilt, and discussed how they would handle these feelings without violating their belief system. Because the feelings were accepted without guilt, they tended to help draw the two closer together. Once married, both felt free to fully express themselves sexually with each other, though it took time to work out how to adjust to their different needs and rhythms. The sexual aspect of their relationship continued to help strengthen the special bond they had together.

On occasion either Drew or Lucia would find themselves aroused by someone other than their spouse. When this occurred, the feeling was accepted and not judged, but neither was it acted upon. At one point, Lucia found that an attraction to someone was more than fleeting. As she became aware of this, Lucia began to realize that she was feeling resentful of the long hours that Drew was now putting into his work, and the extra burden of parenting that she was taking on without sufficient appreciation. Lucia realized that she needed to pay attention to this signal her feelings were giving her, and she brought up this topic with Drew. Several painful discussions ensued, and eventually Drew made some changes that helped the two get through this difficult time. Neither marriage partner heaped guilt upon Lucia for her feelings, but took them as a signal that change needed to be made, and both expected that she would not act out her feelings with the man who was the object of her attraction.

Having looked at how Augustine's views may be lived out, versus how a more contemporary Biblically based view might be lived out, we come to the following question: Is Augustine's view Biblically based? He appears to have drawn his conclusions from the fact that Adam and Eve hid themselves after they had sinned, and because they realized they were naked, and covered themselves with fig leaves. Augustine interpreted this as signaling that Adam and Eve were ashamed of their sexuality, because of guilty feelings connected with sexual arousal.

While there are different theological interpretations possible here, the account of Adam and Eve and their disobedience nowhere suggests that their original sin involved any sexual sin. Rather, the core sin seems to be disobedience of God's instructions—their failure to accept the limits or boundaries that God set forth. By so doing, they in a sense set themselves up as gods. Further, Adam and Eve's desire to hide from God and to cover themselves can be a powerful response to the realization of their unworthiness in general, and not have anything specifically to do with their sexual feelings.

Augustine's view on sexual arousal is nowhere described in the Bible, but was superimposed on it, due to his Platonic philosophical beliefs, and then widely held to be congruent with Biblical teachings. A contemporary understanding of sexual arousal is that sexual responses are first experienced, and then the conscious will is used to decide how to appropriately handle the feelings and what action, if any, to take. This view is compatible with Scripture.

In thinking about Augustine's views, it becomes clear how they helped create a powerful climate in which sexual feelings and their physiological responses were not accepted as a natural, healthy part of human nature. Augustine himself, after his conversion, and many others through the ages who accepted his views or were unknowingly influenced by them, were set up to feel guilty about their sexuality, since sexual feelings are apt to occur whether they are consciously willed or not!

Another influential giant in Western culture and Christian tradition, Thomas Aquinas, in the thirteenth century accepted Augustine's key assumption that sexual arousal should be under the control of the good person's will and had been under this control before the fall. Any sexual arousal occurring not under the complete control of the conscious will was therefore subject to suspicion and probably not pure. Since contemporary understanding of our physiology acknowledges that this cannot be accomplished by us as humans, we are greatly predisposed to shame and guilt if we believe this. Many of us have not understood that this is the underlying assumption concerning uneasiness about sexuality, but have had the guilt, shame, or uneasiness transmitted to us without this explanation. This can make it even easier to be under the influence of the shroud of shame, and more difficult to eradicate.

Just as the Easter cook could discard the habit of chopping off the end of the ham once she understood its origins and that it no longer served a functional purpose, so can we more easily discard our uneasiness concerning healthy sexual expression within Biblical guidelines when we clearly see that it originated from outmoded philosophical ideas, not from Biblical guidelines or physiological reality.

What does this discussion have to do with Mary and her sexual expression? I believe that it has much to do with the schism that can exist between the Biblical record and some beliefs that were adopted about Mary in early Christendom and that can still hold strong influence. Because people who adopted these beliefs about sexuality were therefore uneasy with the sexual part of themselves, they tended to disown this quality and project[8] it onto women, who held less power and were seldom allowed equal education. Men could then own intellect, and assign the baser aspects of emotionality and sexuality to women. Women were therefore often seen as sexual temptresses, luring the men away from higher pursuits.

The church leaders of the day soon became uncomfortable with the idea of a virtuous woman being a sexual woman. The image of the evil sexual woman versus the pure non-sexual woman influenced understanding. Since Mary was surely virtuous rather than evil, it was much easier to think of her as not being sexual. If the early church fathers viewed her as remaining a virgin throughout her life, for them this was a congruent picture of a virtuous woman. Therefore purity, sexual innocence, and perpetual virginity became associated with virtue in a woman.

As a result of this association, many women had to deal with a further double bind. They were expected to marry and bear children, but at the same time this was more base than remaining virginal. Mary was to be their ideal of the godly woman, but Mary was seen as a perpetual virgin **and** a mother, something that was clearly not possible for them. Furthermore, if they dared to enjoy their sexual expression with their husbands, such enjoyment was itself guilt-inducing, because of the idea that the feeling of passion itself was somehow sinful.

No wonder it has been stated that the legends of the Virgin Mary have condemned women to perpetual inferiority![9] One strongly under the influence of Augustine's rationale could renounce marriage and motherhood, choosing to remain a virgin and thereby be "pure," but foregoing the pleasures of family and sexual relations. Another option would be to choose marriage and children, along with a strong dose of guilt about any enjoyment of sexual relations. Or one could give up the struggle for holiness, throw caution to the wind, and be a sensual, sexual wife who enjoyed sexual relations. This would only work if one had a husband who was also accepting of his wife's sexual enjoyment. Otherwise, a woman could find herself looked down upon by her spouse for her pleasurable response.

Our Biblical Roots

It is true that the Biblical view of a virtuous unmarried woman includes virginity.[10] However, it is equally true that the Biblical view of a virtuous married woman is that she enjoys a full sexual relationship with her husband. **To equate a virginal woman as more pure or virtuous than a faithful married woman has no Biblical basis.** Furthermore, such an equation promotes false guilt, and needless psychological difficulties.

Scriptures that support the virtue and health of sexual expression within marriage begin with Genesis 1:27-28, where we are told that God created man (humankind) in his own image, male and female, and then "God blessed them and said to them, 'Be fruitful and increase in number . . .'" Interestingly, this instruction and blessing took place before the fall, and includes the comment that "God saw all that he had made, and it was very good."[11] Thus, sexuality was created by God, was closely linked with God's loving blessing, and was part of what God surveyed and saw as very good.

Paul, though he appears to be ambivalent about the major commitment needed for marriage in a time that he apparently believes is about to pass away, still instructs those who inquire of him that spouses should fulfill their marital duties to each other, and "not deprive each other except by mutual consent and for a time, so that you may devote yourselves to prayer. Then come together again . . ."[12]

How sad that Augustine's synthesis of early Greek ideas with Scripture has been superimposed on the Western world for so many centuries, all too often unrecognized and unexamined, and therefore not corrected. Because it has been so intimately connected to the Christian view of sexuality for many individuals, those who have possessed healthy instincts to discard it have too often been unable to distinguish the dross from the treasure. Too often, scriptural truths have been thrown out along with the misconceptions.

What about those who sincerely hold to the belief that Mary and Joseph never sexually consummated their marriage? Are they able to enjoy a healthy sexual relationship within their own marriages? For those who hold to this belief, it is important to see that if for some reason Mary and Joseph had been called to never consummate their marriage sexually, it would likely have had something to do with the unique circumstances of the parentage of Jesus, and the unique role that Mary played as the mother of the only begotten son of God. Since we are expressly told that Jesus was the only human begotten in this way, it is fairly obvious that none of the rest of us would have this same set of circumstances. Thus, other couples are free to enjoy the usual pattern of sexual fulfillment within marriage, as defined by Scripture. Any guilt about such enjoyment is therefore unhooked from the Biblical model of Mary.

Sexuality as Creative Power

Our sexuality is intricately woven into every portion of our physical being. Doctors point out that the sexual hormones have purposes and receptors throughout our bodies, for example. Further, a person can be either celibate or sexually active and still possess healthy sexuality. Likewise one can be either celibate or sexually active and not possess healthy sexuality. Examples of unhealthy sexuality include sexual repression rather than suppression or when sexuality is expressed in harmful, objectifying ways to self or others.

One purpose for sexuality is to bring forth offspring. Let us now turn to this aspect of Mary's sexuality, especially with regard to Jesus. Here the creative power of her sexuality allowed her to participate in perhaps the most creative act of the universe—that of forming God in human form. Most parents will testify to the awesome, humbling power and privilege of participating in the creation of new human beings. This humbling sense of power and privilege must have been all the more heightened for Mary.

Mary participated in this wonderful creative act in a unique way, and a way that seems to honor women. Jesus was conceived without the benefit of human sperm. It was the genetic material from Mary's ovum that provided the human portion of Jesus, who was both fully God and fully man. Mary has often been called the "second Eve." If sin had entered the world in part due to the temptation and disobedience of one woman, Eve, the means to salvation also entered the world through the choice and obedience of one woman, Mary.[13] There is no indication that Mary in any way flaunted her special role. Instead, as we have seen, she and Joseph shared a common purpose, and Joseph had a crucial role as husband, father, and protector. In fact, it is fascinating that even though God begat Jesus, God chose to have an earthly father for the Messiah. Certainly this truth honors and validates the importance of fathers to the family and growing children.

We have just seen how one purpose of healthy sexuality is to conceive and bring forth children, a powerful and creative act. Another vital purpose is to provide deep and unique bonding between two people committed to one another in love and marriage. This is also a powerful and creative force of giving and of loving. The Bible speaks of two people *knowing* each other when they express sexual love between them. It also speaks of how two people become one when they have sexual relations. In other words, Scripture views sexual relations as a powerful bonding agent between two people that helps them know each other in a unique way. The Bible does not trivialize or minimize the power of sexuality, and provides guidelines where this powerful element in our lives can be used as a comfort and blessing.

Parodoxes of the Pregnant Virgin

In her book *The Pregnant Virgin*,[14] Marion Woodman uses the metaphor of life within the virgin to speak of the integrity of a woman who is whole and creatively growing her own personhood. Such a woman is self-contained, and does not rely on others for her identity. Mary, in this context, would represent the unique reality of a virgin woman actually pregnant with a real child, and would also symbolize a whole woman, creatively developing her own personhood. She can be seen to represent the paradox of a woman totally submitted to God and therefore bearing God within, and yet also complete in herself, pregnant with her own developing wholeness.

Woodman also speaks of the need for the soul and body to be joined. My body needs to inhabit my soul. My soul needs to inhabit my body. Like Jesus's call to "abide in me and I in you," this involves a profound mystery, but that makes it no less a practical imperative. God created us to dwell fully in our bodies in this life. For some Christians, the false prohibition about sexuality set up a perpetual struggle between body and soul. If the body needs to feel no sexual desire or passion in order to be "good," yet defies the best efforts of the conscious soul to bring about this state, one way to resolve the issue is to cut oneself off from body awareness.

Early shaming because of our bodies, whether it be because of our sexuality or other bodily functions and appetites, can lead to disconnection between our bodies and our souls. Experiences of sexual trauma and/or abuse can lead to dissociative states. Patients have described to me the strong sense that they are not in their bodies but are observing the trauma from someplace else in the room, for example.

Woodman also believes that if our parents desired us to be a different gender or did not desire us at all, the developing child may even sense this in utero, and that this can have profound effects in preventing young children from being fully in their bodies—feeling comfortable with their bodies and bodily functions, and loving their bodies. Eating disorders may be a manifestation of such a split. In all such cases, at some point the soul needs to welcome back the body and embrace it lovingly. The body needs to likewise embrace the soul and spirit.

Very little has been said about Mary's body in Scripture. Yet what is there involves profound affirmation of the female body. Her body was a good and acceptable place for God to dwell and to grow. Her body cooperated with the Creator of the Universe to produce the unique god/human that was Jesus. Like a precious jewel covered with scum and cobwebs, this truth endures and needs to be restored to its rightful condition and place. There appears to be no solid scriptural basis for those who would see the female body as less acceptable than a man's body. Both are seen as the temple of God.

SUMMING UP

In summing up, the Mary archetype, when traced back to its Biblical roots, is a powerful model for healthy sexuality and body image. The power is quiet and unassuming, but nevertheless there, as it sheds light on misconceptions. Mary's sexual identity as a woman was a key part of her particular and important life work. Her positive traits as a virtuous woman are equally present in two important phases of her life: as a virgin before the birth of Jesus, and as a sexually active wife after the birth of Jesus. Like Mary, we are free to enjoy sexual comforts and pleasures within the marriage bonds. Mary can be a model both for the unmarried and the married. When her virginity is seen as part of purity and virtue for an unmarried woman, and as vital to establishing the parentage of Jesus, it is seen in its proper light. She models seasons of sexuality, with behavior appropriate to the season.

Chapter Eleven

The Power of Loving Presence in the Midst of Suffering

"This child is destined to cause the falling and rising of many in Israel, and to be a sign that will be spoken against, so that the thoughts of many hearts will be revealed. And a sword will pierce your own soul too."

Simeon speaking to Mary in Luke 2:34-35

Near the cross of Jesus stood his mother, his mother's sister, Mary the wife of Clopas, and Mary Magdalene. When Jesus saw his mother there, and the disciple whom he loved standing nearby, he said to his mother, "Dear woman, here is your son," and to the disciple, "Here is your mother." From that time on, this disciple took her into his home.   John 19:25-27

*T*HE WORDS OF OLD and learned Simeon were spoken at a time of blessing and joy—the consecration of a first-born child. Indeed Simeon has just blessed the new family, and prophesied how Jesus would be "a light for revelation to the Gentiles and for glory to your people Israel."[1] Just as Mary and Joseph are marveling at what has been said about their baby, Simeon speaks again, portending controversy and pain.

Simeon's words come to fulfillment as Mary stands beneath the cross of Jesus, watching her beloved son endure an excruciating death at the hands of the powerful and the religious, as noted above in John 19.

Thus from the beginning of Jesus's life, Mary knew not only

233

that this son was very different, but also had some glimpse that extraordinary pain would be a part of her life because of who Jesus was and what would happen to him. How does a loving, sensitive mother live with such knowledge? To explore this question, let us look at some issues concerning love and the risk it involves.

LIVING WITH FUTURE POSSIBILITIES OF SUFFERING

Loving and Risking

To love someone means to bond emotionally. Inherent in that bonding, so important to love, is the risk of loss, of having the bonds cruelly shattered and being left wounded. This risk is so real that nearly all lovers and parents must come to grips with this possibility at some point in the bonding process. Some literally decide that the risk of enduring such pain is too much, and they pass by the opportunity to love. In the decision to become parents, some decide it is better not to be vulnerable to the heavy grief that such a commitment can bring, since the loss of a child is one of the most difficult to bear.

Those who have healthy children raise them with the knowledge that life and health are not entirely in their control, and that something could happen to dash the hopes and dreams they have for their offspring. Some parents receive the excruciating news that their child has a disease that will mean an early death, and raise the child with this knowledge. For a portion of parents who hear such painful news, the reality of a life-threatening condition in their child is too much. The parent may go through the motions of parenting, but emotionally disengage, holding back from the vulnerability of fully loving, and thereby compounding the tragedy for the at-risk child.

In the animated film *Sleeping Beauty,* an early death is predicted at the christening of a young princess. The princess, the horrified celebrants are informed, will prick her finger on a spinning wheel, and die. Her parents seek to thwart that prediction by banishing all spinning wheels from the kingdom. How tempting it can be to try to eliminate all dangers from a child's life. It is often only when common sense prevails and we realize that this could be just as damaging to a child that we refrain from such measures.

Mary avoided this overly protective approach. She and Joseph went to extraordinary measures to protect Jesus when instructed to by God, as when they left in the middle of the night for Egypt, fleeing the designs of Herod, but otherwise they parented in ways that allowed Jesus to fulfill his destiny, even if it involved danger. Thus Mary neither detached because of fear that something bad would happen, nor over-protected in an attempt to keep Jesus from possible harm as he grew up.

Since we are not told in Scripture, we do not know much of what Mary thought and believed during the active years of Jesus's ministry. For while she was present at the launch of his ministry, and then traveled with him at times, it appears that later she had difficulty, at least for a time, understanding the direction that Jesus was taking, and the sometimes venomous reactions of the religious leaders. We have seen how she went to bring Jesus home, fearing he was out of his mind. Scripture also records that even Jesus's brothers did not believe in him as his work gathered steam and controversy.[2]

Who could have guessed that the Messiah would be like *this*? How could anyone know he would call the religious leaders vipers[3] and that he would overturn the tables of the money-changers, creating a scene in the temple courtyard?[4] Who could have predicted that the people in his own hometown would be enraged and seek to kill him?[5]

Although Mary's Song had prophetic elements to it, she does not appear to have been fully aware of how Jesus would fulfill his ministry. Yet, as a wise woman who was in the habit of pondering about the events surrounding Jesus's life, she must have seen the trends that were occurring during his ministry. Like a storm approaching, the buildup of anger and ill will towards Jesus by the political and religious leaders would likely have become evident to her. How often did she fear for his safety and dread what might be coming?

What about Us?

As we spoke of earlier, for parents, the first crucial part of one's job is to protect our children from harm. It is a strong and compelling instinct for most parents. Other mothers and I have been amazed at the strength of this protective instinct for our newborns. Eager for the births of our children, we took for granted that we would love them, cherish them, and feel protective of them. The force and fierceness of that protectiveness was what took us by surprise, though most of us did not need to act upon it. One friend, a very peaceful person, even related to me how she realized that she would physically defend the safety of her child, with a gun if need be, after bringing him home from the hospital. Since she was returning to her quiet neighborhood with a loving husband, it was not as if she had to strategize such ways to keep her baby safe.

As children reach adulthood, at least some parents are called to release their children and support them on a path that puts them in harm's way. For one of our sons, that was the case for a time, as his dreams and the path he felt led to by God included training as a pilot in the military. The day he told of his acceptance into flight training and the long-term enlistment that necessitated was the day two powerful streams of parental drives collided for me. On the one hand, I was thrilled that he had achieved a difficult-to-obtain opportunity that fulfilled his dream. This is what my husband and I had raised our children for, after all: to be fully who God designed them to be and to fulfill their dreams.

On the other hand, for me, this thrill collided into the powerful force to keep him from harm's way. Because of my brother's death while in the military, not only my intellect, but also my very being, knew to the marrow of my bones that death and loss are associated with being in dangerous positions in the armed forces. Now I was being asked to celebrate sending a son off to unknown dangers where he could be called to put his life at risk and directly in harm's way.

As he went off to basic training, I had a dream of us flying in a plane, with him as a child. As the plane was coming in for landing, someone apparently allowed him to be in a special crow's nest on the outside of the wing, where he could experience the thrill of the wind. Suddenly, the plane approached hurricane conditions, and needed to abort the landing. In the dream, I realized my son would be in danger if he remained in his crow's nest, although he did not see this. I exerted my authority as a parent to get him inside, and held him close to me, both of us appreciating the love and comfort of that embrace.

Upon awakening, I realized that I no longer had such authority, and that in fact, others could now rightfully use their authority to put him in harm's way. My dream was part of my working-through process in adjusting to this new stage of our lives. In very special talks with our son, he acknowledged his own working through of this issue for himself, of facing the danger of his chosen profession, and the paradox of placing himself in God's care and yet also knowing that his life could be shorter because of the risks to which he felt called. As it turned out, this son was released from the military before his training was completed due to a minor medical problem that disqualified him from flight training at the time. This unexpected outcome did not in any way diminish the importance of the process we went through in grappling with such issues.

For myself and countless other parents who must wrestle with the potential or actual loss of children who are put at risk while following their life purpose, there is some inkling of what Mary must have felt. Perhaps many inner streams collided within her at times, as she pondered her beloved son's destiny and how the prophecies might be expressed in his life. We have seen how she was present at the launch of his adult ministry when he performed the first miracle, and noted the enigmatic elements of her dialogue with Jesus at the wedding. We have

238 EMPOWERED WITH MARY

seen how later, she apparently feared for her son's sanity, and
went with family to bring him back from that ministry. Still
later, we see her at the foot of the cross, seeing perhaps her
worst nightmares more than fulfilled.

Coping with the Risk of Loving

How do we cope with this risk of loving? Mary had approximately thirty-three years to relate to Jesus before the crucifixion. There is every indication that she remained emotionally
present and bonded to Jesus during his growing-up years, and
then allowed individuation to take place, allowing both separateness and closeness as Jesus went from adolescence to
manhood.

Whatever she understood about the future destiny of Jesus,
Mary was able to be active in the present, loving and living. She
did not allow any intimations about future suffering to take
away the joys, tasks, and sorrows of the moment. Mary's faith in
God's ultimate goodness and the goodness of his plan for each
one of us was no doubt a major factor in her ability to do this.
She did not have to carry the burden of the future. It was in
God's hands, and she knew he was sufficient for the task. The
ability to be in the present is strengthened by faith in a God
who can be trusted with the future. There is something child-
like in such a faith, because it calls for the complete trust, of
which little children are so capable.

SUFFERING AT THE TIME OF JESUS'S DEATH

Losing a loved one is always very hard. To have an innocent
child executed as a disgraced criminal compounds grief with
unspeakable human anguish. The scene at the foot of the cross
confronts us with that most difficult facet of the Mary archetype: suffering Mary.

Here too, at the foot of the cross, we find a Mary who was able
to be present with Jesus, in an unbearable, painful situation that
breaks one's heart. It is hard to imagine more anguish for a
sensitive and loving mother than to witness the humiliating,

outrageously unfair, intensely physically painful death of her beloved child.

No doubt Mary's worst fears had been exceeded. Her dreams for God's plan for this special son seemed cruelly shattered. How understandable it would have been for her to take refuge from the public eye and to endure the unspeakable grief with friends in private, or to faint from the horror of it all. Yet, not only was she present at the crucifixion, but she also gathered with the disciples after Jesus's death.

It is clear that Jesus tried to prepare his disciples for his impending death, and that it was beyond their capacity to comprehend what he meant. Did he also try to prepare his mother? Like the disciples, was it beyond her capacity to grasp the necessity and purpose of this horrible deed, or did God give her at least some degree of understanding, to help her through this unbearable period? Even if she had some grasp that this crucifixion was necessary and that Jesus would rise from the dead, this would still be a gruesome time. However, real strength and comfort could be drawn from the triumphant results to come. If, like the disciples, she saw this as a terrible and catastrophic dashing of all hopes for the fulfillment of God's plan for Jesus to be the Messiah, her despair and confusion must have been particularly crushing. Whatever we may think about Mary's situation, Scripture is silent on this matter.

If Mary did have some understanding that Jesus was fulfilling his mission by accepting the cross, she nevertheless held a different perspective than all around her, including her other sons. She had to live with that difference in understanding. If, on the other hand, Mary was congruent with the disciples' and her others sons' perspective, how difficult it must have been to wonder what had taken Jesus off track—why weren't things occurring according to the traditional Jewish understanding of a triumphant Messiah?

Suffering Compounded

Suffering because of the death of a loved one is suffering aplenty. However, sometimes the suffering is compounded with

additional factors. Such was the case with Mary, and such has been the case for many a hurting person before and since. Therefore, we will examine a few of these factors for Mary.

Shamed, Rejected, and Despised

If Jesus had died a painful death, that would have been tragic and painful enough. But a heavy added burden was that he was being purposefully killed, having been wrongfully convicted by the government of inciting insurrection, and by the Jewish religious elite of having claimed to be God, a despicable sin in Judaism. A mantle of shame and rejection draped itself over Jesus. When a loved one is viewed this way by society, this can place a heavy burden on those who love that person as well. The mantle of shame covers them too, in the eyes of others as well as themselves. True, God can shield a loved one from the impact of such a burden, but it is important to note that this is a real and painful factor in the situation with Jesus, and in many a situation since then. For a sensitive person, the burden is hard to bear, whether or not the shame and rejection are deserved.

Dreams Gone Awry

Certainly the disciples' grief and despair were compounded by the crushing blow to their dreams and convictions about whom Jesus was and what he was going to do on earth. They were not only crushed by the death and loss of their beloved master, but also by the cruel outcome of their dreams gone awry. They had given up their livelihoods to follow Jesus, and staked their reputations on the validity of his ministry. Now their judgment, their dreams, and their investment of body and soul were all washed away.

Did Mary share in this aspect of suffering? Did she believe that somehow things had gone awry? Did she cling in faith to the promises of God that her son was the Messiah, yet remain in anguish because she did not understand what was happening at

this juncture? Or was she given a peace that passes understanding to protect her from this aspect of the group's anguish? While we do not know the answer to this question, Scripture records that even Jesus went through anguish in the garden, as he contemplated the cup he was to drink. Was there no other way to fulfill his mission? Surely if Jesus went through such agony, it is quite possible that even if Mary understood the necessity of his mission more than the twelve disciples, she still anguished over such a prospect.

When dreams seem to have been murdered, we often question ourselves. We were so certain we had heard God, and yet clearly that was not so, as far as we can tell. Why did God allow us to have this dream and stake our lives on it, believing we were part of his plan and following his will? For some, this can be reason enough to turn one's back on God. After all, he has seemingly abandoned us after promising a different outcome.

When Injustice Triumphs

When wrong wins out and unjust things cause pain, anguish increases. So often there can be not only grief at the pain and loss, but anger and rage at the injustice itself. This is one reason murder can be harder to deal with than a natural or accidental death. Those who knew Jesus realized he had done nothing to deserve death. They could easily have been crushed by the anguish and rage that can come from knowing that evil triumphed, that the plotting of others led to the death of an innocent person. Mary, too, must have had to deal with this issue in some way.

Abandonment by God

Many students of Scripture believe that God **did** abandon Jesus on the cross, because God had to separate himself from the sins that Jesus bore for all of us, and because separation from God is the penalty of sin. What must that have seemed like for Mary and for the disciples? With their leader abandoned by

God, how must they have felt? For many, there is the feeling of abandonment by God when our prayers are not answered in the midst of suffering and pain. This, too, may have affected the feelings of Mary and the disciples, even if it did not affect their deepest convictions. In the cruelest of ways, God seemed to have broken trust. To have faith in the midst of such circumstances is a monumental challenge.

A Precious Gift Rejected

In crucifying Jesus, both the Jews and the Gentile Roman government failed to recognize the greatest and most loving gift bestowed upon a needy world. A life-sustaining gift was rejected. For Mary, as a member of the Jewish community, this tragedy of the failure of the world, her world, to accept the life-giving balm offered in so timely a manner may have been an especially cruel pain to bear.

Imagine, for instance, a missionary who loves the indigenous people she works among. An epidemic breaks out, and people are dying all around her. There is a cure, but it would require that medicine be brought in from the outside world, and be administered by an expert. At great effort, the missionary manages to get the attention of an organization that will fund both the cost of the medicine and the expert physician. She eagerly awaits his arrival, as the people she has come to love languish. Then, to her horror, the tribal guards drag a body into the village meeting area, and proudly present the corpse to the leaders. A mistake has been made, and the one sent to save them has been killed as an intruder. The missionary's pain is overwhelming as she not only grieves at the death of this physician, but also mourns for the tribal members who cannot benefit from the healing the physician desired to bring. Surely Mary felt this type of sorrow.

These factors—feeling shamed, rejected, and despised, the feeling of dreams gone awry, the fact that injustice had triumphed, the abandonment of Jesus by God, and the rejection of a precious gift— all compounded Mary's suffering. We

may brush away some of them, believing that because of her faith and her close relationship to God, she was spared being affected by the rejection of society and religious leaders. If Mary's faith and the grace of God carried her above these factors, it speaks all the more of faith and grace, not less of the trauma of such realities. Further, just as Jesus endured real and agonizing pain on the cross, moving through suffering rather than being lifted above pain, so Mary may have moved through very painful emotions concerning additional factors rather than been sheltered from their blows.

What about Us?

We may experience sufferings similar to Mary's. In her case, several misfortunes occurred together, the impact of each made greater by the presence of the others. For us, they may occur singly or in different combinations. Unless we die a swift and early death ourselves, we will likely not be spared the pain and death of loved ones.

We too may suffer loss of reputation (deserved, undeserved, or some ambiguous combination of the two!), shameful perceptions of others, rejection, and being looked down upon, either of ourselves or of someone we love. An astute and observant businessman recently remarked to me that the media can destroy anyone's reputation, whether deserved or not, so all must be prepared to withstand such onslaughts. Whether the media's glare is involved or not, trouble comes in many shapes and sizes. A reputation that has taken years to build can be damaged suddenly, causing pain not only to that person, but also to family and friends. We can suffer rejection from a parent, spouse, friend, or child on whose love we had counted.

Our dreams may either fade slowly, unfulfilled, or be suddenly wrenched from us. There may be times when we or those we love are unjustly accused, and the wrong fails to be righted. "Where is God when we need him?" we may cry out in our pain, feeling abandoned. Thus, we can relate Mary's suffering to aspects of our own lives. Whether our suffering is similar to Mary's or involves different factors, the extremity of Mary's particular suffering helps us bear ours. That Mary was not exempt provides comfort for us. Somehow, knowing that she was beloved of God and yet suffered can help us to feel comforted rather than abandoned. Perhaps we, too, are still cherished by God even when our calls for healing and aid seem to go unanswered. Let us look a little further at Mary in her suffering.

Called to Be Present in Suffering

We need to be aware that Mary's suffering occurred and was greater precisely because she was close to Jesus. Had she chosen not to say yes to God at the beginning, she would have been spared this particular suffering. Had she chosen to distance herself from God and Jesus at any point along the way, she would have suffered less from this particular pain. Thus saying yes to God and being close to Jesus is not a solution to suffering. We may be spared some sufferings, even delivered from them in miraculous ways, just as Mary's family was guided into Egypt during a time of high danger. At another time, our closeness to God may lead us into suffering.

It is also important to see that Mary chose God, not suffering. However, when suffering was part of the package of following God, she did not avoid it. Healthy people do not seek out personal suffering; neither do they run from it when it is set upon the path where God is leading them. Let us now look at how Mary dealt with the suffering of Jesus, as well as her own suffering.

Physically Present

Mary's ability to be physically present is commendable. For such a horrible event, performed in the cruel public eye, it would have been understandable for her to have been secluded with other family members, as they prayed and mutually consoled each other. However, Scripture indicates that she was standing near the cross, again indicating the strength to be present. From what we know of Mary, she was present both emotionally and spiritually.

Mary may have felt called to be present at the crucifixion, or it may have been simpler and more visceral than that; it may be that as a bonded mother, she could not have stayed away unless restrained. Sometimes, when we are close to someone and suffering occurs, there is no question in our minds and hearts—we simply go. It would be unthinkable not to be there. Other times, we may feel called to be with someone during their period of suffering. And yet at other times, it is possible that others are called, and we are not to be the ones. Discernment is important in such situations.

I recall a surgeon who once described how to know when a patient was nearly terminal. The further from the nurse's station, he confided, the more ill the person was. It was simply too painful to have the dying near on a daily basis, and easier for the staff if the dying person's room and situation was more out of sight and mind. Likewise for us, it can be easier to withdraw than to be present at such times. There is a natural reticence to intrude if one is not within the inner circle of the person and their family. The energy of the suffering one is very limited, and part of the natural process of saying goodbye is to do so by layers, moving closer to the center of one's life at the end. This is why good judgment, common sense, and discernment are called for, even if one is willing and able to be present.

Another factor in being physically present is the preference and capabilities of the person suffering. Some individuals, for whatever reasons, give off strong messages that they want solitude rather than the comforting presence of others. This, too, must be taken into account.

Emotionally and Spiritually Present

It is eight o'clock on a cold, foggy Sunday morning in the new year, and there are six of us at the Formica-topped table in one of our town's popular, plain breakfast spots. My friend is relating some vignettes about loss, gleaned from one of the seminars she has attended. The speaker wraps humor around the truth, she relates, as he speaks about loss and grief. "When my dog died, they said, 'Get another one' to comfort me. 'Don't dwell on it,' they said. It was only when my girlfriend left that I learned she was a fish. 'There are other fish in the sea,' my mother said to me." We chuckled over our eggs, fruit, and crispy grilled potatoes, enjoying the story in a relaxed way because at that moment none of us were suffering the wrenching loss that cannot be comforted by such comments. Our chuckles also acknowledged that we each have this tendency to want to fix things for the hurting one. In our concern, we may give messages not to dwell on the pain and loss, to get a replacement for the loved one or the object of loss, and suggest that because "there are other fish in the sea," the loss of the unique relationship someone had with a special person can be replaced. There can be a tendency to minimize the very real loss, particularly if the other person has left the relationship on his or her own volition.

These humorous comments illustrate how easy it is to avoid allowing someone their pain, and to avoid being with them in that pain. All too often we want to "shoo" someone through grief, perhaps for our sake as much as theirs.

As we have already seen, because of what we have seen of Mary's exceptional ability to be present emotionally and spiritually, I believe that she was present in those ways at the cross. This must have been especially difficult, because she was not able to minister physically to Jesus during his suffering. It is a strong and natural response to wish to touch and soothe a loved one with the stroke of our hand or a gentle kiss when they are in pain. Such comfort was likely not possible. Words are another way in which we may usually comfort a loved one. *I'm here. I care. I love you.* We do not know if words other than those recorded in Scripture were uttered in this most difficult of situations.

In the film *Dead Man Walking*, the young man condemned to

death is assured by the nun who has befriended him on death row that she will be there as one of the witnesses to his execution. Although no contact is possible, her mute presence conveys a love and acceptance that provides a deep emotional and even spiritual support to the man being strapped to the electric chair. The nun's gift of presence is a profound yet mute gift. Her gift to a guilty man is perhaps not unlike Mary's gift to a completely innocent man.

Being present with someone in their pain is in many ways a sacred task. One steps outside the usual busy and practical current of life into a strangely still circle of pain, grief, and suffering. Time and value are measured differently within this circle. We may be aware then or later that we have been privileged to be present in the situation.

When we are bearing our own grief, confusion, and tumultuous feelings within that circle, there can be a dance of comforting, sharing our own pain, comforting some more, and accepting the gamut of emotions and mental states that may swirl within the circle. We may need an extra measure of support and understanding, as we reel from being the comforter to the one in need of comfort. Let us now turn to several sources of comfort and strength for Mary in her grief.

The Comfort of Jesus

We see something important about the way Jesus, in excruciating pain, responded to Mary's presence with him. John records that Mary stood near the cross and that Jesus saw her there, along with John. Jesus addresses her from the cross, "'Dear woman, here is your son,' and to the disciple, 'Here is your mother.' From that time on, this disciple took her into his home."[6]

These words no doubt have various layers of meaning, some of them theological in nature. Yet first and foremost, they speak of the mutuality of comfort and nurture going on between the beloved son and the beloved mother. Deep love and acceptance come from the one suffering, as Jesus expresses his deep appreciation for Mary's presence with him in the hour of extremity and need.

God the father could not be with Jesus during this time, and all but a few of Jesus's disciples fled in fear and despair. But Mary was there. Jesus expresses appreciation and acknowledgment, and also provides her a further source of comfort and protection by saying to John, "Here is your mother." In this brief statement, Jesus has acknowledged Mary as dear to him and as a mother.

The Comfort of Community

Mary's presence at the suffering of Jesus also allows her to comfort and be comforted by the community, which is represented by John, her sister, and Mary Magdalene. Mary is to be John's mother, and he is to be her son. Severe as her pain is, she is surrounded by care. Mutual support no doubt took place.

The Comfort of El Shaddai

Mary had something available to her in this horrible time that Jesus did not. For while the face of God was hidden from Jesus as he took on the sins of the world, the face of God did not need to be hidden from Mary. In the midst of her suffering, God was there. And the God who was there is a multifaceted God, full of mystery, power, and the ability to comfort. The comfort of El Shaddai, the one who is mighty and tender, who contains feminine and masculine aspects, was there for Mary.

El Shaddai is the name of God made known to Abraham when God appeared to Abraham to make the Covenant.[7] As Dr. Daniel Stramara explains, El Shaddai is typically translated "the Almighty" in our English translations. It is a strong and powerful term, with ancient roots. Some scholars point out that *shad* most likely comes from the Hebrew word used for both breast and mountain. Fascinatingly, "El" is an ancient name for a masculine god, and the ending "ai" is feminine, as is found in the ending of the name Sarai, Abraham's wife. Thus the translation "God, the Breasted One," is a blending of the masculine and feminine. El Shaddai speaks particularly to the creative, relational aspects of God.

Stramara notes the descriptions of God's children dwelling under the wings of the Lord in the Old Testament and asserts, "Thus it appears that El Shaddai depicts herself as a mothering bird caring for her young." That this aspect of God is described and affirmed in Scripture—the term El Shaddai is used forty-eight times—gives us a richer, fuller picture of our Lord. Oswald Chambers refers to this name for God in his classic book *My Utmost for His Highest.*[8] "I am the Almighty God—El Shaddai, the Father-Mother God." Both men and women can benefit from becoming acquainted with this name for God, revealed in Scripture, and the reality of a nurturing and comforting God it represents.

Mary had some strengths and comforts during this terrible time of suffering and grief, given to help sustain her. They included her own inner strengths, cultivated over the years, the comfort and dialogue of the suffering Jesus, the comfort and support of other loved ones, and the powerful comfort of God. In our suffering, we too are to draw upon resources given by God.

Resources When We Suffer

When friends and family members go through intense suffering, their inner resources often shine out to us, even when they may be barely visible to the suffering person. Natasha cared for her increasingly frail husband for years as his short-term memory receded more and more sharply. For many reasons, one of which was the fact that her husband had been a prisoner of war during World War II in particularly horrible circumstances, she opted to have him remain at home, where his gentle nature felt most comfortable. Her strong faith and good humor, along with her ability to accept assistance from others, helped her during this long watch of a loved one's decline and her self-enforced severe limiting of her own ability to be out and about. In the midst of this, many noticed an increased radiance about her, restricted though her life was.[8]

The sick or dying person and the ones who love her can often help support and comfort each other. Henri married Thelma, aware that she was in remission of a dangerous form of cancer. When the cancer returned, the communication between the two was a vital part of their love and support for each other. Both were able to discuss hopes and fears for the future and for the dreams they had for starting a family one day. After several cycles of doing better, then worse, it became more and more apparent that Thelma would probably not make it through another year. The blend of humor, good cheer, faith in God, and ability to deeply and freely grieve together helped this remarkable couple to support each other to the end.

Help from the wider circle of loved ones and community also provides vital support to the suffering. Grief and suffering are burdens too large to bear alone, although some are forced to do so by extreme circumstances. Often it is those who have suffered in a similar way who are able to provide unique emotional support to the stricken one. Lolly tells of the pain of losing her only son to a quick-striking illness. Her marriage to the boy's stepfather disintegrated within the year, as he could not handle her overwhelming grief. Within a brief time, Lolly had lost not only loved ones, but her identity as wife and mother. Lolly sought help from the wider community, including seeing a therapist who specialized in grief, and attending a support group in her community for parents who had lost children. She found that while friends and church were supportive, she needed more help. After several years, Lolly continued in the support group—now to help others deal with overwhelming loss.

The grief of a loved one dying when young is a particularly cutting and wrenching one, and one that I know of firsthand. When my brother died in an automobile accident when I was twenty-four, I entered a new land, one with sharper edges and yet more dulling colors than I could have imagined. Years later, when I was given the poignant privilege of helping a young woman at the same stage of life deal with the sudden death of her beloved brother, we spoke the same language of grief. Her metaphors went to a place in my mind and heart that had been scraped open by the jagged edges of grief and allowed me to resonate with her in a different way than would have been possible without those open places.

Nora was at home alone when the phone rang. When she picked it up, she was told that her young daughter had died. Grief overwhelmed her, and she described the next weeks and months of God's tender care for her by saying: *It was as if I was wrapped or swaddled in a big roll of cotton. God allowed the cotton to be unwrapped only as my wounds healed enough to bear it. I felt the tenderness of his love in the midst of all the pain in a way that is difficult to describe.*

Another example from my own life comes to mind. On the first anniversary of my father's death, I was undergoing menopause as well as the resurgence of grief and loss feelings. Cloaked in a cape of hormonal and emotional tumult, I tried to stay with my feelings and allow myself to both express them and be comforted. I lit a candle in memory of Dad, lay on the couch with the covers pulled up, letting feelings and memories wash over me. When my husband could join me, I lay in his arms on the couch and continued the process. At that time, the comfort of the maternal, feminine aspect of God was what reached out to me. The image of the breasted one, El Shaddai, was nurturing, accepting, soothing.

SUMMING UP

Mary's experience shows us that she embraced God's plan for her life, and that part of that plan was a rich, abundant life, a life that also included deep suffering. While Mary did not specifically choose suffering, she did not disengage from a deep, loving relationship with Jesus in order to avoid it.

When suffering came, her ability to be present physically, emotionally, and spiritually allowed her to give profound support to Jesus at a time when he was cut off from other lifelines of support—that of God and that of the larger group of disciples. She was able to give and receive comfort and support during this excruciating time.

From Mary's suffering and from our own seasons of suffering, we see that resources are available to help us in these situations that cut through the bone of our souls and into the very marrow of our being. Inner resources built up within us over the years are available. The interaction with the ill or dying loved one can be a source of mutual comfort and support, giving each the strength to continue through the difficult and new territory. Loving care, acceptance of our feelings, and other types of vital support can be supplied by other loved ones and the larger community. God intends for us to help bear each other's burdens—those things that are too large for us to bear alone. Undergirding and overarching these resources is the love and comfort of God, who keenly understands the depth and sharpness of our suffering.

Not all of these resources are available in each situation of suffering. Some, because of circumstances, are separated from the comfort of others during suffering, and some may have few inner resources to call upon in times of grief. It is the resource of God's care that is the bedrock of support, love, and comfort for us when we call out. Even when no other resources are available, God promises to provide sufficient comfort and grace for us.

Each of us needs to find the balance of resources for his or her particular situation. While it is good to have strong inner resources, God may call us to stretch in our ability to reach out for the comfort of others. At other times, we may find ourselves in a situation where the usual support of friends is not available, yet we are able to draw directly from resources of God's comfort in a new way.

Staying with the Process

Suffering, grief, and loss are processes rather than events. We do not tuck them away after the funeral and go on about our lives with no further work to do. Each person has his or her own particular rhythm of grief and recovery. Staying with the process, accepting the rhythm of one's own grief, is the best way to move through it to healing. Giving ourselves the power of our own loving presence in the midst of our own grief is a powerful healing gift to self that will later allow us to give powerful gifts of our loving presence to others. Being present in our pain allows us to move through and across the river of grief rather than staying mired in it forever.

Being present with others in their suffering, and staying with them in the process, brings a gift more precious than myrrh. It is the gift that Mary brought Jesus at the foot of the cross.

Chapter Twelve

A Balanced Mary—Wholeness and Power

"For nothing is impossible with God".
                        Angel Gabriel to Mary in Luke 1:37
"They all joined together constantly in prayer, along with the women and Mary the Mother of Jesus, with his brothers."
                        Acts 1:14

*T*HE STORY OF MARY does not end at the cross. The last recorded words of Jesus to Mary commit her to the care of John, a loving person in his own right, and also a representative of what would become the new Christian community. After his resurrection, any words that Jesus may have spoken with Mary are kept forever private; we have no scriptural record. The last reference to Mary's life on earth is recorded in Acts 1:14, where the now eleven disciples, plus the women who also sat at Jesus's feet and his close family members, gather in Jerusalem after seeing him ascend into heaven. Here it is revealed that the brothers of Jesus now believe in him and are part of the fellowship, along with Mary. All of them are following Jesus's instructions to pray and wait for the baptism of the Holy Spirit, which was to come in a few days.[1] Mary was surely present when this new stage of faith was ushered in at Pentecost. She was one of the founding members of the new church.

If she was about sixteen when she gave birth to Jesus, Mary

would have been in her late forties or early fifties during these exciting times for the new church. Since we hear no mention of Joseph among the group of believers, it is widely assumed that he had died by this time, and Mary's other children were probably grown. She would have been at a time in her life when she could devote much time and energy to the community of believers. Scripture instructs that the older women are to be models for the younger,[2] and the traits we have been studying in Mary would have made her a powerful example to help women understand what it meant to be a woman of God within the New Covenant. Mary may have lived a very full life during this period, in an explosive time of early church growth and development.

Let us turn now to a look at how the various facets of Mary's personhood combined to make her a crucial model both for those in the early church and for us. We have witnessed a human life move from an innocent young virgin full of faith and hope to a mature, seasoned woman whose heart is pierced by a sword of grief as her firstborn son breathes his last on a lowly cross, and who then goes on to participate in the amazing new church that resulted from his ministry.

As Mary moved through these stages of her life, as recorded in Scripture, we have searched to discover the traits and qualities that formed her personhood. Our search has yielded traits that we may not have noticed previously, perhaps because we were not taught to see them. We have scrutinized these traits, focusing on one at a time in order to better understand that particular trait in Mary, and the possibilities it holds for us.

POWERFUL PROHIBITIONS

As we have examined these traits, we have also noticed that throughout the centuries since her life, cultural and religious factors sometimes were woven together to limit the ideas about who Mary was and correspondingly what the role of women should be. Scholar Jaroslav Pelikan points out that "Mary has been more of an inspiration to more people than any other woman who ever lived."[3] He further notes that at the beginning of the twentieth century, it was traditionally believed that the brief accounts of her in Scripture reflected "what a true woman ought to be."[4] This reality, coupled with what he states "has become a widely held historical consensus that 'the theology of the Virgin Mary has not altered women's inferior status within the Church'"[5] underscores once more the importance of understanding Mary and her archetype.

Recent reexaminations of history have focused on the powerful prohibitions placed on the personhood of women, and many of these prohibitions have been linked to the way Mary has been portrayed historically. It is natural that those who were trying to guide flocks and indeed influence the culture would tend to look for ways to interpret the scriptural record in ways that were congruent with their deepest beliefs and biases about the nature of women, men, and reality. Likewise, it is imperative that these perspectives be reexamined and those that do not stand up to the test of Biblical truth be discarded. This is part of our maturing faith process, both as individuals and as a church body. Numerous women and men still labor to a greater or lesser degree under these constraints, and many times it is their faith that has kept them bound when others have broken free.

Following is a list of prohibitions that have been transmitted to women (and sometimes to men) through the centuries by Christendom and the cultures Christendom inhabited. Not everyone, thankfully, has been exposed to or damaged by all of these rules. Some have been stronger in certain periods of history or in some denominations, and practically nonexistent in others. After this list comes a corresponding list of permissions gleaned by our study of Mary.

1. Die to Yourself

Sadly, the misunderstanding of Biblical principles has often led to the idea that dying to self means that we must give up who we are, and not value the self that God has created. What is closer to the Biblical reality is the idea of dying to or shedding the false self, which we have built up to accommodate ourselves to a world-view that is not accurate. We are to surrender both our false selves and our flawed true selves to God, whose desire is to transform us into the true self that we were created to be. When we look at the Biblical characters chosen by God to be giants of the faith, we see that they are usually well-defined, strong personalities, not empty shells of persons who have never developed talents, likes, dislikes, and passions. In fact, they are a life-loving, passionate group of folks whose unique personhood God shapes, molds, and transforms, rather than obliterates. After all, it was God who created the original person and saw that creation was good.

This prohibition has influenced both women and men. Because of other Biblical and societal encouragement to men to be leaders, to be strong and independent, many men have not been hindered to the extent that women have. Because women have also been bombarded with both overt and covert messages to be submissive, to fit in with their husband's plans, to obey and serve others without proper balances, this message of dying to self has had a much greater negative impact on women. It may be a contributor to the higher rates of depression for women.

2. Give Up Your Own Creative Capacities

This message to women is often given by implication or by default. Because there has been so much emphasis historically on women serving others—husband, children, parents, or church—there is often no time or inner space left to develop creative capacities that do not fit in with the immediate needs of those around the woman.

When Cinderella's wicked stepmother wished to keep her from attending the ball, all the older woman had to do was assign so much work that had to be done before Cinderella could go that attendance was impossible. The overload of menial tasks would have kept Cinderella from her destiny had not the fairy godmother intervened.

Women have received many messages to the same effect. Recall the instructions from a Christian writer that a woman might consider work outside the home only if the household were in such good shape that she had extra time and energy to put towards something else. Given the nature of running a home with children, this instruction seems hauntingly like that of the wicked stepmother!

For women, creativity in those areas considered to be women's domain has been more readily encouraged. Creativity expressed in sewing, playing the piano, cooking, or teaching small children, for example, has been more permissible and praised than creativity expressed in designing a bridge, directing a symphony, or writing a book. The great strides made recently in opening up new areas for women do not immediately sweep away the influence of centuries of this prohibition.

3. Your Mind is Inferior

"Don't worry your pretty little head about this." This type of comment suggests that a woman's head cannot serve two functions at the same time, that a woman's head was not made for thinking, and further, that if she persists in thinking about matters that have been prohibited, she risks losing her allure to men.

Studies on intellectually gifted females indicate that all too often, when girls reach adolescence, they begin to be embarrassed about their intellectual capabilities and focus on being attractive to boys, instead. For too many young women, there is still a dichotomy—they must choose between attractiveness to males and using their intelligence to the fullest.

Such a dilemma only serves to reinforce the idea, firmly held in the centuries the early church was forming, that the female mind is inferior. Why were virtually all of the great composers, playwrights, and artists male? The absence of women in such fields due to cultural prohibitions strengthened the belief in both men and women that females did not have the intellectual capacities to accomplish such feats.

In addition, since women were designed to marry, have children, and help the males succeed, this perspective held that there was no particular purpose in educating women beyond the skills needed to help them do this job well. Education could actually impair their abilities in the domestic arena.

4. Faith Means Blind Obedience

When a culture does not wish to encourage autonomy in a particular group, it often defines virtue in terms of unquestioning obedience from that group. Faith, particularly for women and slaves, has often been emphasized as involving periods of long suffering, patient endurance, and child-like obedience. It means accepting the status quo, with trust that God will take care of things, rewarding the faithful in the next world, if not this one. It means not speaking up in the face of societal injustices, but patiently enduring them, so as to not forfeit a reward in heaven. When faith is defined solely in this way, the boat will not be rocked, and the oppressed will remain in their place.

This belief has contributed to some women not protecting their children or themselves from abusive treatment within the family. Instead, some feel they must not confront such treatment or take steps to keep themselves and their children safe, because to confront their spouses would not be their place. Some even accept such treatment in faith as coming from the hand of God.

5. You Must Choose Between Intimacy and Your Own Identity

Especially in the seventies and eighties, women who desired to succeed in high-powered careers grappled with the question of marriage versus career. A significant number chose not to marry or to remain childless in order to pursue their careers without guilt. Others gave up the idea of significant success, choosing to marry and have children instead. Although not every woman seeks the kind of career that brings up this issue, there are many who have felt they needed to submerge or abandon their own identity in order to have an intimate relationship with a male. This may not be a conscious decision, or one made all at once. It may happen bit by bit, in countless small acts of choosing his likes, dislikes, and scheduling needs over one's own.

As noted earlier, young women often suffer a sharp drop in self-esteem about the time of adolescence, due in large part to the conflict they see between being themselves and attracting young men. The need to be attractive to the opposite sex is seen to be in conflict with allowing the full self to be expressed.

6. The Quiet Woman is the Holy Woman

The virtues of a quiet woman have long been extolled, and this has changed only very recently in history. The prohibition to speak up can therefore be reinforced by likening this behavior to that of Jesus when he was mute before his accusers. There are indeed times when the wise man or woman will choose to be quiet, when it is best not to speak. It is when quietness has been emphasized for women without the balance of appropriate assertiveness that this message combines with other prohibitions to keep women in a limited, unempowered place. Such a message can also contribute to depression and to abusive situations within the work and home settings.

7. Do Not Expect Mutual Dialogue within Marriage

Closely linked to other prohibitions is the notion that women are to unilaterally submit to their husbands, as opposed to the mutual submission that is Biblical. The idea of submission, when linked to the prohibitions about speaking up, can lead to an absence of mutual dialogue between marriage partners. The husband who declared to his wife, "I'll do the thinking for both of us," illustrates in the extreme where this prohibition leads.

8. Submerge Yourself in Motherhood

There have been strong messages to women that fulfillment comes from being a mother, and that a woman should devote herself to this calling, to the exclusion of other endeavors. The idea that a woman who does not feel sufficiently fulfilled caring for her children is somehow deficient as a mother plummets some women into a deep sense of guilt and inadequacy when they find themselves loving their children dearly, yet stifled by an agenda filled with diaper pails, baby formulas, and chauffeuring children to various enrichment experiences.

Who knows what kind of pressure this belief puts on the children who are being raised with this assumption about motherhood? If the self-esteem of the mother becomes tied up with the success of her parenting because this is the only outlet she allows herself, the children are given both power and pressure that may not be in their best interest.

9. Do Not Be Sexual

This prohibition has several facets. Augustine, with his great influence, was uneasy with sexual feelings in any context. Thus, while sex itself was seen as the duty of husband and wife in order to produce children, the pleasure that might be taken even in the act of propagation was seen as sinful. According to this perspective, guilt was a part of even sexual expression within marriage. By some wrongly defining Mary as a perpetual virgin, she was spared having to experience this guilt, and the accompanying sin. It is doubtful that her designation as perpetual virgin would have been necessary or desirable had it not been for this perception about the sinfulness of sexual pleasure, even within marriage.

What many who accepted this view of sexuality found was that mere abstinence from sex did not solve the problem of guilt, because the sexual feelings came unbidden and oftentimes in even greater strength when the opposite sex was avoided, and when there were no sexual outlets. This contributed to a mentality where some of the devout scourged themselves and went to other extremes to purge themselves of that they regarded as their sinful nature.

When there is no way to win, or get out of a dilemma, people have only limited choices. They can accept the belief and remain in a state of uncomfortable guilt, relying on the power of God to continually forgive them. Another alternative is to give up, decide there is no way to meet the criteria, that trying is futile. Such thinking can free the way to toss out all scriptural guidelines regarding sexuality.

10. Do Not Accept Your Body and Its Needs

The idea that the body and its needs were somehow in opposition to being spiritual and holy led to inner conflict about acceptance of the body. The body was seen as tripping up the good intentions of the spirit and soul of the person. Women's bodies in particular were weak and even evil, because they posed temptations to men. Variations of this concept are probably still factors in the eating disorders seen in so many, and in the near universal dissatisfaction women feel about their bodies. Perhaps if they had perfect bodies, women may reason, they would somehow be more acceptable to self and others.

11. Do Not Allow Expression of Grief—A Christian is Always Joyful

This prohibition is one that has probably affected men as much if not more than women. How many children have been told, "Don't cry. Take it like a man," or, "Don't cry. It doesn't really hurt." Such statements invalidate a child's experience, and give instructions to repress feelings. Especially when there has been a tremendous loss, such as the death of a parent, messages of well-meaning relatives that cut the child off from her deep pain and grief can have long-lasting negative effects. When children who have received these messages grow up, they will often find it very difficult to be fully present in situations involving suffering and loss. Adults can also feel the burden to set their feelings aside in an unhealthy way, in order to reflect well their own faith.

12. Limit Your Participation in the Christian Community to a "Woman's Place"

"What are your leadership conferences like?" I once asked a friend, who was active, along with her spouse, in a parachurch organization that worked with youth. She explained to me that the men learned how to lead the meetings, discussed strategy and theology, and bolstered their skills in the above areas, while the women learned about how to support the men in the ministry, including tips for refreshments to serve the youth. No doubt this has changed in the last several decades, but that it occurred in the early seventies indicates how women's talents and service to the church have often been funneled into narrow spaces that ignore their wide range of gifts.

POWERFUL PERMISSIONS

What do Mary and her archetype have to say to us about these concepts? Our study of the scriptural data reveals that Mary, contrary to the messages many have received, gives powerful permissions to women and to men. They act as an antidote for messages that have sprung up reinforcing the application of inferior status to women. These permissions, when we reflect on them, and with God's help claim them as real in our lives, can empower us to be the full persons God created us to be. This empowerment can help equip us for the work we were created to do, fulfilling God's purpose in our lives.

1. Be Inner-Directed—a Strong Self

By saying *Yes* to God after dialoging with the angel, Mary affirms inner-directedness for women and men. This was the first in a series of her actions that demonstrated a strong sense of self and the ability to be true to herself in her decisions, rather than following cultural or peer pressure. Neither God nor Mary felt the necessity to consult with a male authority in this important matter, which lends further support for the value of a strong, inner-directed woman who chooses to follow God's direction.

2. Be Creative

Expression of our creativity is our own stamp of uniqueness. Mary's Song gives us a glimpse into her artistic creativity and affirms the important, nourishing role that tapping into this part of ourselves plays in our lives and in our relationship with God. Expressing our creativity, whether it be by baking a cake, making creative repairs on machinery, designing a building, sculpting a work of art, or delivering a talk, develops our own personhood as well as contributing something to others. Creativity is part of how we are made in God's image.

3. Value and Develop Your Mind and Thinking Capacities

God chose a bright woman who had learned to use her mind and was highly capable of complex thinking to be the mother of the Messiah. This choice affirms the value of learning to use our minds. Developing our minds and thinking capacities is part of using our God-given talents and part of how we glorify God. The developmentally disabled person who labors to keep her own checkbook is acting on this permission just as surely as the intellectually gifted person who embarks on a dissertation. The woman who has not had formal education beyond high school but who reads widely, engages in many intelligent conversations, and thinks through issues carefully also illustrates this trait. This trait is particularly important in a society where we are blessed with the freedom and responsibility to participate in the democratic process of government.

4. Mature Faith Involves Paradox

We are given the powerful permission to grow in faith—not just in quantity, but also in quality, growing into the mature faith that has weathered unexpected gales and dry spells. It is a faith that remains childlike in some aspects but is also able to embrace complexity, uncertainty, and the paradoxical. The crucial role of faith to our personhood and our life purpose is exemplified and celebrated in Mary's life.

5. You Can be Close and be a Separate Person

Mary affirms that we can be close, caring, and intimate with a loved one, and still remain a separate person, with our own individuality and life's work. At times the closeness aspect of our lives will wax and the separate part of our identities may wane. At other times, the reverse may be true. Each person's pattern of this ebb and flow may be unique to them and their circumstances. Unbridled inner-directedness without the balances of both faith and closeness can lead to isolation, arrogance, and unnecessary hurt to loved ones. Thus, while inner-direction is important, it is balanced by relationships with others, both in the family and in the community.

6. Be Respectfully Assertive

Assertiveness as a necessary and powerful tool in expressing who we are and what we and others need is a permission affirmed by Mary's story. Mary demonstrates that we can ask questions about matters that affect our well-being, and that we can make statements about our core selves. Choices about our lives, well-being, and destinies can be made and owned. Creative expression, expressing a range of feelings, and praising God are all forms of assertiveness demonstrated by Mary. We also see that on occasion Mary spoke frankly with family members about the effect of their actions on others.

Assertiveness can be an important tool in ministry as we point out the needs of others, call forth the talents and gifts of others, work to facilitate finding solutions to problems, and provide instruction to others. We see that assertiveness can be a vital way to have influence without imposing control. As we learn to be appropriately assertive, we affirm both our own personhood and that of others, in the context of love and caring.

7. Mutual Dialogue and Mutual Submission—Shared Partnerships are Possible

Marriage relationships can involve two persons with a strong sense of self and a commitment to communicate frankly. The shift in Mary and Joseph's relationship that opened Joseph's eyes to his wife as a full person in her own right, apart from the couple relationship, allowed him to support the work that his spouse was called to do. It transformed the nature of their relationship into one where both had a joint sacred purpose, given by God. Both men and women can be strong, autonomous persons and choose to submit to the discipline of an intimate couple relationship, growing into interdependence. The concept of mutual submission, with both seeking to submit to the will of God, is congruent with Mary and Joseph's relationship. A shared spiritual purpose and mutual submission to God can be the glue that holds together and transforms the union of two strong individuals.

8. Be Yourself and a Loving, Responsible Parent

The importance of motherhood and fatherhood is solidly affirmed by Mary's story. That parenting can receive vital priority and yet help personhood blossom is also affirmed. We receive a *both/and* message rather than an *either/or* message when it comes to being ourselves and making good parenting a priority. Mary emerges from the active years of parenting a strong, individuated woman.

9. Claim and Enjoy Your Full Sexuality

Accepting and celebrating our sexuality is part of accepting who God created us to be. Scripture affirms active sexuality as expressed in marriage. God intends that this be a gift that is treasured and enjoyed. Scripture also affirms the choice of celibacy, whether for a season or for a lifetime. Neither state calls for denying that we are sexual persons, expressing ourselves as females or males, factors that are a key part of our identity.

Mary was equally virtuous as a virginal unmarried woman and as a sexually active wife after the birth of Jesus. Active sexuality can involve creativity at several levels—that of the creativity of forming new life and the creativity of a unique, growing, intimate bond with another person.

10. Celebrate Your Body as Good and Care for It Reverently

Although not much is said about Mary's body, the scriptural record profoundly affirms the female body in the account of Mary. Her female body and its female sexuality were used in God's plan to bring the Messiah, Lord of the Universe, to this planet in human form. God chose to dwell within Mary physically as well as spiritually. What affirmation for the goodness of the female body! Scripture tells us that our bodies are God's temple and as such are sacred to God.[6] We are to cherish and care for our bodies reverently.

11. Expression of Grief is Acceptable to God.

We can be fully present in our experiences of suffering and grief. Jesus experienced fully both the agony of Gethsemane and the agony of the cross. Mary experienced great suffering by choosing to be at the crucifixion of her son. She was physically, emotionally, and spiritually present for a range of experiences in her life, including the suffering of others and herself. God does not always shelter us from suffering; however, he does promise to never leave us, even in the midst of suffering.

12. Claim and Share Your Gifts in the Christian Community

We have seen how Mary bridged the gap between the Old Covenant and the New Covenant. As the new Christian community formed, she was there. That part of her story is recorded in Luke and Matthew indicates that her role and gifts were known. Acknowledging and sharing our full range of gifts within the Christian community is part of investing our talents, as described in the parable Jesus told on this topic.[7] Limits of time and energy may prevent using all of our gifts equally at all times. Being sensitive to God's guidance as to the timing of the exercising of various gifts is a key part of the process. Mary's spiritual gifts included the gift of prophecy, manifested in Mary's Song, and the gift of faith, seen when she said yes to bearing the Christ-child. Gifts of wisdom and discernment are indicated in the episode at the wedding in Cana.

Taking Inventory

This summary of powerful prohibitions, and the powerful archetypal permissions that can correct them, allows us to take inventory. What prohibitions have influenced us? Are we ready to consider whether God is calling us to replace them with a corresponding powerful permission? Both Scripture and sound psychology affirm the importance of doing more than merely giving up a negative. The void needs to be replaced by something positive. Zacchaeus the tax collector illustrated this principle when he stopped cheating his fellows of their taxes and returned four times what he had taken.[8] Thus actively embracing the corresponding permission can be an important part of change and healing.

WEAVING THE STRANDS BACK TOGETHER

We have looked at the life of Mary, focusing on specific traits revealed in Scripture. Each trait has been a vital strand in helping us to define who Mary is. Now it is time to weave the strands back again, and to see their impact as woven together they form the fabric of the person Mary.

More Than the Sum of Our Parts

It is an important principle that the whole person is more than the sum of that person's parts. When the separate traits we have examined are combined in balance in the person of Mary, they form a powerful, healthy whole that is more than any one trait or even the sum of the separate traits. This power is not fully realized in either Mary or in ourselves if some of the traits are omitted. It is the **combination** of the traits we have studied in Mary that is crucial to empowerment in right relationship to God.

We have noted that some views of Mary have emphasized traits that fit the pattern called the traditional view of women— her faith, obedience, humility, purity, and maternal devotion, for example. While these traits are commendable in themselves, they do not form the whole Mary. In fact, the traits traditionally extolled in Mary might indeed "condemn real women to perpetual inferiority," if they are the only traits available to women.

Gestalt theory emphasizes that something occurs in us that is more than the sum of our parts. It is a bit like making a favorite cake recipe. The ingredients may each be good in themselves, but are notably different when combined in the right combination and baked! Then too, most of us have at one time or another inadvertently left out either an ingredient or a portion of an ingredient (now did I put in two cups of flour or three?) after a child has burst into the kitchen, diverting our attention, or the phone has rang, interrupting our concentration. The result can be quite different from the original creation.

When I recently made such an error for the first time in years, the chocolate cake I was intending came out one-third the regular height, had a slightly heavier, gummier texture, and a flatter flavor than was typical. And all I had done was to leave out about a teaspoon of one ingredient. Yet this omission made

the difference between a cake that was enthusiastically consumed and a concoction that no one cared for. How often have we as individuals either failed to nurture or even squelched parts of ourselves that are vitally needed to complete the ingredients of our person because we did not see that this ingredient was part of the recipe? When this is done because of a belief that it is more congruent with Biblical guidelines, it is especially sad. Yet many a woman has felt guilty about key aspects of her true self—her sexuality, her intelligence, her assertiveness—because of misguided understandings of Biblical teachings concerning what a woman should be.

A list of Mary's historically less-noticed traits that has been highlighted in this work includes Mary's inner-direction, assertiveness, creative talent, intellectual giftedness, individuation, and sexuality. Such a list might be compiled by a women's rights group as desirable traits in a healthy woman. Yet this list, too, without the balance of the first list, would be out of skew. Tyrants have had these traits as well as saints, and a host of others in between. The following chart lists the traditional traits on the left and the more newly recognized traits on the right.

MARY'S PERSONAL TRAITS

Traits Traditionally Emphasized (First List)	Traits Newly Emphasized (Second List)
Faith	Inner-Direction
Obedience	Creative Talent
Humility	Intellectual Giftedness
Purity	Assertiveness
Maternal Devotion	Individuation
Strength in Suffering	Sexuality

If the goal is full personhood in right relationship to God, this second list of newly emphasized traits will not suffice. Yet, when these traits are combined with the traditional list, a metamorphosis takes place, and an empowered woman emerges, in balance with her creator, with her family, and with herself.

TRAITS OF EMPOWERED MARY, BASED ON
SCRIPTURAL RECORD

*Combining traits traditionally emphasized and traits discovered from
an examination of the scriptural record produces a portrait of Mary
that models empowerment:*

Faith
Inner-Direction
Obedience
Creative Talent
Humility
Intellectual Giftedness
Assertiveness
Individuation
Purity
Sexuality
Maternal Devotion
Ability to be Fully Present in Joy and in Sorrow

Likewise, if we change *maternal devotion* to *parental devotion,*
the combined list showing empowerment also describes an
empowered male in balance with his creator, with his family,
and with himself. In fact, the list of traits also fits the adult
Jesus. Though Jesus did not display his parental devotion in the
specific way of being an earthly parent of children, he did
display this quality in relation to us all, and in his touching
awareness of the needs of children when he said, "Let the little
children come to me."[9]

Seeing that this set of characteristics describes both Mary and
Jesus underscores an important point. Each of us, male and
female, are to imitate Christ. Thus, Mary affirms for all women
that becoming like Jesus can include the full gamut of their gifts
and talents, the full development of their personhood. What is
true for men in this regard is also true for women. Given
Galatians 3:24, where Paul states that in the New Covenant all are
sons and heirs in Christ regardless of whether they are Greek or
Jew, male or female, slave or free, this should not surprise us.

Also, each of us, male and female, is to be like Mary in that we say *Yes* to God and allow Christ to grow within us.

When Mary's traits are combined, we see a reconciliation of seemingly opposing characteristics. In Mary, faith and intellect are reconciled. In her assertiveness and submission are reconciled. Virtue and sexuality dwell in the same person. Humility and great giftedness are seen together. A devoted mother and one with a strong sense of her own identity are seen as one. The ability for closeness as well as separateness in a relationship is demonstrated. The paradox of being faithfully obedient to God and of being an inner-directed, fully alive person is revealed.

In Mary, body, soul, and spirit are integrated and act together, with God, to produce the Messiah. Emotions, hormones and muscles, thought, and spiritual intent all play crucial roles in this creation. Mary's message of wholeness includes acceptance and celebration of her body, and of our bodies.

How do such combined traits stand the test of time? Our examination of these traits began with Mary as a young woman, perhaps around the age of sixteen. As Mary progressed through her life, we saw that she was able to move into the adult stages of intimacy, identity, and generativity that are described by Erikson as healthy. She is able to form a lasting, intimate relationship with Joseph, her husband. She had a solid sense of her own identity as a capable wife and mother, as well as a member of her community.

Later, after the resurrection, we have intimations that she participated fully in the life of the new community, contributing the fruits of her faith and experience. This is the essence of the stage of generativity, where mature adults, having fulfilled their earlier life tasks, give out of the abundance of their wisdom and talents. Adults share their strengths in a variety of ways, including mentoring, civic service, or powerful praying. Thus Mary's traits were able to continue maturing and developing as she proceeded through the seasons of life. These traits stood the test of time, allowing her to move through the opportunities and challenges of adult psychological development in a graceful and productive way.

Because each of us is a uniquely created person, we will not all have the same constellation of traits that are evidenced in Mary. On his popular radio show, Garrison Keillor used to describe the mythical town of Lake Wobegon as the place where "all the children were above average." His gentle irony pointed out that this phrase was an oxymoron. Not all of us can be above average in artistic and intellectual giftedness, for example. Some of us are probably naturally endowed with a tendency to be more inner-directed than others. Some may affirm that their gifts tend more toward organization, handiness, or some other area than toward artistic creativity or intellectual giftedness. Not everyone is called to be a parent or a spouse. Some who have found themselves incapacitated in numerous ways have found their empowerment in simply but profoundly lifting others up in faithful prayer, or in sharing a gentle sense of humor or simple honesty with those around them. Whatever our combination of God-given traits may be at a particular time in our lives, this combination is what we are called to recognize and use.

The Scriptures about Mary, like much else in the Bible, can be looked upon like a Rorschach test in some ways. In the Rorschach, or inkblot test, the blots are held up to the client, who is asked to tell what this blot might be. Clues about the person's personality makeup and their view of the world can be construed from the answers. There are a few blots that nearly everyone who is not significantly disturbed tends to see in fairly similar ways. With other blots, there is a wider range of perceptions. Information is also obtained about the complexity and richness of the personality of the person by what is seen in the blots. Also, a mature person will tend to see some things that a child will not. Likewise, there is a certain general sense of the Scriptures about Mary being seen differently by not only different persons, but by different cultures and times. Who knows what eludes us that others will someday discover? Our task is to fully see what we are able to at this juncture, and to incorporate our discoveries into our lives and in our communities in ways that affirm the abundant life God has given us.

The Invitation and the Challenge

The woman on the donkey, full of both extraordinary mystery and a clarity of person we have sometimes overlooked, has much to say to us. Those who cried, "Hosanna!" when Jesus passed by on his entry to Jerusalem, also on a donkey, saw him in a loving but limited way, because they did not yet glimpse the mystery and paradox of this Messiah who was about to endure death and resurrection. Some who shouted praise that day, waving palm branches, were later able to embrace a more complex picture of Jesus, as their eyes were opened. Some were not.

Likewise, we have been challenged to take a fresh look at the woman who entered Bethlehem on a donkey. We have dared to part the veil of tradition that has shrouded Mary in loving but limited stereotypes. The reward is to see a powerful, balanced Mary emerge—a Mary who is at the same time both a very real woman and an archetype. Through her example, we are invited to dare to become all God made us to be. We are invited to affirm that God can equip and empower us to fulfill our particular purpose, "for nothing is impossible with God." We are also invited to partake in a celebration, helping to transform that which is ordinary around us, just as the servants at the wedding helped transform water into extraordinarily good wine when they followed Mary's last words in Scripture: "Do whatever he tells you."

We are invited to take Mary's hand and journey to wholeness, sometimes plodding in dusty sandals, sometimes seared by the pain of remaining true, and sometimes soaring in our spirits to the lyrics of angels.

NOTES

CHAPTER 1

1. E.L. Fullam, *Living the Lord's Prayer* (New York: Ballantine Books, 1983).
2. 1 Corinthians 13:11.
3. *Newsweek*, August 25, 1997, 49-55.
4. J.S. Spong, *Born of a Woman* (New York: HarperCollins Publishers, 1992).
5. Since I am not a Biblical scholar, I am not taking a scholarly stand on the various perspectives regarding the historical accuracy of Scripture. I am aware that intelligent, well-educated theologians and pastors take very different perspectives regarding the literalness of the record and the source of the record. Within my field of psychology, it is legitimate to examine the Biblical record as data. Because I am also a woman of faith, my role in this book is one of participant-observer. For me this means that while I strive to be an accurate observer of the data presented as a psychologist, I am also acknowledging and allowing to show from time to time my own personal response to the Biblical account.
6. M. Warner, *Alone of All Her Sex* (New York: Vintage Books, 1983) xxv.
7. Ibid., xxiv.
8. J.S. Spong, *Born of a Woman* (New York: HarperCollins Publishers, 1992) 1.
9 *The American Heritage Dictionary* (Boston: Houghton Mifflin Company, 1982).
10 H. Cloud and J. Townsend, *Boundaries* (Grand Rapids, MI: Zondervan Publishing House, 1992).
11 This does not mean that we don't set appropriate limits on other's inappropriate behavior; that may be an important part of taking care of our own yards. It also does not imply that we don't show love and concern for other's feelings in appropriate ways. It refers instead to the reality that we cannot control how another person feels, thinks, and behaves. We can influence these things by our own healthy behavior, but we cannot control them. For example, Jesus himself was not able to control the feelings, beliefs, and behaviors of others. In spite of the fact that he was without sin, some hated him, some thought he was of the devil, and the behaviors of some ended his life.

CHAPTER 2

1. The annunciation refers to the announcement or proclamation by the angel Gabriel that Mary was chosen to bear the Christ-child. The whole passage quoted above is referred to as the annunciation in this book.

2. Luke 1:11-19.
3. Matthew 1:20-25.
4. Luke 1:29.
5. Exodus 3.
6. 1 Samuel 3.
7. Acts 9:1-9.
8. Matthew 3:13-17.
9. Matthew 20:16.

CHAPTER 3

1. Luke 1:42-45.
2. Luke 1:46.
3. Some believe the account as written. Others have stated, for example, that they believe that Mary never created the song. Instead, they believe the Scripture writer later added this song to embellish the story and/or to further illustrate truths in a mythological sense. Others may believe that the song was added later but still see analyzing the data as a valid way of examining whatever has been included in the scriptural record.
4. This definition is paraphrased from *The American Heritage Dictionary*, 2nd Ed. (Boston: Houghton Mifflin, 1985).
5. This is seen as only one facet of our being created in God's image. Since we seem to differ in types and degrees of creativity, this in no way suggests that someone with a high degree of creativity is somehow created more in the image of God than someone who may have a lesser degree.
6. E. Polster and M. Polster, *Gestalt Therapy Integrated* (New York: Vintage Books, 1973) 215.
7. Ibid., 235.
8 C.P. Estes, *Women Who Run With the Wolves* (New York: Ballantine Books, 1992) 318.

CHAPTER 4

1 Tos. Ber. 7:118, as quoted in Joseph Bonsirven, *Palestinian Judaism in the Time of Jesus Christ* (New York: Holt, Rinehart & Winston, 1964) 100.
2. From *Women and Capitalism,* by Jeanette Thomas.
3. Cognitive can be interchanged with intellectual. The stages used here are based on those developed by Jane Loevinger and described in her book *Ego Development* (San Francisco: Jossey-Bass Inc., 1976), and *Measuring Ego Development* (San Francisco: Jossey-Bass Inc., 1970).
4. Adolphe Tanquerry, *The Spiritual Life: A Treatise on Ascetical and Mystical Theology* (Westminster, Md, 1930) 232.
5. M. Fox, *Original Blessing* (Santa Fe: Bear and Company, Inc, 1983).
6. S. de Beauvoir, *Memoirs of a Dutiful Daughter* (New York:World Publishing Company, 1959).

7. M. Pipher, *Reviving Ophelia* (New York: Ballantine Books, 1994).

8. Greenberg-Lake/American Association for University Women, *Shortchanging Girls, Shortchanging America* (Washington, DC: AAUW, 1991).

9. J. Loevinger and R. Wessler, *Measuring Ego Development* (San Francisco, CA: Jossey-Bass, Inc., 1970).

10. Mark 9:35.

11. Matt. 5:5.

12. Of or relating to Greek history from the time of Alexander the Great through the first century, BC.

13. Matthew 25:14-30.

CHAPTER 5

1. Matthew 19:24.

2. C. ten Boom, *Clippings from My Notebook* (Minneapolis, MI: World Wide Publications, 1982) 56.

3. Luke 2:35.

4. E. Erikson, *Identity—Youth and Crisis* (New York: Norton & Company, 1968).

5. J. Fowler, *Stages of Faith* (New York: HarperCollins, 1981).

6. See p. in Chapter Four

7. Fowler, 184.

8. Ibid., 201.

9. Hebrews 5:12.

10. Communicated at a conference held in Granby, Colorado, in June 1997. Rev. Fullam is a noted author and speaker, known for both the power of his intellect and his faith.

11. John 10:14.

12. Mark 13:26-27.

13. From Luke 1:38.

14. Communicated at the conference held in Granby, Colorado, June 1997.

15. Luke 1:28, 30.

16. Hebrews 13:20-22, 2 Timothy 3:16-17, and Ephesians 2:10.

17. These stories are told to illustrate the link between faith and action, and do not imply anything about the faith or alertness of others who lost their lives in the flood. Many of firm faith and good judgment perished in that tragedy. This is akin to the mystery alluded to in Corrie ten Boom's statement, quoted earlier in the chapter.

18. Hebrews 6:12.

19. Luke 1:46-47.

20. Luke 1:45.

CHAPTER 6

1. Thanks to Diana Lee Christen, whose 1984 unpublished senior honor thesis for the Department of History at Colorado State University is entitled

"The Genesis of Misogynism and Woman's Subordination within the Christian Church."
2. R. J. Stoller, "A Contribution to the Study of Gender Identity," *International Journal of Psycho-Analysis:* 45, 220-226.
3. C. Gilligan, *In A Different Voice* (Cambridge, MA: Harvard University Press, 1982) 8.
4. Matthew 1:18-24.
5. Luke 2:48-52
6. John 2:1-12
7. Mark 3:20-32
8. John 19:25-27
9. M. Woodman, *The Pregnant Virgin* (Toronto: Inner City Books, 1985) 155.

CHAPTER 7

1. *The American Heritage Dictionary,* Second College Edition (Boston, MA: Houghton Mifflin Company, 1982).
2. Seeking professional help may be indicated if feelings are disrupting one's personal, family, or work life. It can also be a helpful support for those who feel strong inhibitions about accepting or expressing their own feelings.
3. Luke 1:26-38.
4. Luke 1:5-22.
5. Luke 2:41-52
6. John 2:1-11
7. Mark 7:24-30
8. John 2:12
9. Mark 3:20-35

CHAPTER 8

1. Matthew 1:18-2:23
2. Adultery is the term used, even though Mary and Joseph were betrothed. A woman who was unfaithful to her betrothed was considered adulterous.
3. We are analyzing Joseph's choices here. This does not rule out the possibility that another person might not make a different choice in a similar situation and also have healthy boundaries.
4. D.S. Garland and D.E. Garland, *Beyond Companionship: Christians in Marriage* (Philadelphia: Westminster Press, 1986).
5. Ephesians 5:32.
6. D. Dumm, *Flowers in the Desert* (New York: Paulist Press, 1987).
7. D.S. Garland and D.E. Garland, *Beyond Companionship: Christians in Marriage* (Philadelphia: Westminster Press,1986).
8. The Garlands' work may have particular significance coming from a religious tradition that has often been considered a champion of the more traditional, hierarchical perspectives on the marriage relationship.

9. Narcissism refers here to someone who focuses on their own needs, with little ability to see the view point or perspectives of others.

10. J. Bernard, *The Future of Marriage*, 2nd Ed. (New Haven, CT.: Yale University Press, 1982).

11. D.S. Garland and D.E. Garland, *Beyond Companionship: Christians in Marriage* (Philadelphia: Westminster Press,1986) 51.

12. H. Hendrix, *Getting the Love You Want* (New York: HarperPerennial, 1988).

CHAPTER 9

1. *American Heritage Dictionary*, 2nd Ed. (Boston, MA: Houghton Mifflin, 1985).

2. Deuteronomy 6:5.

3. Luke 2:47.

4. Luke 2:22-24.

5. Matthew 2:13.

6. Luke 4:1-13

7. John 2:12.

8. This gentleman was later grounded before his mission, after a change in his health disqualified him, due to the rigorous health requirements for astronauts.

9. Mark 3:20-21.

CHAPTER 10

1. B. Manning, *The Ragamuffin Gospel: Embracing the Unconditional Love of God* (Portland, OR: Multnomah, 1990).

2. Matthew 1:24

3. Matthew 1:25

4. Mark 6:2-3

5. J. Burnaby, "Saint Augustine of Hippo," in *Encyclopedia Britannica*, Vol. 2 (Chicago, IL: Encyclopedia Britannica, Inc., 1976) 364-65.

6. B.H. Jones, "Anger: Psychological and Biblical Perspectives" (Unpublished dissertation, Colorado State University, 1990) 41.

7. Augustine, *The City of God* (M. Dods, Trans.), in R. M. Hutchins (Ed.), *Great Books of the Western World* (Chicago: Encyclopedia Britannica, Inc. Original work published circa AD 420) 390.

8. The term project refers to a defense mechanism where we are uncomfortable owning some trait in ourselves, so we deny its reality in our own person but place or project it onto another person, more than reflects reality.

9. From the back cover of *Alone of All Her Sex*, by M. Warner (New York: First Vintage Books Edition, 1983).

10. When paired with spiritual or moral virtue, it is important to note that the term virginity thereby takes on a different meaning in contemporary religious circles than simply an intact hymen or a woman who has not had sexual

intercourse. For example, a woman whose hymen may have broken due to other causes such as sports participation would still be considered a virgin in this context. Likewise, a virgin who is sexually assaulted remains a virgin in God's eyes and the church's eyes, according to most enlightened religious clerics. This is an extremely important point for believers who are concerned about this issue after enduring such a trauma.

11. Genesis 1:31.

12. 1 Corinthians 7:5

13. This parallels 1 Cor. 15:22: "As in Adam all die, so in Christ shall all be made alive."

14. M. Woodman, *The Pregnant Virgin* (Toronto: Inner City Books, 1985).

CHAPTER 11

1. Luke 2:32.

2. John 7:5.

3. Matthew 12:34.

4. Mark 11:15-16.

5. Luke 4:23-30.

6. John 19:26-27.

7. D.F. Stramara, "El Shaddai: A Feminine Aspect of God," Dove Leaflet #28 (Pecos, NM: Dove Publications). The remainder of the material on El Shaddai is referenced to this article. The interested reader is also referred to the *Encyclopedia Judaica* for further information. Via personal communication, Dr. Stramara informs me that "El Shaddai" also has links to the ancient precursor of Hebrew, a language known as Akkadian. It is this language that is the source of the feminine endings for both Sarai and El Shaddai.

8. This example is not meant to encourage the choice to keep someone at home under such circumstances, as each situation is different.

CHAPTER 12

1. Acts 1:4-5.

2. Titus 2:3.

3. J. Pelikan, *Mary Through the Centuries* (New Haven and London: Yale University Press, 1996) 2.

4. Ibid., 3. He is quoting F. Adeney Walpole, *Women of the New Testament*, (London: James Nisbet, 1901) 835.

5. Ibid., 3. His quote is from Alvin John Schmidt, *Veiled and Silenced: How Culture Shaped Sexist Theology* (Macon, GA: Mercer University Press, 1989) 95.

6. I Cor. 3:16-17.

7. Matt. 25:14-30.

8. Luke 19:1-9.

9. Luke 18:16.

BIBLIOGRAPHY

Augustine. *The City of God*. M. Dods, trans., In R. M. Hutchins, Ed., *Great Books of the Western World*. Chicago: Encyclopedia Britannica, Inc., 1953. Original work published circa A.D. 420.

de Beauvoir, S. *Memoirs of a Dutiful Daughter*. New York: World Publishing Company, 1959.

Bernard, J. *The Future of Marriage*, 2nd Ed. New Haven, CT: Yale University Press, 1982.

ten Boom, C. *Clippings from My Notebook*. Minneapolis, MI: World Wide Publications, 1982.

Cloud, H. and Townsend, J. *Boundaries*. Grand Rapids, MI: Zondervan Publishing House, 1992.

Dumm, D. *Flowers in the Desert*. New York: Paulist Press, 1987.

Erikson, E. *Identity—Youth and Crisis*. New York: Norton & Company, 1968.

Estes, C. P. *Women Who Run With the Wolves*. New York: Ballantine Books, 1992.

Fowler, J. *Stages of Faith*. New York: HarperCollins, 1981.

Fox, M. *Original Blessing*. Santa Fe, CA: Bear and Company, Inc., 1983

Fullam, E.L. *Living the Lord's Prayer*. New York: Ballantine Books, 1983.

Garland, D. S. and Garland, D. E. *Beyond Companionship: Christians in Marriage*. Philadelphia: Westminster Press, 1986.

Gilligan, C. *In A Different Voice*. Cambridge, MA: Harvard University Press, 1982.

Greenberg-Lake/American Association for University Women. *Shortchanging Girls, Shortchanging America*. Washington, DC: AAUW, 1991.

Hendrix, H. *Getting the Love You Want*. New York: HarperPerennial, 1988.

Loevinger, J. *Ego Development*. San Francisco: Jossey-Bass Inc, 1976.

Loevinger, J. and Wessler, R. *Measuring Ego Development*. San Francisco: Jossey-Bass, Inc., 1970.

Manning, B. *The Ragamuffin Gospel*. Portland, OR: Multnomah, 1990.

Pelikan, J. *Mary Through the Centuries*. New Haven and London: Yale University Press, 1996.

Pipher, M. *Reviving Ophelia*. New York: Ballantine Books, 1994.

Polster, E. and Polster, M. *Gestalt Therapy Integrated*. New York: Vintage Books, 1973.

Spong, J.S. *Born of a Woman*. New York: HarperCollins Publishers, 1992.

Warner, M. *Alone of All Her Sex*. New York: Vintage Books, 1983.

Woodman, M. *The Pregnant Virgin*. Toronto, Canada: Inner City Books, 1985.

Index

Alone of All Her Sex, 23-24, 26
Annunciation, 37, 52-53
Archetype, 15-
    Defining, 24-26
    Desire for, 15
Assertiveness, 151-69
    Need for, 152-53
    Concerns about, 153-54
    Defining, 155
    Foundations of, 155-57
    Of Mary, 157-68
Augustine,
    Views regarding sexuality,
        219-23
Aquinas, T., 226

Balance, 23, 72-75
    Relation to health, 23
Betrayal of the father, 82
Beyond Companionship, 181
Body,
    Female, 232, 268
    Mary's female, 232, 268
Bonding, 109
Boundaries, 28

Chambers, O., 249
Chain of authority, 52-53
Cinderella Complex, 82
Cloud, Henry, 28
Cognitive developmental stages,
        85-89
Creative thought, 18
    Creativity, 62
    Definition, 62-63
    Guideposts for, 67-72
    Ingredients fostering, 66-67

    Relation of training and
        discipline, 64
    Union of awareness and
        expression, 63
Cultural developmental stages, 19-20

Dante, 50
De Beauvoir, Simone, 82
Dead Man Walking, film, 246-247
Developmental psychology, 19
Diana, Princess of Wales, 19-20, 26
Discerning, 118
    New wineskins, 20-21
Dowling, Colette, 82
Dumm, Demetrius, 182
Dying to self, 257-58

El Shaddai, 248-49
Elizabeth, 44-45, 49
Empowerment, 27-30
    Boundaries of, 28
    Defining, 27
Erickson, E., 109, 198, 273
Estes, Clarissa Pinkola, 73
Eve, 78

Faith,
    As organizing principle, 108
    Foundations of, 109-111
    Structure of, 111
    Developmental stages, 111

Flowers in the Desert, 182
Fosdick, Harry Emerson, 17
Fowler, J., 111
    Stages of faith development,
        111-13

Fox, Michael, 81
Fromm, Erich, 18
   New systems of thought, 18
Fullam, Everett L., 18, 118, 123

Gabriel, Angel, 44, 47-48
Garland, Diana and David,
   181-82
Generativity, stage of, 273
Gilligan, C., 139
Grief,
   As process, 252-53

Hendrix, Harville, 187
Holy Spirit, 59, 65
Horner, M., 83
   On fear of success, 83
Humility, 80-81

Individuation, 131-147
   Definition, 132
   Differences in men and
      women, 138-40
   Cultural perspective, 140-42

Inner-direction, 38-55
Intellectual giftedness, 77, 91
   Cultural influences affecting
      gifted women, 82-85

Jesus, 96, 120, 142, 161-62, 191,
   272
   And paradox, 89
   Comfort of, 247
   Development as a child, 191-98
Joseph, 44-45, 256
   As parent, 192-98
   In relationship with Mary, 171
   Personal qualities, 174-78
Jung, Carl, 24-25
   Regarding archetypes, 24-25

Keillor, Garrison, 274

Lewis, C.S., 127
Loevinger, J., 85
Lost self, 66
   Reclaiming, 67-68

Magnificat, 57
   authorship, 59-61
   originality, 59-60
   revealing Mary's intellectual
      gifts, 79-81
Manning, Brennan, 214
Marriage relationship,
   Flexible, 181-82
   Interdependent, 179-80
Mary and Joseph, 179-89
   Persistance, 178
   Stages in, 186-88
   Steadfastness, 178
   Styles of, 182-86
Mary,
   As healthy role model, 24
   As mentor to Jesus, 206-08
   As parent, 191-212
   As virgin, 48
   Body of, 232
   Dangers of idealizing, 145-46
   Fully present, 28, 47-51
   Inner-directed, 38-39
   Present in suffering, 244
Mary's Song, 57, 65, 77-81, 90
Moses, 50
Mutual submission, 52
My Utmost for His Highest, 249

Outer-direction, 39-40

Paradiso, 50
Paradox, 88-90, 112
   Of choice and obedience, 43-44
Parenting,
   Eagle, 204-05
   Foundation for, 198-200
   Goals, 192-98
   Principles of, 200-11

Paul, 20, 52, 113, 228
Pelikan, Jaroslav, 256-57
Peter, 21
Permissions,
    Of the Mary archetype, 264-69
Phillips, J.B., 17
Pipher, M., 83
Polster, Erving and Miriam, 63-64
Pregnant Virgin, 231
Progressive revelation, 18-19
Prohibitions,
    On personhood of women,
        257-64

Ragamuffin Gospel, 214
Reasoning powers, 18

Samuel, 50
Saul, 51
Self-esteem,
Study of young women, 84
Sexuality,
    Adam and Eve, 220, 225-26
    Ambivalence toward, 213-15
    Aquinas, 226
    As creative power, 229
    Augustine's view, 219-223

Paul and marriage, 228
Platonic Greek tradition,
    218-19
Purpose of, 230
Shaming,
    Of our bodies, 231-32
Siblings of Jesus, 217
Simeon, 233
Spong, J.D., 25-26
Stramara, D., 248-49
Submission, 182-85
Suffering, 233-53

ten Boom, C., 107
Teresa, Mother, 19-20, 112
Townsend, John, 28

Virgin Mary,
    Legends of, 23-24
Virginity of Mary,
    Perpetual virginity, 227
    Purpose of, 216

Warner, Marina, 26
Woodman, M., 146, 231

Zechariah, 48, 59, 158-60